What others are say

"James and Colleen Heater have done a magnificent service for anyone wanting to visit the heart and soul of France. Everything a pilgrim needs is right here—directions, history, secret places, and high inspiration."
—Jyotish Novak, author of *How to Meditate*

"In a very inspirational, informative and practical way, the Heaters help others to reach the deepest level of experiencing the true beauty of the sacred places they visit, and to know more personally the holy people who helped make them sacred."
—Br. Daniel Geary, OFM Conv. Pilgrimage Tour Leader

"The Pilgrim's France is adept at providing the essential information, both practical and historical, to an impressive array of pilgrimage sites dating from every Christian era. With this guide in hand, the traveler to France becomes not only a knowledgeable pilgrim, but an inspired one as well."
—Father Hugh Feiss, OSB, author of *Essential Monastic Wisdom*

"My only consolation for not having had *The Pilgrim's Italy* when I visited Italy last year is that when I return, I most certainly will. For the moment, I'm thoroughly enjoying reading *The Pilgrim's France* and recommend taking it on any trip to France. Splendidly executed!"
—Carol Lee Flinders, Author of *Enduring Grace: Living Portraits of Seven Women Mystics*

"When I began my practice of pilgrimage, I went forth to find myself. To my surprise, I found the saints as well, acting as hidden lodestones in my experience. *The Pilgrim's France* is a tonic for the memory, making the saints alive again for the modern pilgrim."
—Robert Tindall, Pilgrim

"I could really go on and on and on about how fantastic *The Pilgrim's France* is—suffice it to say, I'm glad the Heaters are doing more!"
—Amy Louise Ralston, Pilgrim

The Pilgrim's
FRANCE

A TRAVEL GUIDE
TO THE SAINTS

JAMES & COLLEEN HEATER

The Pilgrim's
FRANCE

A Travel Guide
to the Saints

JAMES & COLLEEN HEATER

Foreword by Phil Cousineau

Inner Travel Books
Nevada City, California

Front Cover: Laugeé & Jehenne, 'Bernadette bergère', chromolithograph, from Henri Lassarre, Notre-Dames de Lourdes, 1878.

Cover Design: Colleen Heater, Lito Castro
Interior Design: James & Colleen Heater, Stephanie Steyer
Maps: James Heater
Photographs by the authors unless otherwise noted

Printed in Canada
ISBN 0-9719860-1-0

Inner Travel Books
14618 Tyler-Foote Road, Suite 171
Nevada City, CA 95959 USA

Toll free telephone: 866-715-8670
info@innertravelbooks.com
www.innertravelbooks.com

Publisher's Cataloging-in-Publication
(Provided by Cassidy Cataloguing Services, Inc.)

Heater, James
   The pilgrim's France: a travel guide to the saints /
James and Colleen Heater. – 1st ed.
   p. ; cm.
   Includes bibliographical references and index.
   LCCN 2003110310
   ISBN 0-9719860-1-0

   1. Christian pilgrims and pilgrimages—France—
Guidebooks. 2. Christian shrines—France—Guidebooks.
3. Christian saints—Cult—France—Guidebooks. 4. France
—Guidebooks. 5. Christian saints—Biography. I. Heater, Colleen. II. Title.
BX2320.5F8 H43 2004   2003110310
263/.04244–dc22   0401

Scripture quotations are taken from *American Standard Version Bible*, unless noted (NIV), in which case they are taken from the *Holy Bible, New International Version*, 1984 by International Bible Society.

Every effort has been made to provide accurate information. The authors and publisher accept no responsibility for loss, injury, or inconvenience sustained by any person using this book. Please reconfirm details before making your trip.

To the Blessed Virgin Mary
For her boundless love and compassion

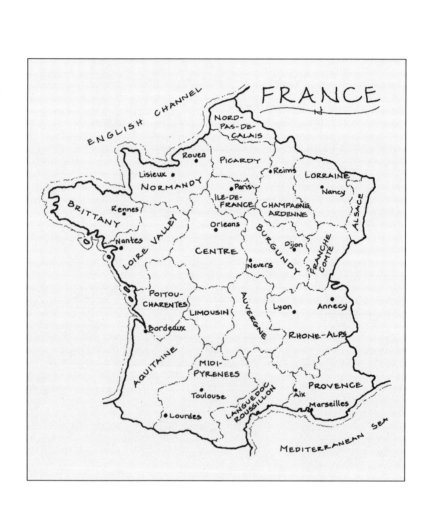

Contents

Rhone Alps (Rhône-Alpes)

Foreword

According to the World Tourism Association, France is the most popular destination in the world. More people visit there than any other country in the world, partly because of its geography, which places it at the crossroads of Europe, but also because it has been the center of artistic and political revolutions for the last several centuries. To paraphrase the old Romans, there are as many different ways and reasons to visit France as there are roads to Paris.

For those who love the arts, it is the home of Cezanne, Delacroix, and Rodin, and for writers, it is the home of Rimbaud, Colette, and Simone de Beauvoir. France also gave birth to the Lumiere Brothers, who screened the world's first movies, and to the first restaurants and cafes in the world, where *la bonne vie* has been carefully cultivated. All of these sites, and hundreds more like them, have been attracting cultural pilgrims for centuries, which is to say, travelers with a deep sense of purpose. But below these secular forms of pilgrimage, like the Roman ruins that lie below so much of today's France, is a much older tradition, the spiritually inspired journey. I believe the two overlap. They are both transformative journeys to places that may be personally or collectively sacred, and both renew our spirits, though in different ways.

For thirty years, I have been making both kinds of journeys to this country that happens to be my ancestral land. With a name like Cousineau, the reader might suspect that I have a vested interest in the subject of special journeys there. *C'est vrai*. It's true. My own ancestor, Jean-Baptiste Cousineau, left the tiny hamlet of Périgueux, in the Dordogne, in 1678, and settled in Ontario, Canada. In the spirit of pilgrimage everywhere, I retraced his footsteps back to the cathedral where he prayed before he left for a new life in the New World. But I've also taken soulful journeys to scores of other sites, such as Reims, Tours, Le Thoronet, Taizé, and Lourdes, which deeply moved me.

One of the most unforgettable moments of my French travels came on a lone journey to the magnificent cathedral at Chartres, an hour outside of Paris. As I walked its famous labyrinth I was approached by Monsieur Boisvieux, an elderly Frenchman, who bore an uncanny resemblance to my great-grandfather, Charlemagne Cousineau. He tapped me on the arm with the crook of his oak walking cane, and asked me, *"Pouvez-vous m'aider à trouver Dieu?"* "Can you help me find God?" He was perfectly serious, like a medieval pilgrim who has temporarily lost his way. He was also waiting for a well-considered response.

Suddenly, a ray of blue light slanted in from the brilliant rose window and landed directly in the center of the labyrinth, the ancient symbol for the long and winding road of the soul, the path that leads in and out of the center of our lives. As the old pilgrim waited for my response, I knew it would not require words. Only a gesture, a recognition, an opening of the heart.

I simply pointed over my shoulder to the whorling pattern of black and white flagstones behind me. The old Frenchman nodded knowingly, touched the edge of his beret, in gratitude, let out a long Gallic sigh, and entered the labyrinth.

The old pilgrim's question was asked in what I have come to think of as the pilgrim mood. That is why I took it seriously and tried to respond to him honestly. It is a question that has been posed by spiritual seekers all over the world for at least the last 40,000 years, since Australian aborigines began their walkabouts, and in France, where pilgrims have been trekking to the ancient megalithic sites for probably the last 6,000 years.

If a traveler were to look at a map of medieval pilgrim routes across France it would resemble a spider web. These well-trodden roads led from Paris to Santiago de Compostela in western Spain, and from Paris to Rome and Jerusalem, replete with pilgrim's inns, shrines, etc. Other beloved routes led to the shrines of visionary saints, such as Jehanne d'Arc, whom we know as Joan of Arc, Francis de Sales, and the Curé d'Ars and the many shrines to the Virgin Mary. All those souls who have sought out the transcendent dimension of life, asking: "Where can I find God? Where can I encounter the divine? Where can I *experience* the sacred?"

For centuries, pilgrims ventured to these sacred sites at great cost and in great danger. Yet they believed in the vital importance of acts of gratitude to the saints they prayed to on a daily basis, and in the spirit-renewing power of taking pilgrimages.

Unfortunately, many of those shrines, routes, and the rituals that accompanied them have long been forgotten, paved over, or ignored in modern times, especially in comparison to the attention lavished upon the cultural accomplishments of France. I strongly feel that to appreciate France in all its glory, it is important to pay attention to its cultural, political *and* religious dimension, otherwise it is a false façade.

However, that gap in knowledge and ceremony has at long last been filled. *The Pilgrim's France* fulfills a sacred function, which is providing us, in the form of the pilgrim's guides of old, with the means to complement any visit to France with some attention to its sacred history, or inspire a pilgrimage to the sites of the saints for its own sake. More than a mere listing of sites, this guide offers inspiring biographies of the saints, the location of relics, suggestions for meditation and contemplation and prayer, maps and directions, and even lists lodging in places that are amenable to the pilgrim mood, such as retreat centers and monasteries.

Beyond the utilitarian function of their book, James and Colleen Heater also write with reverential attention about the ultimate motivation for taking seriously the lives of saints. They show that pilgrimage need not be slavish devotion or rote ritual, but in its ideal form is an act of humility, and a humble recognition of the deeply real spiritual renewal that is possible through contemplation of the saints and experiencing *their living presence* at their shrines.

As a visit to Truffaut's grave in Paris may ignite the passions of a young filmmaker, or a visit to Renoir's home in Nice may inspire the imagination of a young artist, so too, the Heaters show, a visit to the shrine of a saint may rekindle one's spiritual fire.

Remarkably, this is a book for the times. It has been created for people of all faiths, encouraging respect, reverence, curiosity, and compassion for saints and holy ground the world over.

The immortal French writer, Victor Hugo, wrote, in *Contemplations*, "The word is the Verb, and the Verb is God." This maxim has multitudinous meanings, but one way of reading it is this: The sacred word is not just passive, it is active; spiritual life is not just thinking about one's faith, but requires acting upon it. Faith in action is the source, solace and strength of pilgrimage.

The Pilgrim's France shows us an important aspect of that great country's sacred history, but also how we might make that difficult but ultimately inspiring move from tourist to pilgrim, from admiration to contemplation, and from contemplation to exploration.

Phil Cousineau
Author of *The Art of Pilgrimage*

Introduction

Before our trip to France in May 2003, some of our friends questioned our visiting at a time when our respective national leaders were not getting along. In a post 9-11 world, with an impending war in Iraq, tensions between the two powers were anything but cordial. Because we thought that what is played out in the political arena is not necessarily reflected in the everyday lives of ordinary people, we had no misgivings concerning our trip to research pilgrimage sites. Our instincts turned out to be correct. The French people were exceedingly sweet and inviting everywhere we went. Even though we spoke only rudimentary French, everyone we met attempted to have long conversations with us, using their sometimes-limited knowledge of English. We had expected the devout individuals at the shrines to be accommodating, but our entire experience was consistently positive.

One of our favorite sanctuaries was in Nevers, where St. Bernadette is enshrined. After she left Lourdes, she spent the last thirteen years of her life here, and her sanctity can still be felt at her shrine and throughout the grounds. To walk where she walked, to pray where she prayed, was a special privilege we cherished. We also felt Lourdes, one of the most popular shrines in the world, was exceptionally uplifting—just to be surrounded by thousands of people from all over the world who simply love God. Even in Paris, a city famous for its worldly pleasures, we found the popular shrine of St. Catherine Labouré of the Miraculous Medal, a testament to modern day faith. In the middle of this big city, it is a refuge with obvious devotion, alive and active.

Then there was Ars where St. John Vianney lived and died. This little town is a great place for retreat, with comfortable lodgings and the shrine of St. John Vianney always available for prayer and meditation. A surprise blessing awaited us from St. Edmund of Abingdon, who resides in a mostly ignored crypt in the abbey of Pontigny. His love for this abbey and the rich monastic history of the Cistercians could still be felt in this ancient church. Likewise, Pellevoisin at first appeared to not have much to offer, until we sat and meditated in the room where Estelle Faguette had visions of the Virgin Mary. The sweetness of this holy site, and the religious order that caretake the shrine, touched our hearts and left a lasting memory.

France has been particularly favored with many apparitions of the Virgin Mary. The five Marian shrines in this volume represent some of the more inspirational sites in the entire country and every year attract increasing numbers of pilgrims from around the world. Many of the routes to Santiago de Compostela in Spain are part of the history of French pilgrimage, as they originate on French soil. There are shrines that were stopping points for pilgrims along these routes since the eleventh century, and continue to accommodate those brave souls making the sacred journey today. France has some of the most beautiful cathedrals ever constructed on the planet. From Chartres to Reims to Notre-Dame of Paris, France is bejeweled with Gothic wonders, making even an architectural pilgrimage an exceptional experience.

Our goal is to provide enough information on each shrine to enable you to design your own pilgrimage adventure, tailored to your own needs. Some people told us Lourdes was a disappointment because it was so crowded and commercialized, but we felt special blessings there and would return again. La Salette, in the Alps, looked too distant on the map, but we are so happy we ventured there because it was a delight walking the beautiful hills where the Blessed Virgin Mary appeared. These were two very different experiences, but each was rewarding in its own way. There are tangible blessings to be received at each and every shrine—we have only to be open to the possibility.

We have discovered that we feel a saint's spiritual power and blessings more easily when we create an inner environment that invites them to visit. For this very reason, we include a chapter in the back of the book entitled: *How To Meditate with the Saints*. Here we give instructions for stilling the heart and mind through meditation. When we are receptive, the saints transmit their love of God to us as a taste of what awaits us if we stay centered in God. Many spiritually minded people are seeking profound and transformational experiences to inspire them on their spiritual paths. To assist in their efforts we offer straightforward tools that have helped us realize this goal. Even without visiting a shrine, we have often found inspiration when reading about the life of a saint, beginning to imagine how it would be to live for God alone, as they have done.

Though the saints in this book are Roman Catholic, we have written for people of all faiths. In this age of expanding spiritual awareness and interest in understanding different religions, it becomes apparent that most faiths share basic beliefs. We believe that Truth is universal and transcends religious boundaries. God-realized souls, or saints, can share that Truth with us, regardless of their, or our, particular faith.

While France is known worldwide for the romantic grandeur of Paris, beautiful chateaux, lush vineyards and gourmet cuisine, it also offers an exceptional opportunity for spiritual enrichment. Our hope is that this travel guide will provide the inspiration, tools and information you need to create a more meaningful, and possibly profound, experience when visiting the saints and shrines of France. May the saints of all religions bless you on your spiritual journey.

James & Colleen Heater
Nevada City, California

History of Pilgrimage

In our busy world many people are searching to find balance between their inner spiritual lives and their outer material ones. Pilgrimage is one way to energize our search for deeper meaning and purpose in our lives. Through pilgrimage, the spirit is renewed and our general outlook becomes uplifted, changing the way we look at everyday life. The footsteps of pilgrims have echoed continuously through the halls of time, for by visiting sacred sites we are able to immerse ourselves in their powerful vibrations and have a direct personal experience of divinity. This experience is the power of pilgrimage and why it is a major tenet of most religions.

Pilgrimage has been practiced since the sun first rose on human civilization. Before recorded history, the faithful devotees of the Indus Valley, people now known as Hindus, made sacred treks to the revered sites of India. The Hindu spiritual life is a process of reaching complete union or oneness with the Divine. This state of consciousness is known as *samadhi,* and pilgrimage has historically been a means of seeking this deep connection. Modern Hindus continue to take pilgrimage very seriously, often traveling to one of the seven sacred rivers, seven liberation-giving cities, or other spiritual sites found throughout their ancient land. For the Hindu, where one "goes" on pilgrimage is not as important as how one follows the "way of the pilgrim." The goal is to have a personal experience of God through a life-changing encounter with the Divine and to experience God as an inner reality.

While pilgrimage in Hinduism relates to universal sacred sites and temples of the deities, the Buddhist tradition of pilgrimage is associated with the specific places important to the life of the Buddha. Following the death of Buddha in 544 B.C., the sites marking the four sacred events of his life were enshrined. These four primary sites of veneration are the birthplace of the Buddha in Lumbini, Nepal; the site of his enlightenment under the Bo Tree located in Bodh Gaya, India; the locale of his first teaching in Sarnath, India; and the place of his death, or final *nirvana*, in Kushinagar, India. In addition, the ashes from his funeral pyre were distributed to eight stupas, or burial mounds, throughout India, which have also become pilgrimage destinations. A Buddhist pilgrim seeks to abandon the material world and to dive into a deeper understanding and assimilation of the teachings of the Buddha. The sacred journey is a means of purification which eliminates karma due to past actions, and leads to enlightenment, or nirvana, the ultimate goal for every Buddhist. With the blessings of the Buddha and all the great souls that pay homage at these shrines, the holy sites continue to be places of spiritual power and enlightenment, even 2500 years after the Buddha's exit from this world.

Every aspirant in the Islamic tradition is encouraged to make a once-in-a-lifetime pilgrimage to Mecca, if physically and financially feasible. One of the Seven Pillars of Islam is Hajj, or pilgrimage to the Haram mosque in the Saudi Arabian holy city of Mecca, in order to pray and commune with Allah. Muslims descend on Mecca from all over the globe to commune together in peace, for peace is the dominant theme of their pilgrimage. They seek peace with Allah, with their own souls, with one another, and with all living creatures.

This search for peace actually has its roots in Judaism, as the prophet Abraham and his son Ishmael originally founded the Ka'ba in Mecca two

Cliffside Sanctuary of Rocamadour

millennia before Christ. They initiated the rituals that are now an integral part of Islam. Following their inception, these rites were practiced in increasingly lower degrees of devotion until the time of the Prophet Mohammed in 622 A.D. Mohammed re-introduced the importance of pilgrimage and specifically the holy significance of Hajj in Islamic life. The Hajj is the peak of religious experience for the Muslim, and over four million pilgrims partake in the rites every year. Jerusalem is also an important pilgrimage destination for followers of Islam, for The Dome of the Rock is the site of Mohammed's ascension into heaven to commune with Allah, Abraham, Moses, Jesus and other prophets, and is said to be the place of Final Judgment.

Pilgrimage in the Jewish tradition also began with Abraham, as he was the earliest to journey into the desert to seek communion with God. Centuries later, Moses led the definitive pilgrimage when he guided the children of Israel out of Egypt and into the Sinai desert in search of the Promised Land. This pilgrimage was a way of life for forty years, and formed the very basis of the Hebrew nation.

The history of Jerusalem also plays an important role in the life of the Jewish people, for it parallels their history as a people and relates directly to their practice of pilgrimage. The repeated cycle of construction and destruction of their temple coincided with the acceptance and rejection of the Jewish people: a cycle that has repeated itself throughout history to the present day.

David first conquered the Jebusite city of Jerusalem in the eleventh century B.C. His son Solomon erected the first temple to house the Ark of the Covenant in the tenth century B.C. Jerusalem became a primary pilgrimage destination of the Jewish people, for all devout Jews were expected to visit the holy site yearly. In 586 B.C., Nebuchadnezzar of Babylonia destroyed the temple and the Jews were exiled from the city. But fifty years later, the Persians gained control of Jerusalem and welcomed the Hebrews back, allowing them to rebuild the temple. Thus, the tradition of faith and pilgrimage was maintained, and even flourished, over the next four centuries, culminating with the rise in prominence of a Roman Jerusalem under the leadership of Herod the Great at the time of Christ. A new and lavish temple was constructed during Herod's reign and this was the site of many visits by Jesus, as he attended holy days in Jerusalem with his family and later with his disciples.

This temple, too, was destroyed and burnt to the ground when the Romans attacked the rebellious city in 70 A.D. The Jews were exiled from Jerusalem in 135 A.D. following another uprising, and were not allowed to return until the Muslims captured the city in 638 A.D. The Jews did not rebuild the temple, but did build an underground synagogue at the West Wall of the old temple. Their peaceful coexistence with the Muslims lasted another four centuries until, in 1099, the crusaders conquered the Holy Land and decimated the Jewish population, again exiling them from their sacred place of pilgrimage. They were allowed to return after ten years, and were accepted into the city on a limited basis, but did not regain control of their homeland until the mid-twentieth century. Even with the forming of the state of Israel in 1947, the temple has never been rebuilt, but the West Wall is still an active and revered shrine, a central focus of Jewish pilgrimage.

The first Christian pilgrims were those early members of the Christian community who sought out the sites of the martyred apostles and their slain followers. This outward veneration was an infrequent occurrence, as it often involved traveling long distances and meeting in great secrecy. With the acceptance of Christianity by the Emperor Constantine in 312 A.D., and the pilgrimage of his mother, Helen, to the Holy Land, many Christians came out of hiding. Helen traveled to Jerusalem and Galilee, being one of the first to seek out the sacred sights of Jesus' life. She encountered the original cross and many relics of his life and death, and returned to Constantinople with these treasures.

Abbey Cloister of Mont Saint Michel

After the fifth century, the Church of Rome began to separate from the patriarchates of Constantinople, Jerusalem, Antioch, and

Carved wooden statue of St. James

Alexandria. By 1054 A.D., the Church of Rome broke off permanently, becoming the Roman Catholic Church, with the four patriarchates forming the Eastern Orthodox Church. Many of the same pilgrimage destinations are shared by both churches, most notably, Jerusalem, but there are many sites that are unique to Eastern Orthodoxy. These sites include St. Catherine's Monastery on Mount Sinai, Mount Athos in Greece, and Aegina, a Greek island where the relics of St. Nectarios are found. Orthodox pilgrims typically attend religious services, partake of the sacraments of Confession and Communion, and venerate the holy icons and relics of the saints.

The Middle Ages were arguably the golden years for Christian pilgrimage in Europe. Christianity was at the center of the Western world in both political and religious terms. The roads of Western Europe were trod by countless pilgrims traveling to sites such as Rome to visit the relics of Saints Peter and Paul, to Santiago de Compostela to visit the tomb of St. James, to Loreto, Walsingham, Monte Sant' Angelo, as well as countless other places. People were eager for direct contact with holiness and for Divine intercession in their lives. This desire was fulfilled by visiting the holy sites, and by praying for forgiveness, grace and miracles in the presence of the saints' relics. The relics carried back from the Holy Land by the Crusaders enlivened the spiritual ambiance of many churches and created vortices of power and prayer. Many roads were built, and inns and churches erected, to accommodate the multitudes traversing the continent in search of inner peace and a touch of sanctity.

Pilgrimage to Santiago de Compostela in Spain began in the

eleventh century and had a significant impact within France, because this is where all the major pilgrimage roads to Spain began. The four primary routes wound their way through the French countryside and turned small forgotten towns into thriving spiritual centers. Among these were Conques, Rocamadour, Le Puy-en-Velay and Nevers. The endless streams of pilgrims making their way to the shrines also contributed to the evolution of the great Gothic cathedrals of France by financially supporting their construction. As a result, today we can still visit the wonders of Chartres, Notre-Dame, Reims, Mont Saint Michel and many others.

This popularity of pilgrimage continued until the advent of the Protestant Reformation at the end of the fifteenth century. With Martin Luther's separation from the Roman Catholic Church and the beginning of the Protestant movement, many people began to look anew at the practices of the Church. Many Protestants held the act of pilgrimage as useless and felt the worship of saints was misguided. Their misunderstanding of the heart-felt devotion of many true pilgrims dampened the pilgrim spirit for years and placed a negative connotation on sacred travel. The ancient tradition was again bolstered by the Catholic Counter-Reformation of the sixteenth century, although the numbers of pilgrims never again approached those of the Middle Ages.

The beginning of the industrial revolution and the age of scientific thought produced another low ebb in spirituality, and it took Divine intervention to awaken those with spiritual inclinations. Many highly publicized apparitions of the Blessed Virgin Mary occurred in the mid-nineteenth century, raising the spiritual consciousness of the masses and starting a new

Espace Bernadette Soubirous Nevers

flood of pilgrims to these "modern" holy sites. Blessed Mary's appearance in France at Rue de Bac in 1830, La Salette in 1846, at Lourdes in 1858 and Pontmain in 1871, sparked a renewed interest in pilgrimage. After the turn of the twentieth century, the apparitions of the Blessed Virgin Mary spread to other countries, at Fatima, Banneau, Beauraing, and later, Medjugorje, inspiring many people to visit new lands and discover the depths of the pilgrimage experience.

Now, in the twenty-first century, this quest for a personal experience of the Divine continues to magnetically attract people of all religions and beliefs. Pilgrimage was enjoying an all-time high in the

latter part of the twentieth century until the terrorist attacks of September 11, 2001, when the world of travel was abruptly derailed. We believe terrorism or any other obstacle to travel creates only a temporary barrier, for pilgrimage. It will always be a source of inspiration as it has been since the dawn of spiritual aspiration. For a time, the pilgrimages may be more of the heart than of the body, but the longing for God will continue uninterrupted. Whether we travel to a sacred site or stay home and read about a saint, our prayers and focused meditations are the

Hiking to Santiago de Compostela

most important aspect of inner pilgrimage. The true essence of pilgrimage is always centered at home in one's own heart.

When God spoke to St. Catherine of Siena as recorded in her *Dialogue*, He said, "The eye cannot see, nor the tongue tell, nor can the heart imagine how many paths and methods I have, solely for love and to lead them back to grace so that my truth may be realized in them!" God, the Father, Mother Divine, offers us many paths to satisfy our inner yearning for spiritual wholeness, but it is up to each of us to seek out that infinite source of love, embrace it as our own, and awaken the saint within.

How to Use this Guidebook

The intention of this book is to provide all the information needed to plan a journey of pilgrimage to the shrines of France. Before determining the minute details of your pilgrimage, read about the various saints to discover which ones speak to you personally and call you to visit. Then start planning your personal adventure.

The chapters are organized by region and include the cities that are home to the saints and their shrines. The life of each saint is described in a biography, followed by details about the shrines, points of interest, maps and information on getting there. Finally, there is a guide to basic meditation techniques and how to experience the saints. This travel guide is essential to making your pilgrimage a deep, personal experience.

This book is not intended to be a complete travel reference with lodging, dining, and other general tourist advice. We suggest you purchase a guide that is published yearly; giving all the pertinent and up-to-date information you will need to plan your trip. There are many excellent guidebooks that cater to different budgets and interests, so visit a bookstore with a large travel section and purchase a book that appeals to your brand of travel.

While researching the lives of the saints, we discovered countless interesting facts and numerous discrepancies. The details of the saints' lives, especially those of antiquity, tend to become "legend" over time. We have attempted to be as true to fact as possible. What is important is the inspiration we receive from their lives.

Below is a short description of some of the information provided in each chapter and how it is best utilized.

English/French Names First we list the English name of the region, city, saint, and shrine, followed by the French name. When the names are the same in English and French, they are listed once.

Maps We have included regional maps to help you get your bearings, and city maps to get you to the shrines. The regional maps are located at the beginning of each chapter and the cities discussed in this book are underlined. The city maps follow the shrine information and the names of the shrines are underlined. If you are driving, purchase a more detailed map, such as the *Michelin France Tourist and Motoring Atlas*. Refer to "Travel Tips" in the appendix for information.

Speaking French It is wise to know a little French when you travel to France, even if it's only "please – s'il vous plaît" and "thank you – merci." Purchase a small English/French phrasebook before you go. You will be glad you did, especially in small towns where English is not usually spoken. We like Rick Steves *French Phrase Book & Dictionary* that has phonetic spellings. Pronunciation of French can be difficult. We suggest listening to French language tapes well in advance of your trip to understand pronunciation and for training the ear to hear the language. Libraries usually have a selection of language tapes. We have included useful French phrases in each chapter to help you navigate the shrines themselves. Many French people know some English, and are eager to help, especially once you try to speak French and they don't understand your pronunciation. If your French is not getting anywhere, ask if they speak English; "Parlez-vous anglais?" When all else fails, show them the questions written in French, and point! A helpful note: The French are formal in their greetings and always say either "Bonjour Madame/Monsieur" or "Bonsoir Madame/Monsieur" "Good day Madame/Sir" or "Good Evening Madame/Sir." These words will get you far, along with "please" and "thank you," and are a must to learn. Bonne chance (Good Luck)!

English Spoken We note under "Shrine Information" if English is spoken at a shrine, using the following scale: rarely=most likely not; occasionally=sometimes; and typically=most likely, yes. We are using these vague terms because we have found that the priests and nuns who caretake these shrines are frequently reassigned, and we cannot be sure if an English-speaking person will be there when you visit. In general, the larger the shrine, the greater the likelihood of finding

English-speaking personnel. Usually, you won't need to speak to anyone, but always have your phrase book handy.

Websites The websites listed in each chapter and in the appendix are in English, unless we make a note of them being "French." On the Internet, the British flag is used to indicate the English version of the website, and more and more French sites are incorporating English sister sites. Sometimes a website in French will have English for portions of the site while the rest is in French. At times the English icon is at the bottom of the page, or hiding out in some odd place, so be adventuresome. If you really want the information on a French-only site, you can copy and paste onto a website that translates French into English. Two websites are: www.freetranslation.com and www.Systransoft.com. The translations are not perfect, but you can get the idea.

Kilometers/Miles and European Time We list both miles and kilometers because you will need kilometers while traveling, while miles give you an idea of how far it is in your own frame of reference. Europeans use a 24-hour clock while Americans use a 12-hour clock. We list American time (AM and PM) but you can easily convert to European time by adding 12 hours to the PM times. For communication purposes, France is 9 hours ahead of California, 7 hours ahead of Chicago, 6 hours ahead of New York, and 9 hours behind Tokyo.

Accessibility for Travelers with Disabilities More and more travelers with disabilities are making their way to Europe, so we have tried to give as much information as possible on the accessibility of the shrines. We list, to the best of our knowledge, if a shrine is accessible under "Shrine Information." If there is any doubt, please contact the shrine before visiting so you will not be disappointed. If you do not speak French, contact the helpful local tourist agencies. Some of the shrines and cities also offer tours planned especially for accessibility. See Resources for "Travelers with Disabilities" in the appendix.

Update/Correct/Contact If you find information in this book that has changed or is incorrect, we would appreciate hearing from you at info@innertravelbooks.com. This is a work in progress, so we are always open to improvements. Also, if you discover a shrine that you feel should be a part of our book, please let us know so we can try to include it in the next edition or add it to our website. We want to provide the most up-to-date information, and we are grateful for your input and feedback! Merci beaucoup!

Auvergne

The Massif Central, in the Auvergne Region, is located in the southern interior part of France. It is the country's most geologically diverse region, including the largest national park and four volcanic mountains. The rugged scenery is contrasted by a number of thermal hydrotherapy spas that serve more than 70,000 enthusiasts each year. For those who seek Romanesque architecture, five hundred churches from the eleventh and twelfth centuries remain in the area. The most famous of these structures is in Le Puy-en-Velay, a city built among the many chimneys of volcanic rock that rise above the valley floor. The inhabitants of the city have enhanced these stone edifices by placing a chapel on the peak of one, and on another, a towering statue of Notre Dame de France, which keeps watch over the city below. Pilgrims have made the Auvergne region a spiritual destination since the tenth century, when Le Puy became one of the four French starting points for the route to Santiago de Compostela in Spain.

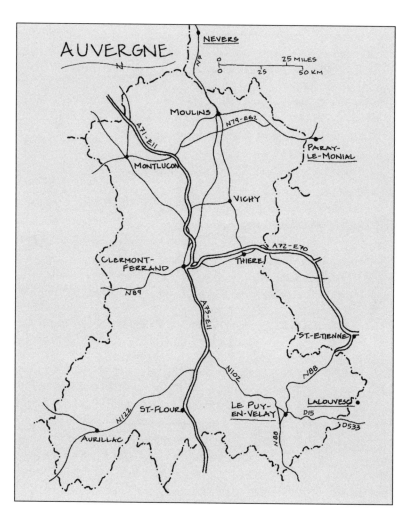

LE PUY-EN-VELAY
Our Lady of Le Puy

Le Puy-en-Velay
Population 22,000

Located in the southwestern part of the Massif Central of France, 325 miles south of Paris, Le Puy-en-Velay was founded on Mount Anis, one of the many volcanic peaks that rise above the fertile plain of Velay. Pagan in origin, the town was converted to Christianity in the third century. By the fifth century, it was well known in Europe for its shrine to the Black Virgin. In the tenth century, Le Puy became one of the four starting points on the pilgrimage route to Santiago de Compostela, the shrine of St. James in Spain, after Bishop Gothescalk first completed the trek in 951. After miraculous healings on Fever Rock (Pierre des Fièvres), an ancient Druid ceremonial stone, and a number of apparitions of the Virgin Mary many spiritual seekers were attracted to the area. The cathedral of Notre Dame was built in the twelfth century to receive the increasing numbers of pilgrims. Today, more than 700,000 visitors annually travel through the mountains to Le Puy. Specialties of the city include "Fuseau" lace, which you will see being made by hand in front of shops around the city, and a green digestive liqueur called "Verveine verte," famous since the nineteenth century.

OUR LADY OF LE PUY
Notre Dame du Puy

The dramatic volcanic peaks rising above the plains of the Velay have been sites of spiritual ceremonies for more than two millennia. The Druids were known to congregate on Mont Anis, where the current Basilica is located, and a temple honoring Jupiter was built here during the Roman occupation. But with the introduction of Christianity into the valley in the third century, the tenor of the worship changed dramatically. There are many versions of the legend of Mont Anis, but they all tell of the Virgin Mary appearing on separate occasions to several women and healing their maladies. One of the stories told is of a woman the Virgin told to lie on the black dolmen, an ancient Druid ceremonial stone, so that she could be healed. After the miraculous healing, the Virgin appeared again and asked that a chapel be built on the site. News of the miracle swept the area, and the Bishop himself investigated the claims the following summer. Legend has it that he witnessed a freak snowfall in July, and saw a deer trace the outline of a chapel in the snow. Convinced of the authenticity of the apparition, he ordered the building of the church.

Another woman was healed following an apparition of the Blessed Virgin in the fifth century, after which the veneration of Mary became even more pronounced in the region. Le Puy began to see a great increase in pilgrims coming to the city and a hospice was built at the cathedral to receive them. Over the coming centuries, the cathedral was enlarged and remodeled several times, as the site at Mont Anis became a center for pilgrimage activity. Charlemagne visited Le Puy twice in the 770s and many popes came to venerate the Virgin.

Our Lady of Le Puy

Veneration of the Black Madonna began in the tenth century after the arrival of the mysterious statue at Le Puy. The statue came from the East, perhaps brought from Palestine by a crusader. The Black Madonna drew a great influx of pilgrims in the eleventh and twelfth centuries, as Le Puy became a major city on the route to Santiago de Compostela.

Following the French Revolution, in 1794, the Black Madonna was removed from the sanctuary and desecrated, guillotined, and burned by the civil authorities. A copy of the Black Madonna was reinstated in the Cathedral in 1844, and has remained an object of veneration. In modern day Le Puy, the statue of the Black Virgin is carried in procession through the streets on August 15th, the feast of the Assumption. Thousands attend this ceremonial walk. (When the feast of the Annunciation on the 25th of March coincides with Good Friday it is known as the Jubilee. The next occurrence of this event takes place in 2005.)

CATHEDRAL OF OUR LADY OF LE PUY
Cathédrale de Notre Dame du Puy

As the legend relates, the Virgin Mary appeared to a woman, who was healed of her fever, and requested that a church be built on the spot. This Fever Stone (La Pierre des Fièvres) is currently in front of the

Golden Gate of the main entrance of the Cathedral. The Cathedral of Our Lady of Le Puy was initially built in the fifth century on Mt. Anis, and became the seat of the bishop for a time. In the eleventh and twelfth centuries the church was enlarged to accommodate the growing number of pilgrims. While the original structure was built on the rock of Mt. Anis, the additional bays were later added to the western end of the nave, where they hover over the rocky mount, supported

Cathédrale de Notre Dame du Puy

by many stone pillars. This unusual design results in a long series of stairs that lead from the Golden Gate and the streets of Le Puy, climb up under the Cathedral, and enter the church in the very center of the Nave, facing the altar and the Black Madonna. It is one of the most unique cathedral entry sequences in the western world, and is worth the long ascent up the stairs.

The style of the Cathedral is Romanesque with Moorish elements, producing an interesting juxtaposition of East and West. The interior stonework is somewhat austere, but the towering structure displays soaring vaults and cupolas. The many additions over the years include the Cloister, Chapel of the Relics, the bell tower, and Baptistry. The focus of the Cathedral is the statue of the Black Madonna with the baby Jesus, which sits on the main altar dressed in all its finery. During regular hours, the access to the Cathedral is directly up the stairs that rise above the main entry, but during Mass, signs will direct you to the right and up ancillary stairs to a side entrance.

CLOISTER OF THE CATHEDRAL
Cloître de la Cathédrale

As you exit the Cathedral to the left of the main altar, you will come upon the Cloister on your left. Listed as a historic monument, the Cloister was built in the eleventh century for secular canons (religious who lived in the world) who formed the bishop's advisory council. Ongoing restoration from the fourteenth century through the twentieth centuries has resulted in a display of wondrous medieval stone carving and decorative arts. The cloister exhibits many beautifully carved capitals above the columns with unique themes and ornamentation. Upstairs is the Museum of Religious Art in the Etats du Velay room, and, in the Chapter

Cloister column capital

House, a thirteenth century fresco of the crucifixion. Entrance fee: for adults €4.60; 18-25 yrs old €3.10; 17 & under free. Tours are sometimes available; ask at the entrance. Your ticket also admits you to the Chapel of the Relics and Treasury of Religious Art. Open 9AM-12PM and 2PM-6 except Thursday.

STATUE OF OUR LADY OF FRANCE
Statue Notre Dame de France

The Statue of Our Lady of France is hard to miss in Le Puy, as it stands high on the Corneille Rock (Rocher Corneille) overlooking the city. This rock, like many of the chimney-shaped outcroppings in the valley, is the core of an ancient volcano. The statue's history began on September 8, 1855 when General Pélissier won the siege of Sebastopol during the Crimean War. Pélissier asked the Bishop to request some of the cannons taken from the enemy to be used for construction of a statue dedicated to Our Lady of France. Emperor Napoleon III granted the appeal and 213 cannons were melted down to build the statue that

Statue Notre Dame de France

measures 52.5 feet high, without the pedestal, and weighs 835 tons. From the valley floor to the top of the statue is 2,484 feet and a considerable climb for some, but many pleasant resting places are placed along the way. There are tiny stairs that curve up the inside of the statue, like a miniature version of the Statue of Liberty in New York. Tours are sometimes available; ask at the entrance. Spring, summer and fall, open daily from 10AM-5PM; closed December and January, except on Sunday afternoons. Check the website www.ot-lepuyenvelay.fr for more information. Phone: 33 (0)4 71 04 11 33; Email: info@ot-lepuyenvelay.fr.

CHAPEL OF ST. MICHAEL D'AIGUILHE
Chapelle Saint Michel d'Aiguilhe

In 951, Bishop Gothescalk became one of the first pilgrims to walk from Le Puy to Santiago de Compostela, Spain. After his return to Le Puy, he constructed a small chapel dedicated to St. Michael the Archangel on the volcanic peak, Rocher Saint Michel d'Aiguilhe, not far from Mont Anis.

In this ancient sanctuary, sunlight filtered through rustic stained glass illuminates a twelfth century fresco and a tenth century wooden crucifix. If you are interested in more primitive architecture, it is worth the climb up hundreds of steps. Open daily 10AM-12PM and 2PM-6; summer 9AM-12PM and 2PM-7. Closed November to mid-March, except for Christmas holidays, when it is open all but Christmas and New Year's Day.

Adults €2.50; children under 14 yrs old €1. Tours available in French. Saint Michel d'Aiguilhe/43000 Le Puy-en-Velay Phone: 33 (0)4 71 02 98 74.

SANTIAGO DE COMPOSTELA

Le Puy is one of the four original starting points on the pilgrim's walking route to the shrine of St. James in Santiago de Compostela, Spain. (This route is also called "Via Podiensis" and "Chemin de Saint Jacques.") The pilgrim can obtain a pilgrimage certificate

Chapelle Saint Michel d'Aiguilhe

(créanciale) at the Cathedral after a meeting with an official representative of the church, and receive a parting benediction at a 7AM Mass. The certificate is subsequently stamped at all official towns along the route, with the goal of receiving the final stamp of the journey at Santiago de Compostela. Pilgrims can also arrange to meet others who have already completed the route to Compostela. Special parking rates (tarif spécial randonneur) are given to the pilgrims in the town of Le Puy-en-Velay. Call Le Breuil underground car park for more information and reservations: Phone: 33 (0)4 71 02 03 54.

There is a Reception Center for pilgrims hiking the Santiago de Compostela at Accueil Saint Jacques, 15, Avenue de Mondon in Espaly-Saint-Marcel. Former pilgrims meet to share their experiences. Open from April 1 to October 1 at 6PM in the evening. Call 33 (0)4 71 09 66 42, or 33 (0)4 71 66 63 12.

Where is the Cathedral with the Black Virgin?
Où est cathédrale avec la Vierge Noire?

Where is the Chapel of St. Michael d'Aiguilhe?
Où est Chapelle Saint Michel d'Aiguilhe?

SHRINE INFORMATION

Shrine: Cathedral of Our Lady of Le Puy (Cathédrale de Notre Dame du Puy)

Address: Rue des Tables/43000 Le Puy-en-Velay/France

Phone: 33 (0)4 71 05 98 74 **Fax:** 33 (0)4 71 09 38 41

E-mail: None

Website: None

Quiet areas for meditation: There is a quiet, beautiful chapel in the middle of the Cathedral on the left as you face the altar. The crowds are moderate depending on whether there are services.

English spoken: Occasionally

Hours: Daily 8AM–6PM

Mass: In July and August, pilgrims' Mass every day at 11AM, brief processions (3 hours), meetings with priests and confessions.

Feasts and festivities: March 25 — Feast of the Annunciation; July 1 — Feast of the Visitation; August 14 — 8:30PM procession with the Black Virgin; August 15 — Feast of the Assumption, 3PM procession with the Black Virgin; September 8 — Nativity of the Blessed Virgin Mary; Thursday before Easter — Procession of the Penitents.

Information for Pilgrimage: Haute-Loire Terre Mariale, 4 rue St. Georges, 43000 Le Puy-en-Velay Phone: 33 (0)4 71 09 69 94 Fax: 33 (0)4 71 09 93 17. The Isabelle Romèe day Centre is a welcome center with lodging for pilgrims walking the Santiago de Compostela. Address: Rue Isabelle Romée/43000/Le Puy-en-Velay/France Email: ddp.lepuy@wandadoo.fr. Phone: 33 (0)4 71 09 73 45 Fax: 33 (0)4 71 05 78 08 Tours: Free tours in summer at 11AM and 3:30PM in French.

Bookstore: Cloister bookshop.

Recommended books: *Le Puy-En-Velay: Cathedral, Cloisters, Penitents, N.D. de France* by Louis Comte. Available at Cloister bookshop.

Lodging: Haute Loire Terre Mariale/Maison Saint Françoise/rue Saint Mayol/43000 Le Puy-en-Velay/France Phone: 33 (0)4 71 05 98 86 Fax: 33 (0)4 71 05 98 87.

Directions: The Cathedral is high on Mont Anis, in the center of town, just below the large statue of Mary with the baby Jesus. Follow the signs to the Cathedral. There are several confusing entrances, so try to enter from the front of the church on rue des Tables.

COMING AND GOING

LE PUY-EN-VELAY

Car: Le Puy is off the beaten track, 80 miles (50 km) southwest of Lyon, a two-hour drive. Just south of Lyon on A7, take A47 to St. Etienne, then N88 to Le Puy. From the south of France and A7, take D333 west at Valence all the way to Le Puy. This is a very curvy mountain road, so allow three to four hours to reach Le Puy once you turn off A7. From the west and Clemont-Frerrand, take A75, then N102 to Le Puy. This is an 80-mile (50 km), two-hour drive.

Train: From the Lyon Perrache station, take the train to Le Puy via St. Etienne. Another option from the Paris Gare de Lyon station is to take the train to Clermont-Ferrand, continuing to Le Puy via St. George d'Aurac.

Bus: Main bus station at Pl. M. Leclerc, Phone: 33 (0)4 71 09 25 60.

Taxi: 24 hour Phone: 33 (0)4 71 05 42 43.

Air: Le Puy en Velay/Loudes airport ten minutes from Le Puy. Weekday only service with Paris Orly Sud.

TOURIST INFORMATION

✻ Office du Tourisme/Place du Breuil/43000 Le Puy-en-Velay Phone: 33 (0)4 71 09 38 41 Fax: 33 (0)4 71 05 22 62 Email: info@ot-lep-uyenvelay.fr Maps and tours are available. www.ot-lepuyenvelay.fr/ Comprehensive website: go to "History and Heritage" then "monuments" for descriptions of the sites in Le Puy.

❈ Haute-Loire Comité Départemental du Tourisme/1, place Monseigneur de Galard/43011 Le Puy-en-Velay/cedex France Phone: 33 (0)4 71 07 41 54 Fax: 33 (0)4 71 07 41 55 Email: cdt@mididelauvergne.com www.mididelauvergne.com/accueil.html French.

❈ Official Site of Le Puy-en-Velay Town: www.mairie-le-puy-en-velay.fr Limited info in English.

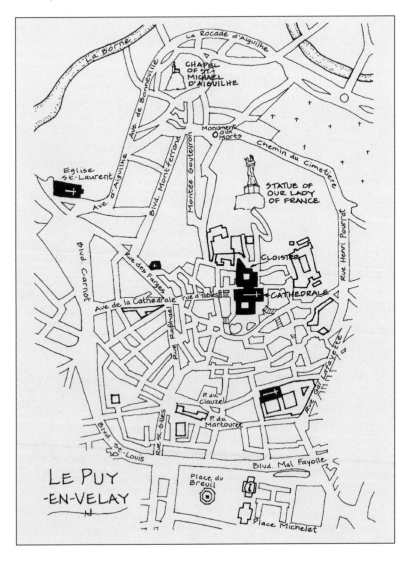

WEBSITES

Department Tourist Office www.ot-lepuyenvelay.fr — Comprehensive website: go to "History and Heritage" then "monuments" for descriptions of the sites in Le Puy. Also, tours of the town are listed in detail and a page on the Compostela lists resources and everything you need to hike the Chemin.

La Maison du Pèlerin www.lourdes-fr.com — Information about the major shrines in France and Europe, including Le Puy.

Town of Le Puy-en-Velay www.mairie-le-puy-en-velay.fr — Limited info in English.

Villes Sanctuaries en France www.villes-sanctuaires.com — The Association of Shrine Towns in France with a suggested tour and contact information.

PLACES OF INTEREST NEAR LE PUY-EN-VELAY

LA LOUVESC
The Basilica of St. Regis

The Basilica of St. Regis (Basilique St. Régis) and the Chapel of St. Therese Couderc (Maison Thérèse Couderc) are both in La Louvesc, about 45 miles (72 km) northeast of Le Puy. There is no easy way to reach La Louvesc. The mountainous roads lead to beautiful vistas, but traveling is slow, so take your time and enjoy the scenery. Refer to the chapter on Rhone Alps for more information.

Brittany

Bretagne

This westernmost region of France is a diverse mix of rugged coastlines, ancient towns, magical islands and inland woods. The Celts called this region home for many centuries and it only became a part of France when annexed in 1532. The Bretons pride themselves in their heritage and work hard to maintain their native culture. This makes a visit to this remote area a real treat and one of unique adventures. The man-made features include the ancient stone megaliths of Carnac and the architecture of Quimper, Auray and Vannes. Natural splendor is the greatest calling card of Brittany, as attested to by the works of Picasso, Matisse, Gauguin, and Monet, who all came here to capture the picturesque landscape and seaside in paint and canvas. Religious history is also a part of Brittany, as small chapels dot the countryside and granite churches reach towards the heavens in St. Thegonnec, Guimiliau, Lampaul-Guimiliau, and in St. Anne d'Auray, where the mother of Mary, St. Anne, has been venerated since the sixth century.

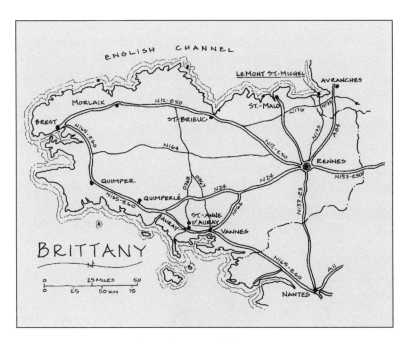

ST. ANNE D'AURAY
St. Anne of Auray

St. Anne d'Auray

Population 2,000

St. Anne, the mother of the Blessed Virgin Mary, was first venerated in St. Anne d'Auray around the sixth century, when the first missionaries to bring Christianity to the area dedicated a chapel to her. Although the chapel was later destroyed by fire, the village retained the name of Keranna, meaning "village of Anne," in Breton. St. Anne appeared to Yves Nicolazic in 1623 and 1624, asking him to rebuild the chapel. A new chapel was built, and later replaced with the current Basilica. Since then, this small town in Brittany has become a major pilgrimage destination, hosting more than 800,000 visitors a year. The hospitable Bretons open their town and hearts to all those seeking the blessings of St. Anne and the Blessed Virgin Mary.

ST. ANNE D'AURAY

"I am Anne, the mother of Mary."

The sleepy village of Keranna was populated by only fifty hard working Bretons in the early seventeenth century—farmers and laborers

Yves Nicolazic

who worked the land to support their families. One such laborer, Yves Nicolazic (1591-1645), was a devout man who daily put in many hours working with his team of oxen, but who also made time to recite his daily prayers. His small village had been a sacred place of veneration for St. Anne, the mother of Mary, since the sixth century when the first missionaries to Brittany had erected a chapel dedicated to the Virgin's mother. The chapel had since burned to the ground, and by 1600 the only remaining memory of St. Anne was the name of the village, Keranna or "village of Anne." Still, Yves said his prayers and kept a place for St. Anne in his heart.

One evening, in August of 1623, Yves and his brother-in-law Le Roux were taking their oxen to drink at the watering trough at the end of their long day. As they approached their usual watering hole, they were startled by the presence of a lady they had never seen before— a majestic lady filled

Altar of St. Anne

with a radiant light. The image said nothing to the two dumbfounded men, and soon disappeared into the twilight. Returning home to their families, the men did not speak much of the incident but wondered at the significance of the meeting.

Yves' life went on as usual for the next year, but in July of the following summer, a brilliantly illuminated figure appeared once again to the devout man. As Yves was working in his barn during the evening of July 25, 1624, the lady appeared to him again, this time carrying a candle. She spoke to him in the native Breton language saying, "I am Anne, the mother of Mary. There was a chapel here before that was dedicated to me. I ask you to build it again and to take care of it, because God wants me to be honored here." Again, Yves did not take the apparition very seriously and continued to go about his daily chores as before.

On the night of March 7, 1625 Yves was once again blessed with an apparition, this time in the form of the flame of a single candle. His neighbors also witnessed the appearance of this ethereal light, and they all followed it to the field of the Bocenno, the location of the original chapel dedicated to the mother of Mary. Here they uncovered in the ground an ancient statue of St. Anne and marveled at their uncanny discovery. Yves finally realized the true nature of his apparitions and committed himself to building a chapel dedicated to St. Anne.

But, before Yves could begin the new project, the Bishop of Vannes instituted a strict investigation of the apparitions, and the young laborer was questioned thoroughly about his visions. The Bishop finally acknowledged the validity of the apparitions and authorized the construction of the new chapel, subsequently appointing a community of Discalced Carmelite friars to serve as caretakers of the shrine. Yves moved from St. Anne d'Auray once the chapel was completed, but returned here to die on May 13, 1645 at the age of 54. He is buried in the new Basilica, and a statue of him stands inside the church.

The legacy of St. Anne is celebrated each year on July 26th, when pilgrims come from all over the world to Sainte-Anne d'Auray to receive the Great Pardon of St. Anne by climbing the Scala Santa on their knees.

THE BASILICA OF ST. ANNE
Basilique Sainte Anne

The chapel first built in 1625 was soon too small to handle the increasing number of pilgrims, so plans were made for a larger church. In 1865, the present church was begun in the same location as the original sixth century chapel. Built from 1865–1872, entirely of granite, the church is Gothic in style, with elements of Renaissance decoration. The church was declared a minor basilica in 1874. As you enter the Basilica, on your right are the remains of Yves Nicolazic, buried beneath the St. Yves altar. On your left as you enter, is the tomb of Pierre de Keriolet, a disbeliever who had led a corrupt lifestyle until visiting the shrine, and subsequently became a convert and later a priest.

The south arm of the transept, on the right of the main altar, contains the altar of St. Anne. The original wooden statue found by Yves Nicolazic was destroyed during the French Revolution, but another statue was carved in the saint's honor in 1825, and now resides in the niche of this altar. In the altar's plinth is a fragment of the original statue. A statue of Yves, dressed as a Breton of the seventeenth century, also stands at this altar. To the left of the altar is a reliquary containing a fragment of St. Anne's arm, a relic brought from Constantinople during the Crusades, and presented to the church by Louis XIII.

MONUMENTS AROUND THE BASILICA

There are several monuments and places of interest on the grounds surrounding the Basilica. On the left, as you face the Basilica, is the fountain where Yves had the first apparition of St. Anne. The fountain is capped by a statue of Anne and Mary, shown welcoming arriving pilgrims. Adjacent to the fountain is a memorial for the 240,000 Bretons who gave their lives in WWI. Across the large lawn from the front of the Basilica is the Scala Sancta, a stairway that was originally part of the first chapel, designed to connect galleries on each side of the chapel. Pilgrims would climb the stairs on their knees as a form of penance. When the new basilica was constructed, the Scala Sancta was dismantled stone by stone and reconstructed in its present location.

The fountain and Basilique Sainte Anne

THE HOUSE OF YVES NICOLAZIC

Across from the Tourist Information Office, and adjacent to the Basilica, is the house of Yves Nicolazic. The original home was destroyed by fire in 1903 and restored four years later. Although it contains no personal belongings of Nicolazic, you can get a feel for life in Keranna in the seventeenth century. There are two rooms, a chapel and living area. Look for a light switch (minuterie) in each room and watch your head for a very low doorway.

The reconstructed house of Yves Nicolazic

Where is the Basilica of St. Anne?
Où est la Basilique Sainte Anne?

Where is the house of Yves Nicolazic?
Où est la Maison de Nicolazic?

SHRINE INFORMATION

Shrine: The Basilica of St. Anne (Basilique Sainte Anne)

Address: 9, rue de Vannes/BP 16 / 56411 Ste Anne d'Auray/France

Phone: 33 (0)2 97 57 68 80 Fax: 33 (0)2 97 57 63 35

E-mail: basilique.ste.anne.auray@wanadoo.fr

Website: www.sanctuaire-ste-anne-dauray.com — Official website. Comprehensive website in French. Directions to St. Anne d'Auray under "Renseignements pratiques."

Quiet areas for meditation: The Basilica is quiet unless there is a celebration or other festivity.

English spoken: Rarely

Hours: Daily 8AM–10PM; July-August: 8AM–7PM.

Mass: Daily 9AM, 11, 6:30PM; Sun 9:30AM, 11; Sat 9AM, 11, 6:30PM. Refer to website under "Nouvelles et agenda" for more celebrations.

Feasts and festivities: March 7 — Anniversary of the discovery of the statue of St. Anne; April 14-21 —Week of the Saint; July 25-27— Festival of St. Anne; August 15 — The Assumption of the Virgin Mary.

Accessibility: The Basilica is accessible on the west (left) side.

Information office: Secrétariat de la Basilique Phone: 33 (0)2 97 57 68 80; Fax: 33 (0)2 97 57 63 35 Email: basilique.ste.anne.dauray@wandadoo.fr French only. Or, contact the tourist office below to communicate in English.

Tours: Guided visits to the Basilica are available for groups through the secretariat and through the Tourist Office in St. Anne d'Auray.

Bookstore: 9 rue de Vannes/ Sainte Anne D'Auray, inside the south side of the Sanctuary.

Recommended books: *Sainte-Anne d'Auray* by Jean Le Dorze is a guide available in tourist shops.

Lodging: None

Directions: The Basilica is on the north side of rue de Vannes in the center of town. Follow signs to "Sanctuaire de Sainte Anne." Don't confuse the larger nearby city of Auray with this small town of St. Anne d'Auray.

COMING AND GOING

SAINTE-ANNE D'AURAY

Car: Highway N165-E60 runs east and west from Vannes to Auray. East of Auray, take D17 or D17 Business Route north to Sainte-Anne d'Auray. Follow signs to the town center and "Sanctuaire de Sainte Anne."

Train: Direct link by TGV (high speed train) all year. SNCF station Auray; Paris-Auray, 3 hours 30 min.

Air: Airport Lorient Lann-Bihoué 45 minutes from St. Anne d'Auray. Phone: 33 (0)2 97 87 21 50. Take a taxi to the city.

TOURIST INFORMATION

✳ Office du Tourisme/12, place Nicolazic/56400 Sainte Anne d'Auray/France. Open from May to September. Phone: 33 (0)2 97 57 69 16 Fax: 33 (0)2 97 57 79 22 Email: tourisme.steanne@wanadoo.fr www.sainte-anne-auray.com French.

✳ Comité Départemental du Tourisme du Morbihan/Hôtel du department/BP 400/56009 Vannes cedex/France Phone: 33 (0)2 97 54 06 56 Fax: 33 (0)2 97 42 71 02 www.morbihan.com French.

Basilique Sainte Anne

WEBSITES

La Maison du Pèlerin www.lourdes-fr.com — Information about the major shrines in France and Europe, including St. Anne d'Auray.

Sanctuaire Sainte-Anne d'Auray www.sanctuaire-ste-anne-dauray. com — Official website for the Sanctuary of St. Anne d'Auray in French.

Villes Sanctuaries en France www.villes-sanctuaires.com — The Association of Shrine Towns in France with a suggested tour and contact information.

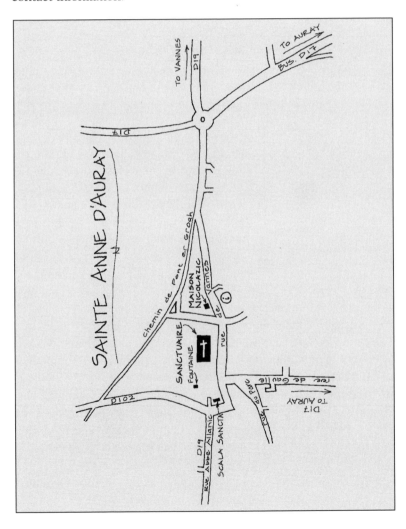

Burgundy

Bourgogne

Burgundy is the wealthiest region of France, due to the worldwide notoriety of its wines and gastronomical treats. Located in the central eastern part of the country, Burgundy consists of lazy rolling hills laced with fields and wine vineyards. The region is historically known for its religious culture, its spiritual wonders lying within the stonewalls of its Cistercian abbeys and medieval cathedrals. The abbeys of Cluny, Citeaux, Fontenay and Pontigny date from the eleventh and twelfth centuries, and are central to the long history of monasticism in the area. During its zenith, the Cistercian culture exerted a tremendous influence in the Western world but kept its roots in Burgundy. In the middle ages, the Basilica of St. Madeleine in Vézelay was one of the great places of pilgrimage as it was one of the primary starting points for pilgrims taking the road to Santiago de Compostela, in Spain. Today, the spirituality of the region is alive in the community of Taizé, in the Sacred Heart chapels of Paray-le-Monial, and at the crypt of St. Bernadette in Nevers.

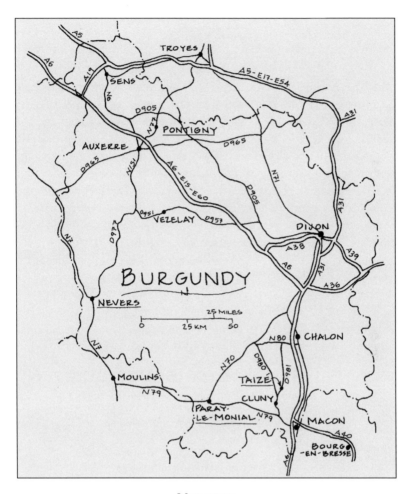

NEVERS
St. Bernadette Soubirous

PARAY-LE-MONIAL
St. Margaret Mary of Alocoque
St. Claude de la Colombiere

PONTIGNY
St. Edmund Rich

TAIZÉ
The Taizé Community

Nevers

Population 46,000

As the Loire River winds through the gentle landscape of Burgundy, it joins the Nièvre and Allier Rivers at the city of Nevers. The city center is located on the north bank of the Loire and is punctuated by meandering streets lined with a mixture of modern and ancient architecture. One of the stopping points on the road to Santiago de Compostela in Spain, Nevers has welcomed pilgrims for the last eight centuries. The twentieth century Cathedral St. Cyr-St. Juliette with its modern stained glass windows, and the nearby Ducal Palace, are the major points of interest in the historical center of town, and are typical examples of period architecture. This center is dotted with cafes and shops, many of the latter featuring the fine faïence pottery for which the city is known. As a whole, the city is another nice little town in Burgundy; what makes it special is the presence of the relics of one of the great saints of France—St. Bernadette. Her relics are found in the Chapel of Espace Bernadette Soubirous Nevers, a short walk northwest of the city center. St. Bernadette lived there her final thirteen years after leaving Lourdes. (pronounce Nevers: Neh-vay.)

ST. BERNADETTE SOUBIROUS

Sainte Bernadette Soubirous 1844–1879

*"Come! We must learn to do everything for
God alone in order to deserve Heaven."*

The appearance of the Virgin Mary at Lourdes is one of many apparitions in the history of spirituality. In each instance, there is necessarily someone to serve as a channel, and at Lourdes, Bernadette Soubirous was that special soul. In most accounts of apparitions, the person receiving the vision fades into the background of the story because the message of the vision is of prime importance, not the messenger. What makes the story of Bernadette so intriguing is that she left behind her experiences at Lourdes and became a highly venerated saint on her own merits. She was not canonized because she witnessed the apparitions, but due to the life she led and the souls she touched. She was a living example of absolute devotion to God, for she took all that God placed before her and saw it as a blessing—whether it was a vision of Our Lady, a harsh reprimand from a superior, or severe pain and suffering. Her willing acceptance of all circumstances was based on the understanding that all things of this temporal world will pass, but our life in God is eternal. As Our Lady told her, "I do not promise to make you happy in this life, but in the next."

Bernadette's life began very inauspiciously. She was born on January 7, 1844 in the small town of Lourdes as the first child of François and Louise Soubirous. Louise would eventually bear eight more children, though only four would survive to adulthood. At the time of Bernadette's birth, the family lived in a flourmill, which they worked for their sustenance. Before Bernadette was even a year old, her family life became disrupted when her mother severely burned herself while tending the fire. She was unable to continue nursing her ten-month-old child, and arranged to send Bernadette to the nearby village of Bartrès to be wet-nursed by a friend of the family who had just lost a baby. Bernadette remained at Bartrès for ten months before returning to her own family.

Life in the Soubirous family was not easy, for the flourmill was often unprofitable and illness frequently plagued the family. Young Bernadette contracted cholera at the age of two, and shortly thereafter had a bout with tuberculosis. She also developed a chronic asthma, which would cause her much suffering throughout her life. Bernadette survived all these trials of the body, but as a result she was very small,

The reliquary of St. Bernadette

looking much younger than her age. As she grew older, the other girls of Bernadette's age were in school and taking catechism classes, but she had to remain home most of the time to care for her younger siblings and help with family chores. Bernadette was a bright and cheerful child, but her academic development was much neglected, and she longed to study and prepare for her first communion.

In 1857, the Soubirous family was sinking ever deeper into poverty as millwork was unavailable, and both mother and father had to find day work to feed the children. The entire family was now living in a single room—a dark, damp place that had been a dungeon. In their despair, they sent the thirteen-year-old Bernadette back to Bartrès to work for her old friends and help care for their children. It was hoped she would also be able to attend school and prepare for her first communion. As it worked out, Bernadette became a shepherdess for the family—tending the lambs and spending most of her time alone in the

pastures. It was a solitary life for the young girl, but also a time when she could be alone with God. She built a little altar at the foot of a tree and prayed often while she watched over her flock. Still, a girl of her age gets homesick, so she

Replica of the Lourdes grotto in Nevers

returned home in January of 1858, just one month before she ventured to the grotto at Massabielle and first experienced her Lady. (Refer to the chapter on the Midi-Pyrenees and Lourdes to read the story of the apparitions of Bernadette.)

For five months Bernadette was blessed with visions of the Blessed Virgin Mary—eighteen apparitions in total. With each one she experienced an ecstatic state. Bernadette admitted, "When one has seen Her, one cannot love the world." Though transformed by these raptures, Bernadette still had to function in the "real" world. She had to withstand the condemnation of the local authorities, the threat of imprisonment, doubt from her own church and constant harassment from all those wanting to see her and touch her.

Bernadette's life became that of a modern superstar—everyone literally wanted a piece of her. In one instance, she was surrounded by curiosity seekers who began to cut at her veil to procure "relics." Perhaps her most difficult ordeals were the incessant interviews she held with members of the clergy and aristocracy who wished to hear her story directly, and who would often doubt and question her. Bernadette later told a confidant, "God alone knows how I hate presenting myself to bishops, priests and people of high society." In one of these interviews, a parish priest questioned her for two hours, and then demanded that Bernadette give him the rosary she had used while praying with Our Lady. She obeyed. He then demanded her to give up her scapula, but Bernadette respectfully refused. Though she had a right to feel the indignity of her treatment, Bernadette always remained calm and poised, with a humble spirit, charming all those she met with her open sincerity and honesty.

To escape notoriety, Bernadette became a boarder at the Hospice of Lourdes, which was run by the Sisters of Nevers. It was two years after the apparitions, and she was ready for some peace. The continual interviews were still a part of her life, but she was able to have a little time to herself. At the Hospice she attended school, worked in the kitchen and performed various other duties. She was happy being just one of the school children, and finally had the opportunity to develop her skills in French, reading and writing. But her favorite activity was visiting the grotto. Twice a week, a Sister would take her to Massa-bielle for prayers and meditation, and Bernadette would kneel in her usual place and pray deeply to her Lady. There were few people coming to the grotto at this time, as the chapel was still under construction, so Bernadette was able to pray without being disturbed. This was the last period of her life in which she directly enjoyed the blessings of the grotto.

Bernadette continued to battle her weak body and was so ill from pneumonia in April of 1862, that she was given last rites and expected to perish during the night. Coughing up blood and experiencing great pain, she finally asked for blessed water from the grotto. A few small droplets were trickled down her swollen throat and she was instantly relieved. These constant bouts with illness also kept Bernadette from participating in many activities, including the installation of the statue of Our Lady at Massabielle in 1864. When asked if she liked the statue, Bernadette said, "Having seen Our Lady Herself, I find no statue of the Virgin beautiful."

By now, Bernadette was over twenty years old and it was time for her to decide what to do with her life. Since the time of her visions she had wanted to become a nun, but was never clear as to what order would suit her needs and temperament. Sisters and priests were ever approaching her to join their community, but she always felt it was because of her notoriety that she was sought out. She wished to become a nun, but one of complete obscurity. In 1864, she met with the Bishop of Nevers and finally decided to join the Sisters of Charity at Nevers so that she could serve the poor and nurse the sick. However, physical weakness kept her from leaving Lourdes then, and for two years she fought to regain her vitality. Finally, in the summer of 1866, she was ready to leave Lourdes for her new home. Her last public act in Lourdes was attending the consecration of the crypt and a Mass at the grotto in May of that year. When she left for Nevers on July fourth, she knew she would never return to her earthly birthplace or the site of her spiritual awakening.

The Convent of St. Gildard's at Nevers was the Mother House for the Sisters of Charity. Their mission was to work in the local hospitals, serving the poor and needy. Soon after Bernadette arrived, she took the religious habit and was given the name Sister Marie Bernarde. It was clear to her from the beginning that she would be treated as no one special—simply another child of God. Just what she had prayed for! Bernadette was permitted to tell a gathering of her sisters the story of the apparitions one time only, and then was ordered to never again mention those events unless requested by a superior. The Mistress of Novices was very hard on Bernadette, for she did not want Bernadette to fall into the trap of feeling special. Although this was difficult at first, Bernadette eventually welcomed the treatment with understanding and acceptance. When she was reproved or humiliated by her Superior, she would say, "I have just been given a sweet."

Illness still haunted Bernadette's life. Within three months of her arrival at Nevers, she had a nearly fatal asthma attack. She again received last rites and, with special dispensation, took the vows of her order. The next morning she related to a sister who was surprised to see her alive, "I am better. Almighty God did not want me; when I reached the gates of heaven, he told me to go away; it is too soon." Physical suffering was the hallmark of Bernadette's life for it was her way of purifying herself and helping others. Her charge from the Blessed Virgin was to do penance and pray for sinners. As she said to one sister, "My job is to be ill." And to another, "Suffering passes, but to have borne suffering remains."

A prayerful life was equally Bernadette's mission and she practiced it with zeal, often remaining in the chapel long after Mass to meditate deeply. She would pray for sinners and unite her consciousness with that of her Lord. "I imagine that Our Lady herself is giving me the Child Jesus. I receive Him … I speak to Him and He speaks to me." When speaking of prayer and inner contemplation she said, "We must receive Our Lord with love and make him feel at home in our hearts, for then He is bound to pay the rent."

Bernadette's poor health came and went over the years, so at times she was in charge of the sick room, and at other times, she was the patient. Through all her trials, one thing remained constant—her sweet humility. "I was able to admire her deep piety, her extraordinary evenness of temper, her childlike simplicity and above all her profound humility," related a fellow sister. As the years passed, Bernadette became more of a patient than a caregiver, and finally became a permanent resident of the infirmary. Beside severe asthma, a tumor found root in her right knee and completely de-voured the flesh. To say it was intensely painful is to put it mildly. She had no painkillers—nothing but pure faith to combat the anguish. But she did so with grace. When the

Espace Bernadette Soubirous Convent

pain became too intense, she offered it to God crying, "Oh, my God! I offer them to you! Oh, my God! I love you!"

As death approached, Bernadette had all the pictures of saints and loved ones removed from her curtain around her bed, saying, "He is all I need," while pointing to a crucifix. In the days following Easter of 1879, her suffering grew ever more intense, and she relinquished herself to her Beloved. Lying on her deathbed she called out, "Oh! My God! I love you with all my heart, with all my soul and with all my strength." She held her crucifix and slowly and devoutly kissed the five wounds. Then, raising her eyes to heaven, she stretched out her arms as if on the cross herself and cried out, "My God!" As soon as her spirit left the body, the face of Bernadette became young and peaceful. At last she was finished with earthly suffering and could live in the arms of her Blessed Lady.

Bernadette, Sister Marie Bernarde, passed on April 16, 1879 and was buried in the St. Joseph chapel on the grounds of St. Gildard. Her body remained buried in the chapel until 1909. At that time, the corpse was exhumed and inspected as part of the initial steps in the process of canonization. It was discovered that her body was incorrupt—still in perfectly supple condition. Sister Marie Bernarde was declared venerable in 1913 when the body was again examined and found to still be incorrupt. In 1925, for the final time, her body was examined, relics were taken, and a wax covering was made for her

face and hands. In June, she was proclaimed Blessed, and on August 3rd, her body was transferred to the Espace Bernadette Soubirous Chapel and placed in a glass urn. This is where it remains and is venerated by pilgrims to this day. On

Espace Bernadette Soubirous Chapel

December 8, 1933, Sister Marie Bernarde Soubirous was canonized as a saint.

ESPACE BERNADETTE SOUBIROUS CHAPEL

The Espace Bernadette Soubirous Chapel was originally constructed as the Mother Center for the Sisters of Charity in 1850, and was built over the ruins of an ancient abbey—the resting place of St. Gildard of the seventh century. The Convent, now known as Espace Bernadette Soubirous Nevers, has always maintained its position as the Mother Center, and was home to Bernadette from 1866 until her death in 1879.

After her death, St. Bernadette was buried in the St. Joseph Chapel within the Convent's grounds, but her body was moved to the Chapel of St. Gildard and placed in a glass urn in August of 1925. This was shortly after she was declared a Blessed. Her incorrupt body has resided in this urn ever since, and it is visited by half a million pilgrims every year. This side chapel is small and intimate—a quiet place to pray and meditate on the life of the saint. Tour groups of pilgrims frequent the chapel, but early morning is always a time of limited activity.

The Espace Bernadette Soubirous is encircled by several acres of beautifully maintained grounds and has many private areas for meditation. The tiny Chapel of St. Joseph, where Bernadette was initially buried, is located directly behind the main building, in the lower garden area. In the far right corner of this garden area, by the outside stonewalls, is a statue of the Virgin Mary—Our Lady of the Waters. This is the statue that Bernadette declared was the most like the Lady in her vision, and she would often go here to pray. Just outside the Chapel is a scaled-down replica of the Massabielle grotto of Lourdes and a statue of the young Bernadette. This is a gathering place for pilgrims and presents an opportunity to experience the power of Lourdes. A museum and bookstore are next to the Chapel and worth a visit. The Museum has many personal articles of Bernadette's and the bookstore has books and brochures in English.

The Espace Bernadette Soubirous Chapel is one of the most powerful places in France, attracting over 500,000 visitors a year. It is one of our favorites because we were able to stay in the convent where St. Bernadette lived, walk the halls she walked, pray in the gardens where she prayed, and meditate quietly in the chapel with her relics. If you are looking for a place for spiritual retreat, this is an ideal location.

Where is the Sanctuary of St. Bernadette?
Où est le Sanctuaire Sainte Bernadette?

Where is the crypt of St. Bernadette?
Où est la crypte de Sainte Bernadette?

SHRINE INFORMATION

Shrine: Espace Bernadette Soubirous Nevers

Address: 34, rue Saint-Gildard/58000 Nevers/France

Phone: 33 (0)3 86 71 99 50 **Fax:** 33 (0)3 86 71 99 51

E-mail: ebsn@wanadoo.fr

Website: www.sainte-bernadette-nevers.com — Official website

Quiet areas for meditation: The chapel containing the body of St. Bernadette; Our Lady of the Waters in the garden; the grounds in good weather.

English spoken: Typically from May to September; Occasionally in the winter.

Hours: April through October, Daily 7AM–12:30PM; 1:30PM–7:30; November through March, 7:30AM–12PM; 2PM-6.

Mass: Daily 8:00AM, 11:30; Sun 10AM.

Feasts and festivities: February 11 — Our Lady of Lourdes; February 18 — Feast of St. Bernadette; April 16 — Anniversary of St. Bernadette's death; July 7 — Anniversary of St. Bernadette's arrival at Saint-Gildard.

Accessibility: The Chapel and Convent lodging are accessible.

Tours: By reservation between May and September, Sisters and laypeople are available to guide groups on a walk in the footsteps of Bernadette as a spiritual endeavor (not a sight-seeing tour). These guided groups will visit, among other places, the Chapel of the Holy Cross where St. Bernadette died, and the welcome chapel, formerly the novitiate room. For individuals, there is a welcome packet at the reception desk with the *Walk in Bernadette's Steps* booklet.

Bookstore: Next to the Information sign, there is a bookstore with brochures and books in English.

Recommended books: *Saint Bernadette Soubirous* by Abbé François Trochu

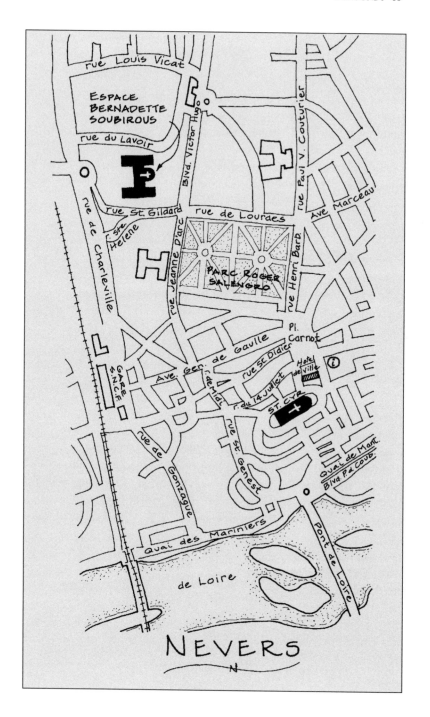

NEVERS

N

is published by Tan Books & Publishers. *Some of Bernadette's Sayings,* published by the Saint-Gildard Convent, is available at their bookstore among other books in English.

Lodging: Pilgrim lodging is available for individuals or groups. They stress that it is not a hotel, but available for retreat. They have two hundred rooms with showers/toilets down the hall and five dining rooms. There are also conference rooms available. The Gîte Saint-Michel is a separate building provided to accommodate up to thirty young people. Check-in for lodging is at the Information desk inside.

Directions: Espace Bernadette Soubirous Nevers is across from the northwest corner of Parc Roger Salengro, at the corner of rue St. Gildard and boulevard Victor Hugo. It is north of the train station (Gare SNCF), enclosed by walls and easy to miss. Park on boulevard Victor Hugo and enter the small gate on the right of the large gate, or go around the corner and enter on rue St. Gildard. If you are staying there, once you check in, they will tell you how to enter the convent with your car for overnight parking.

COMING AND GOING

NEVERS

Car: From the North take A77-N7 and exit #33 at sign for town-centre. From the South take N7 from the town of Moulins and follow signs for Paris, then Fourchambault that is north of Nevers. Exit at #34 and follow signs to town-centre and Saint Bernadette's Shrine. The Convent is about half a mile from the train station (Gare SNCF). Nevers is 144 miles (232 km) from Paris; 143 miles (230 km) from Lyon; 112 miles (180 km) from Dijon.

Train: From Paris Gare-de-Lyon station take Paris-Marseille via Clermont-Ferrand; Nantes-Lyon via Saincaize. The train station (Gare SNCF) is half a mile from Espace Bernadette Soubirous Nevers. SNCF Phone: (0)8 92 35 35 35 Taxi: (0)6 87 03 08 07.

Bus: For bus hours call the STUNIV 33 (0)3 86 59 72 00.

Plane: Nevers-Fourchambault is a small airport. Phone: Air Normandie 33 (0)2 32 85 38 53.

TOURIST INFORMATION

✲ Office de Tourisme/Palais Ducal – BP 818/ 58008 Nevers cedex/France Phone: 33 (0)3 86 68 46 00 Fax: 33 (0)3 86 68 45 98 E-mail: contact@tnevers-tourisme.com www.ville-nevers.fr French.

WEBSITES

Espace Bernadette Soubirous Nevers www.sainte-bernadette-nevers.com — Official website of the Sanctuary.

La Maison du Pèlerin www.lourdes-fr.com — Information about the major shrines in France and Europe, including Nevers.

Villes Sanctuaries en France www.villes-sanctuaires.com — The Association of Shrine Towns in France with a suggested tour and contact information.

MORE ST. BERNADETTE SHRINES IN FRANCE

LOURDES
Sanctuary of Our Lady of Lourdes

Lourdes is where St. Bernadette was born and where she witnessed the eighteen apparitions of Our Lady of Lourdes. It is in the southwest part of France, and is one of the largest pilgrimage centers in the world. In planning your pilgrimage, it would be ideal to combine Nevers and Lourdes. Refer to the Midi-Pyrenees chapter under Lourdes for more information.

Paray-le-Monial
Population 10,000

Located in the south of Burgundy, Paray-le-Monial has been a magnet for religious orders in various historic periods. Its earliest religious structures were built around a Benedictine monastery in 970 A.D. In the twelfth century, the Romanesque basilica, now named the Sacred Heart Basilica, was built as a smaller version of Cluny III. From Pope Pius IX's visit in 1850, to the first pilgrimage in 1873, the Chapel of the Apparitions began to attract ever-increasing numbers of pilgrims to Paray-le-Monial. Following St. Margaret Mary Alacoque's canonization in 1920, the Sacred Heart Basilica has been second only to

Lourdes in attracting pilgrims to France. The town offers little for the general tourist, but for the 500,000 spiritual travelers a year, Paray does not disappoint, featuring enough sites and activities for a full one-day visit. However, two days would be preferable, to allow time to meditate and pray in the different chapels and in the Park of the Chaplains.

ST. MARGARET MARY ALACOQUE
Sainte Marguerite Marie Alacoque 1647–1690

"I seem to be as a little drop of water in the ocean of the Sacred Heart."

Devotion to God comes in many forms, and these various forms evolve through the deep commitment of disciples and their personal relationships with God. Sometimes, these forms of devotion become universally known and practiced, as in the case of St. Margaret Mary of Alacoque. Devotion to the Sacred Heart of Jesus was central to the life of St. Margaret Mary, and developed over years of intensely personal contact with her Lord, through numerous visions and frequent occurrences of inner communication. Her mystical life was

one of both joy and sorrow, as she reveled in the peace of soul communion with Jesus Christ, yet suffered great physical torments while paying for her sins and taking on the sins of others.

Born in eastern Burgundy, in the small town of Janots, Margaret was the fifth of seven children born to a wealthy notary and his wife. From her earliest recollections, the young child was aware of her love for the Blessed Virgin

St. Margaret Mary Alocoque

and Her son. Desiring at the tender age of four to give her life to God, the girl was drawn to promise, "Oh my God, I consecrate to Thee my purity, and I make Thee a vow of perpetual chastity." Margaret was too young to comprehend the meaning of her vow, but it was something she felt called to pronounce from the depths of her heart. In her eighth year, Margaret's father died, and she was sent to the convent of the Poor Clares in Charolles to receive an education. Here she witnessed the piety of the nuns and longed to follow their example. The Sisters were likewise impressed by the devout young girl and allowed her to take her first communion when she was only nine.

Two years later, Margaret became very ill and was bedridden for four years. After the first two years she was sent home from the convent, and convalesced with her family. No cause or cure was determined and the sickly girl was left to suffer on her own. Finally, she prayed to the Blessed Virgin and promised to become "one of her daughters" if she would institute a cure. "Scarcely had I made this vow, than I was cured and taken anew under the protection of Our Lady. She made herself so completely Mistress of my heart ... teaching me how to do the Will of God."

Now fifteen years old and living at home, Margaret was under the rule of her family—governed by an aunt and uncle who had commandeered the estate of her father. The family was very hard on Margaret and her mother, treating them as servants. She had to seek permission for every action and was in constant conflict with her keepers. The most difficult situation was their refusal to allow her to go to Mass, as they suspected her of going off to meet boys. This caused Margaret much pain, and she would hide in the garden and cry day and night without eating. Though often dejected from her inability to attend Mass, Margaret dove more deeply into the inner reaches of her soul and there, freely communicated with the Blessed Virgin and Jesus. She gave up her free will to be guided by the Divine Will, and inwardly received answers to all her yearnings.

The family situation improved when Margaret was seventeen, as her elder brother came of age and gained control of the family estate. When she became an eligible young woman of twenty, Margaret was persistently pressured by her mother to seek marriage. She flirted with these wishes, but finally realized that her true calling was that of a religious. Still fighting the will of her family, Margaret ultimately was guided to join the "Holy Marys" at the Visitation convent at Paray-le-Monial. When entering the parlor of the convent for the first time, she heard an inner voice say, "It is here I would have thee to be." She left her family behind and entered the convent on June 12, 1671, at the age of twenty-four.

Life in the monastery was a blessing for Sister Margaret Mary, but not in the usual way. Margaret Mary was a mystic in the true sense of the word, for she had frequent mystical experiences of communicating with Christ and the Blessed Virgin, often hearing their voices and receiving their guidance. Upon taking the final vows of her profession in 1672, Margaret Mary heard these words from Christ, "I will make my abode in thee that I may be able to hold familiar converse with thee." She later wrote of this incident: "From this time forward, He allowed me continually to enjoy His divine presence… I saw and felt Him close to me, and heard His voice much better than if it had been with my bodily senses." These episodes became apparent to her fellow Sisters and she was often humiliated and ridiculed for her behavior. They felt it was improper for a simple nun to receive such graces, and her Superior would openly deride her. But for Margaret Mary, the humiliation was a blessing, for she saw it as a means of relating to the humiliations and sufferings of Jesus.

She was also mocked for her inability to perform verbal prayers with her Sisters, but for Margaret Mary, her silent prayers in the presence of Christ were much more powerful and fulfilling. "I know only what He had taught me concerning prayer," she wrote, "namely; to abandon myself to all His holy inspirations, whenever I was able to shut myself up in some little corner alone with Him."

Mystical experiences with Christ continued for Margaret Mary and, in 1673, they began to clarify her specific mission. Late in the evening of December 27, Margaret Mary was praying alone before the Blessed Sacrament when Christ appeared to her and opened his glowing heart before her saying, "My Divine Heart is so full of love for all, and for you in particular, that it is unable to contain within itself the flames of its burning love. Its needs must be spread abroad by means of yourself, and so manifest itself to all to enrich them with the treasures this heart contains." He asked Margaret Mary for her heart, then took it and placed it within the glowing furnace of His own heart. He finally placed it back in her breast, saying, "My well-beloved, I give thee a precious token of My love," and named her "beloved disciple of My sacred Heart."

Margaret Mary had several more revelations concerning the Sacred Heart of Jesus over the next eighteen months. Christ told her of the contempt and ingratitude he received from mankind when He offered all His love and compassion to them. He asked Margaret Mary to lovingly commune with Him specifically on the first Friday of every month, and for an hour every Thursday evening to commemorate His time of agony and abandonment in Gethsemane. This she did faithfully with great fervor and was witness to the Sacred Heart as a "resplendent sun" which united with her own heart. But she also felt the pain, for she so deeply communed with the spirit of Christ that she experienced His dire

Reliquary of St. Margaret Mary of Alocoque

pain and suffering. But to Margaret Mary, this was all a blessing, for she lived that much closer to her Lord. During the final apparition regarding the Sacred Heart, Jesus asked that a feast of reparation be celebrated on the first Friday after the octave of Corpus Christi. This has become the modern feast of the Sacred Heart.

Though Margaret Mary received the visions of Christ with an open heart, her fellow Sisters had varying reactions to her experiences. Many believed in the sanctity of the revelations, while others were skeptical and thought she was full of self-importance and only desirous of attention. On one occasion, after experiencing the burning heart in her own breast, Margaret Mary fell very ill with a fever. Her Superior,

Mother de Saumaise, questioned the authenticity of the visions and told Margaret Mary that she must be healed of her fever in order to convince the Mistress of the truth of her message. Margaret Mary prayed and was instantly healed, for Christ always stressed to her the importance of obedience and following the commands of her superiors.

To help verify the validity of Margaret Mary's call for creation of the new devotion to the Sacred Heart, two visiting theologians were invited to interview her. After hours of grueling questioning, they declared that Margaret Mary was simply delusional and that the visions were not from God. This threw Margaret Mary into despair and turmoil, for she knew the truth of her experiences, but also realized how extraordinary they were. She began questioning her own sanity, suffered greatly from doubt, and had many temptations from Satan. But God promised her that he would send one of his servants to comfort her and support her in spreading the doctrine of the Sacred Heart. This servant was Reverend Father de la Colombiere, a priest who was Superior at the local Jesuit school. Margaret Mary had met the Father years before, but now he was assigned as confessor to the

St. Claude de la Colombiere and St. Margaret Mary

Visitation Sisters at Paray-le-Monial. As Margaret Mary heard him speak, she heard inwardly, "He it is I send you."

After several meetings, Margaret Mary confided completely in the gentle priest, telling him of all her mystical experiences, along with her fears and doubts. Father la Colombiere felt the truth in Margaret Mary's story, and became her staunch supporter and a primary advocate of the celebration of the

Sacred Heart of Jesus. She said of the Father, "He taught me to cherish the gifts of God and to receive His communications with faith and humility." The Father and Margaret Mary developed a very close relationship, for they were equally dedicated to the Sacred Heart, but the Father was soon sent to England to act as priest for the Duchess of York. Here he spread the message of the Sacred Heart, but was eventually forced to leave the country. He returned to Paray-le-Monial, where he died in 1682. (For more information, refer to the biography of St. la Colombiere later in this chapter.)

Margaret Mary remained at the convent and continued to commune frequently with her Beloved, although she had no more direct visions concerning the Sacred Heart. The years were spent in a mixture of bliss and suffering, for the Lord blessed her with great inner joy, but He also asked her to take on the expiation of the sins of her fellow Sisters. This she accomplished through austerities and mortifications. As a result, she was often ill, unable to eat or drink. But still, she took on all that was given to her, for she lived to do God's will. During these trials, there was still much resistance to Margaret Mary within her Order, especially because of her acts of expiation. The reaction of her fellow Sisters is understandable, for they were openly confronted with their shortcomings and told to go to confession. Furthermore, this judgment came from a junior nun who had been in the convent for only five years!

In 1683, the atmosphere at the Visitation convent changed dramatically as Mother Merlin became Superior, and appointed Margaret Mary as Assistant Superior with approval of the Order. Margaret Mary served well in her new role, and was also named mistress of the novices. Everyone in the convent knew the secret of her devotion to the Sacred Heart, but the Sisters did not openly practice it. Soon, Margaret Mary introduced the devotion to her novices, and in 1685, they privately celebrated the feast. The following year, on June 21st, the whole house participated in celebratory devotion to the Sacred Heart. Just two years later, a chapel was built in Paray-le-Monial dedicated to the Sacred Heart, and the feast was consequently celebrated by other houses of the Visitation Sisters, and at other religious houses throughout France.

Margaret Mary continued to serve her sisters as Assistant Superior, until she fell deathly ill in the autumn of 1690. The doctors did not think she was seriously ill, but Margaret Mary said, "I shall not live, for I have nothing left to suffer." The following week, on October 17th, she asked for the last sacraments and said, "I need nothing but God, and to lose myself in the heart of Jesus." While receiving the last rites, she left her body with the name of Jesus on her lips. By now, devotion to the Sacred Heart of Jesus was celebrated throughout the region. Today, it is celebrated around the world and lives on as a significant devotional practice that brings many souls closer to the living presence of Jesus. Margaret Mary was beatified in 1864 and was canonized in 1920.

CHAPEL OF THE VISITATION
Chapelle de la Visitation

During the years of 1673, 1674 and 1675, Christ appeared to St. Margaret Mary in this Chapel. Over the front door, the inscription reads, "In this church Our Lord revealed His Heart to Saint Margaret Mary."

The Chapel of the Visitation was originally built in 1633 in a simple style to serve the nuns. Through the years, the original building was altered many times. In the aftermath of the Revolution, starting in 1792, it was used as a dwelling and warehouse. The nuns returned in 1823, enlarging the building. A complete restoration, retaining the original walls and roof, was completed in 1856. Another renovation was made in 1926, to create a side chapel for the saint's body to the right of the main altar. The arch over the saint's reliquary quotes Jesus' promise to Margaret Mary, "I make you the heir to my Heart." Other words spoken to St. Margaret Mary during her visions are displayed on the walls and crypt. St. Margaret Mary's bones are underneath a wax figure in the glass reliquary.

The new main altar was consecrated in 1965, with a wrought iron screen to the right of the altar allowing the cloistered Sisters of the Visitation to participate more fully in the Mass. The nuns, currently numbering twenty-five, sometimes lead the pilgrims in prayer from here. Inside the concealed nuns' choir, behind the crypt, is the incorrupt brain of St. Margaret Mary, preserved in a beautiful reliquary. The fresco on the wall behind the altar was completed by Luc Barbier in 1973 and represents the second apparition. In this apparition, Jesus revealed his Heart surrounded by a "devouring fire" and asked for a feast to be dedicated to his Sacred Heart. The painter integrated saints of the Order and apostles of the Heart of Jesus into the fresco, including St. Francis of Assisi, whom Christ named to Margaret Mary as her spiritual guide.

The nuns of the Visitation Order, founded by St. Francis de Sales, follow the rule of St. Augustine. Except for the period after the Revolution, the nuns have been in this location since the monastery was built in 1632. St. Margaret Mary entered the convent in 1671. The Convent garden where some of the visions took place is only open to the public on the joint feast day of the Sacred Heart and Margaret Mary (Oct. 16). The pilgrim's tour of the convent includes the hazel tree grove where Margaret Mary talked with Jesus while she tended a donkey and its foal, and the courtyard called "cour des Séraphins" where she experienced a vision of the heart of Jesus at the center of

Chapelle de la Visitation

flames of love, surrounded by seraphim singing. There is also the chapel built in honor of the Sacred Heart in 1688 where St. Margaret Mary went into ecstasy while attending the dedication.

THE BASILICA OF THE SACRED HEART
Basilique du Sacré-Cœur

The Romanesque Basilica of the Sacred Heart was constructed in the eleventh century, built to replicate Cluny II and III. The building is a study in simplicity, with its use of classical elements such as flat, fluted pilasters typical of Cluniac design, and the tall arcade with its small clerestory windows. Pope Pious IX named it the Basilica of the Sacred Heart in 1875, but today its value is more historical than theological, as the real treasures of Paray are found in the shrines and chapels directly associated with St. Margaret Mary Alacoque. The Basilica is open from 9AM-7PM.

PARK OF THE CHAPLAINS
Parc des Chapelains

Behind the Basilica of the Sacred Heart is a park with an outdoor chapel, Diorama and shelter for pilgrims. At the entrance to the park, on the left, is the Chapel of the Relics that offers a 23-minute video in English (donations accepted), and a museum with mementos of St. Margaret Mary's. It is open from 9:30AM-12PM and 2-6PM. Phone: 33 (0)3 85 81 62 22. The Chapel of St. John (Chapelle St. Jean) is above the Chapel of the Relics and is a quiet place to pray and meditate. The chapel is dedicated to St. John because the first apparition of Christ to St. Margaret Mary took place on the feast day of St. John, Dec. 27, 1673, and also because Christ invited Margaret Mary to rest in his Heart, as he had invited St. John to do at the Last Supper.

ST. CLAUDE DE LA COLOMBIERE
Saint Claude de la Colombière 1641–1682

We are all instruments of God, but some of us have very specific missions to accomplish within God's plan. The mission of Claude de la Colombière was to help proliferate the practice of devotion to the Sacred Heart of Jesus, and specifically to act as confessor, friend, and confidant to St. Margaret Mary Alacoque. The success of his mission has resulted in the widespread use of this sincere devotional practice.

Claude was born into a family of French nobility near Lyons, and was well educated from an early age. He chose the religious life at eighteen when he was ready to attend university, and entered the Society of Jesus in Lyons. His novitiate was spent in Avignon, where he went on to teach grammar and the humanities at the city's college. While in Avignon, Claude was called upon to speak at the celebration of the canonization of St. Francis de Sales. His stirring sermon touched many hearts and promoted his image as a magnificent preacher.

Paris has historically been the center of intellectual life in France, so Claude was sent there to complete his theological studies. He was awarded the great honor of being the personal tutor to the children of a highly placed minister, but he unwittingly offended the magistrate, and was forced to return to his home province. Once again in Avignon, Claude was appointed preacher to the college church in 1673, and became widely known for his inspirational sermons and dissertations.

Prior to his final vows in February of 1675, Claude had the

St. Claude de la Colombiere

opportunity to take a month of reclusive retreat, during which he made several personal commitments to his spiritual life. He spent his days meditating on the life of Jesus and upon his own life as a loving disciple. During this retreat, on his thirty-third birthday, Claude consecrated himself with new zeal to his Lord Jesus, and specifically to the devotion of the Sacred Heart. He wrote in his spiritual diary, "It seems right, dear Lord, that I should begin to live in Thee and for Thee alone, at the age at which Thou didst die for all and for me in particular." At this time, he also took solemn personal vows to live by the very strictest interpretation of the Rule of the Jesuit Order.

Two months after his spiritual renewal and final vows of profession, Father la Colombiere was appointed as Superior of the Jesuit house in Paray-le-Monial. This seemed a strange appointment at the time, for there were only a handful of fathers at the house, but the true mission of Father Colombiere was soon to be revealed. Included in his duties were ministerial instructions and confessions for the Sisters at the Visitation Convent, where he was introduced to Sister Margaret

Mary of Alacoque. (Refer to the biography of St. Margaret Mary earlier in this chapter.)

At the time of their meeting, Sister Margaret Mary was in deep turmoil, for other theologians had recently discounted her mystical visions of Christ and many religious people considered her to be delusional. Upon hearing the Father speak, Margaret Mary was much relieved to hear an inner voice say, "He it is I send you." Father la Colombiere immediately felt the sincerity and depth of the visionary and the validity of her mystical experiences. He found in Margaret Mary a soul mate who was similarly devoted to the Sacred Heart. Father la Colombiere and Sister Margaret Mary developed a close spiritual relationship and were mutual supporters. The Sister said of Father la Colombiere, "He opened out my heart and showed me its depths, good and bad. He consoled me greatly and told me not to fear God's leading as long as I was obedient."

Father la Colombiere did not remain long in Paray, for he was soon sent to London, where he was appointed the preacher to the

Chapelle la Colombière

Duchess of York. The Duchess and her husband were Catholics in the then Protestant country of England, so the job of Father la Colombiere was complicated. His skills as an orator became well known as he fervently preached on the qualities of the Sacred Heart and, subsquently, converted many souls. His notoriety and Catholic allegiance also brought upon him the wrath of the King, and he was soon sent to prison, accused of conspiring to overthrow the monarchy. Fortunately for Father la Colombiere, he was also well known to Louis XIV of France. Through the French King's influence he was eventually released from prison and exiled from England.

Returning to his native land in 1679, Father la Colombiere attempted to continue his preaching, but his body was too weak from his time in prison. He was sent to Lyon to regain his strength, and then to Paray-le-Monial, where he spent time with his fellow disciple, Sister Margaret Mary. On his second convalescent visit to Paray in 1682, he was counseled by the Sister to remain in that city to await his death. This he did, and he passed on February 15th. The following morning, Sister Margaret Mary had a vision of Father la Colombiere residing in heaven, and knew no prayers were needed for the reclamation of his soul.

CHAPEL OF ST. COLOMBIERE
Chapelle la Colombière

This Jesuit chapel was built in 1929 for the beatification of Claude de la Colombiere. The main altar is very colorful and inspirational, being built within the last century. On the left-hand side of the church is a reliquary with the saint's relics on display. It is a quiet church and a fine out-of-the-way place for prayer and meditation.

Where is The Chapel of the Visitation?
Où est la Chapelle de la Visitation?

Where is the Chapel of St. Colombiere?
Où est la Chapelle la Colombière?

SHRINE INFORMATION

Shrine: Director of Pilgrimages (Directeur du Pèlerinage)

Address: Place Cardinal Perraud/B.P. 104/71603 Paray-le-Monial cedex/France

Phone: 33 (0)3 85 81 62 22 **Fax:** 33 (0)3 85 81 51 67

E-mail: sanctuaries.paraylemonial@free.fr

Website: www.paray.org — Official website French.

Quiet areas for meditation: The Chapel of St. John (Chapelle St. Jean);

Chapel of St. Colombiere (Chapelle la Colombière); Chapel of the Visitation (Chapelle de la Visitation) when not crowded.

English spoken: Rarely

Hours: Chapel of the Visitation: 7AM–9PM; Chapel of St. John: 1PM–7:30, Thurs to midnight; Chapel of St. Colombiere: 8AM–7PM.

Mass: The Chapel of the Visitation: Weekdays 9AM, 11, 6PM summer; 9AM, 6PM winter, Fri 11AM, Sun/Hol 9AM, 6PM; Chapel of St. John: 7AM, Exposition of the Blessed Sacrament: 8:30AM–7PM.

Feasts and festivities: February 15 — Feast Day of St. Claude de la Colombiere; Sunday after Easter — Sunday of Mercy; Third Friday after Pentecost — Feast Day of the Sacred Heart; October 16 — Feast Day of St. Margaret Mary.

Accessibility: The Chapels of the Visitation, St. John, St. Columbiere and the Basilica of the Sacred Heart are all accessible for wheelchairs.

Information office: For tourist information (in English) visit the tourist office listed below. For pilgrimage information (in French) visit the "espace Saint Jean" behind the Basilica. Both are very close to each other.

Tours: Guided tours in English when available. Contact the pilgrimage office above.

Bookstore: The Chapel of the Visitation has a good bookstore before you enter, to the right.

Recommended books: *Saint Margaret Mary and the Visitation in Paray*, by Jean Ladame, a booklet available in the church bookstore; *The Autobiography of St. Margaret Mary*, TAN Publishers, a small book.

Lodging: There are four religious houses and many hotels. The Maison du Sacré Coeur and Foyer du Sacré Coeur are connected with the sanctuaries. The hotel Le Prieuré du Coeur de Jésus offers lodging for large groups. Inquire at the tourist office for contact information and book early for July and August, their busiest times.

Directions: The Sanctuary is located on Rue de la Visitation in the center of town, just around the corner from the Basilica. Follow signs to "Centre Town" and the Basilica. The town is small, and there are many one-way streets, so be patient. It easy to walk around and parking is free.

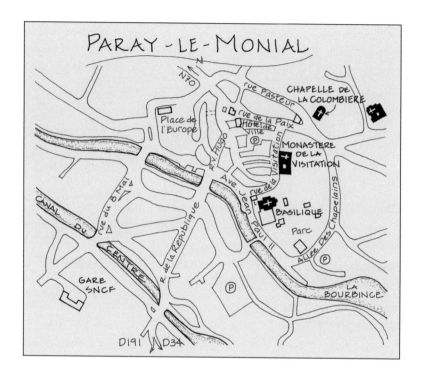

COMING AND GOING

PARAY-LE-MONIAL

Car: Paris is 236 miles (381 km), Nevers is 69 miles (111 km), and Le Puy is 106 miles (170 km) from Paray. From the east and A6, exit at Macon and take N79 west to Paray. From the west and Moulins, take N79 east to Paray. From Nevers, take N7 south to Moulins, then N79 to Paray. Follow signs to "Centre Town."

Train: From Nevers, take the local train to Paray. Or from Paris take the TGV from Gare de Lyon to Le Creusot, then a bus to Paray. SNCF buses go to Paray-le-Monial.

Bus: The town of Le Creusot has bus service to Paray-le-Monial.

TOURIST INFORMATION

❋ Office de Tourisme/25, Avenue Jean-Paul II/B.P. 119/ 71603 Paray-Le-Monial/France Phone: 33 (0)3 85 81 10 92 Fax: 33 (0)3 85 81 36 61 Email: ot.paray@wanadoo.fr http://perso.wanadoo.fr/richez/Burgundy/Paraye.htm.

❋ Sâone-Loire Department www.southernburgundy.com — Department tourist information.

WEBSITES

Angel Fire www.angelfire.com/ar/tjhsaints/mmary.html — The promises Jesus made to St. Margaret Mary for souls devoted to his sacred heart.

Eternal Word Television Network www.ewtn.com/library/christ/firstfri.txt — Text of the apparitions.

Home with God http://my.homewithgod.com/israel/margaretmary — Letters written by St. Margaret Mary.

La Maison du Pèlerin www.lourdes-fr.com — Information about the major shrines in France and Europe, including Paray-le-Monial.

Let's Go www.letsgo.com/FRA/17-Burgundy-154 — Tourist information for Paray-le-Monial.

Paray-le-Monial Pèlerinages www.paray.org — Official website for the Sanctuaries French.

Pontigny
Population 750

In the northernmost section of the Burgundy region, the small town of Pontigny rests in the rolling hills of the Serein River valley. A lovely drive brings you to Pontigny. The town is not much more than a wide spot in the road, so keep your eyes and map open. The tourist office is directly across from the Abbey. Pontigny is but one of many religious sites in the area, with much to see within a short driving distance: the ancient pilgrimage town of Vézelay, the well-preserved abbey of Fontenay, and the mother abbey of the Cistercian order at Citeaux.

ST. EDMUND OF ABINGDON
Saint Edme d'Abingdon 1180–1240

"I have sought nothing else but You."

Though buried in Pontigny and enshrined in the ancient Cistercian abbey there, St. Edmund of Abingdon is primarily known as the Archbishop of Canterbury and a nemesis of King Henry III of England. St. Edmund was a man of strong principles and an iron will. These traits served him well in his religious life, but put him at odds with his King and led to the tumultuous end of his life. Though a native of England, St. Edmund spent some years in France during his youth, and eventually returned to the French countryside, where he died and was buried.

Abingdon, England, was home to Edmund Rich, and here he lived in the pious household directed by his mother Mabel. The family owned several properties, so they were members of the small middle class of twelfth century England. None-the-less, austerities were a way of life for the family, as they typically fasted on Saturdays, and often wore hair shirts. Edmund's father was desirous of the religious life, and in his later years, with full consent of the family, entered the monastery in Oxfordshire.

Edmund grew up with his brother and sisters, and received an excellent education, leaving home at the age of twelve to attend school in Oxford. One day, while walking

Reliquary of St. Edmund of Abingdon

alone through a field, Edmund had a vision of the young child Jesus. This was a profound experience for the young man, and he wished to keep the encounter alive for himself. To accomplish this, he made a vow of chastity and acquired two rings: one he placed on the finger of the statue of Our Lady in St. Mary's Oxford, and the other he placed on his own finger. He also began the custom of praying to Jesus at bedtime and tracing the words "Jesus of Nazareth" on his forehead as a form of blessing and protection.

Side Chapel, Abbaye de Pontigny

After three years at Oxford, Edmund and his brother left for Paris, where they planned to continue their studies. Edmund was soon called back to Abingdon to the deathbed of his mother, where he received her final blessing. When he asked her to bless his siblings she replied, "I have given them my blessing in you, for through you they will share abundantly in the blessings of Heaven." As his father was already in the monastery, Edmund was put in charge of his family. He placed his two sisters, who desired to be nuns, in a Benedictine convent, and then returned to Paris. The next few years were spent studying in both Oxford and Paris, followed by stints of teaching at each university. He finally settled down in Oxford and became regent of the arts.

Edmund taught mathematics and became deeply engrossed in his studies and lectures. One night, he had a dream in which he saw three intersecting circles—then his mother appeared to him and asked the meaning of the rings. When he replied that they represented the topic of his lectures, she admonished him and said it actually represented the Trinity—the only topic truly worthy of study. From this time forward, Edmund dedicated his life to theology and preaching—obtaining his doctorate and becoming an ordained priest. For eight years he taught theology at Oxford, where he was renowned for his skill at preaching, attracting many students to his classes.

During this period, Edmund wrote his lone book, *Speculum Ecclesie* or *Mirror of Holy Church*. This treatise, written in Latin, was originally intended for cloistered brothers and sisters, but eventually became translated into more parochial English and was read by lay members of the church. The book consists of exercises in living the devout life, and concludes with instructions on contemplation and meditation. The third stage of meditation is "infused contemplation," where the aspirant is taught to forget body consciousness, and concentrate solely on the will and presence of God. "Expel from your heart all bodily images and forms and allow your understanding to fly, above all human reasoning, up to heaven, and there you shall find such sweetness in the secrets of God as no man can know, unless he has tasted it."

In 1222, when Edmund was 32, he accepted the post of treasurer at the nearly completed cathedral of Salisbury and became pastor of the neighboring rural parish at Caine. Five years later, he was directed by the Pope to preach for a crusade against the Saracens and was promised stipends for his services from each church at which he preached. Edmund preached for the cause with great vigor and aroused the congregations into action. Miracles were reported to occur in several parishes, and his fame spread throughout the nation. Through all this, Edmund refused to accept any stipends and also donated most of his salary to the poor, leaving him destitute.

Heartfelt prayer was key to the inner life for Edmund. He considered it his duty to teach his congregations how to pray with deep conviction and sincerity. He wrote, "A hundred thousand persons are deceived by multiplying prayers. I would rather say five words devoutly with my heart, than five thousand, which my soul does not relish with affection and intelligence. Sing to the Lord with understanding: what a man repeats by his mouth, let him feel in his soul." Edmund lived to pray very deeply and was known to levitate in ecstasy while engrossed in devotional prayer.

The height of Edmund's ecclesiastical power came in 1234, when Pope Gregory IX consecrated him as the Archbishop of Canterbury.

His first duty was to act as emissary for King Henry III, and negotiate a peace between the throne and rebellious English and Welsh barons who were threatening civil war. A staunch proponent of the Magna Carter and English rule, Edmund quelled the uprising with his peaceful yet forceful nature. He is well remembered for averting a disastrous war and reorganizing the government.

Though a supporter of the King in secular arenas, the position of Archbishop placed Edmund in direct opposition to Henry III in matters regarding Church and State. The monarch was attempting to usurp the power of the Church and place it under control of the State, but Edmund upheld a strict and just interpretation of the law, and would not bend under any pressure—either from the King or his own compatriots. In response, King Henry III requested the appointment of a papal legate, and Cardinal Otto was selected to balance the power of the Archbishop. Edmund soon left for Rome for his tri-annual visit, and took his cause to the Pope. He was supported by Rome but, upon returning home, Edmund found a large contingent of his monks had turned against him and his interpretation of the Order's rule, and he excommunicated seventeen of the rebels. This was a time of tumult for Edmund as he was constantly fighting with the King and members of his own order. It took a toll on his health, but he never wavered from his principles. In 1240, he was again called to Rome and, in the fall, he left England for the papal state.

Edmund and his staff landed in France and made their way towards the Italian peninsula. King Louis IX and the Queen Mother graciously received them when they stopped in Senlis. He then traveled on to Pontigny, where he had stayed on previous pilgrimages to Rome. The Abbey of Pontigny was dear to the heart of Edmund as he was appreciative of the Cistercian way of life, and because of the hospitality the Cistercian Brothers had shown to St. Thomas Beckett and Archbishop Stephen Langton in earlier times. During his brief stay, Edmund attended a chapter meeting, gave a sermon to the Brothers, and asked to become an honorary member of the order. After resting in Pontigny for several days, Edmund became ill. His condition deteriorated quickly, and it was decided that the group should return to England.

Heading home, Edmund made it to Soissy, where it became clear to his attendants that he was not long for the body. He spent three days here, writing letters of testimonial for his staff and seeking complete absolution. When his condition continued to worsen, he was given his last sacrament. At this time he said, "It is you, Lord, in whom I have believed, whom I have loved, about whom I have preached and taught. You are my witness that I have sought nothing on earth except you." On November 16, 1240, Edmund died peacefully after receiving last rites and consoling his companions, which included his brother Robert, and other long-trusted friends.

Edmund wished his body to be buried in Pontigny, and it was transported here immediately after his death. The funeral procession took days to travel the many miles from Soissy to Pontigny, and crowds of people lined the roads to acknowledge the saint. Miracles were reported along the route, so larger crowds began gathering to witness the procession. At times, the people became raucous and threatened to abduct the body from the small band of clerics. The superior of the Abbey of Pontigny became concerned and prayed to St. Edmund to stop the miracles. The miracles did cease, and the entourage made it to the Abbey without further incident. Edmund was buried in the Abbey as he requested, and was here venerated by the cloistered monks. Within six years, the Pope canonized St. Edmund, and his relics have remained forever enshrined in the Abbey of Pontigny.

THE ABBEY OF PONTIGNY
Abbaye de Pontigny

Founded in 1114, the Abbey of Pontigny was the second of the four daughter abbeys of Cîteaux. As part of the pioneering efforts of the new Cistercian Order, the Abbey was established at the beginning of the return to strict observance of the rule of St. Benedict and monastic asceticism. The new leaders, Stephen Harding, followed by Bernard of Clairvaux, built the abbeys with simple lines and devoid of decoration. This was in stark contrast to the abbeys of the opulent Cluny Order that preceded the Cistercians. Built in the time of transition from Romanesque to Gothic style, the Abbey is constructed of white limestone with a simplicity that reflects the Cistercian austerity. The columns of the side aisles are capped with clean arches that support the gallery of glazing, lighting the ceiling high above. Unfortunately, the dark Gothic choir, added in a later era, disrupts any mental image of the simple early days of this order.

The Abbey is known for three Archbishops of Canterbury who stayed here. They were Thomas Becket, who spent four years here, Stephen Langton, and St. Edmund of Abingdon. Before his death, Edmund requested to be buried at Pontigny.

St. Edmund's remains were initially placed in a plain stone sarcophagus, but with permission from the Pope, were later moved to an expensive shrine with gold and precious stones. This shrine is no

Abbaye de Pontigny

longer in existence (probably to the relief of St. Edmund) and has been replaced by a more discreet but elegant shrine resting high above the floor at the end of the choir, behind the main altar. The body remains incorrupt (although thought to be embalmed) except for his right arm, which was removed and now resides at St. Edmund's Retreat on Enders Island, Connecticut, USA. You must walk behind the altar to reach his crypt, and unfortunately, there are no chairs. However, to the right there is a simple side chapel used by the local parishioners, and it is a good place to pray and meditate.

The Abbey was plundered and burnt by the Huguenots in 1569, and only the relics of St. Edmund were saved. Following restoration, the Abbey continued to function until the French Revolution, after which it was placed under the care of the Fathers of St. Edmund in 1843. Today it is open to the public, acting as a tourist attraction for those interested in Cistercian architecture, and it is still used as a sanctuary by the local parish. The blessings of St. Edmund of Abingdon can still be felt here and this shrine deserves more attention from pilgrims seeking to touch the sanctity of those who have come before.

Where is the Abbey of Pontigny?
Où est l'abbaye de Pontigny?

SHRINE INFORMATION

Shrine: The Abbey of Pontigny (Abbaye de Pontigny)

Address: Amis de Pontigny/B.P.6/89230 Pontigny/France

Phone: 33 (0)3 86 47 54 99 **Fax:** 33 (0)3 86 47 84 66

E-mail: amis.de.Pontigny@wanadoo.fr

Website: None

Quiet areas for meditation: The Abbey is not busy and there is a side chapel on the right hand side that is quiet.

English spoken: Rarely

Hours: April–Sept, Daily 9AM–7PM; October–March, 10AM–6PM.

Mass: Sun 11:15AM.

Feasts and festivities: Celebration of the Pentecost (seventh Sunday after Easter) with guided visit in French, and concert.

Accessibility: Yes

Information office: The tourist office is across the street from the Abbey. It is a small town, and the Abbey is set back off the street, so it is not obvious, but there are signs as you pass by. They speak French only.

Tours: There are guided tours in French during the tourist season by reservation only. Ask in French at the tourist office.

Bookstore: Inside the Abbey to the left as you enter. There are no books in English about the Abbey or St. Edmund.

Recommended books: *The Life of St. Edmund*, by C.H. Lawrence, Alan Sutton Publishing Limited, Oxford. Not available at the Abbey.

Lodging: None

Directions: N77 goes through this small town. The Abbey is across from the Tourist Office.

COMING AND GOING

PONTIGNY

Car: Pontigny is on N77 between Auxerre (A6) and Troyes (A5). Take N77 11 miles (17km) north of Auxerre, or 37 miles (60km) south of Troyes. The Abbey is across from the Tourist Office on rue Paul Desjardins.

Train: The closest station is in Auxerre, 11 miles (17km) south of Pontigny.

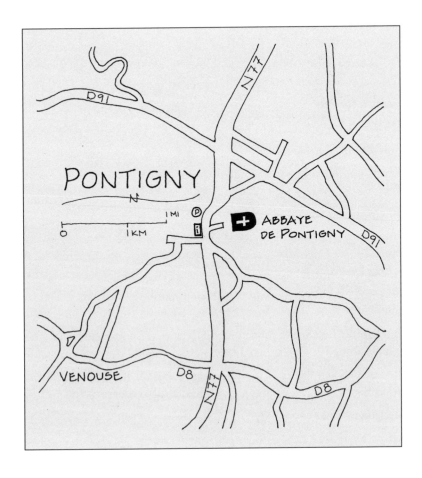

Tourist Information

❋ Office du Tourisme/22, rue Paul Desjardins/89230 Pontigny/France
Phone: 33 (0)3 86 47 47 03 Fax: 33 (0)3 86 47 58 38, French only.
There is no city map since the town is so small.

❋ Yonne Tourist Board www.tourisme-yonne.com — Tourist info.

Websites

Enders Island www.endersisland.com — A retreat center in Mystic,
Connecticut, USA. A biography of St. Edmund is under "About Us"
at the bottom of the page, under links.

The Society of St. Edmund www.sse.org — The religious society of
St. Edmund in Colchester, Vermont, USA. A biography of St. Edmund
is under "Our Patron."

More St. Edmund Shrines

St. Edmund's Retreat
Enders Island, Connecticut, USA

Founded by the Society of St. Edmund, a Catholic order of priests and
brothers who operate this retreat just off the Connecticut mainland at
Mystic, on Enders Island. They offer spiritual retreats, adult education,
and an institute of Sacred Art. Although the Edmundites are
Catholic, they offer their facilities to people of all faiths. The facilities
include a turn-of-the-century mansion, modern meeting room,
overnight accommodations, a new chapel that has been called "a
pilgrimage destination in its own right" and the tiny Fisherman's
Chapel. The formal gardens and coastal vistas provide a peaceful and
reflective atmosphere. The new chapel is where the relic of the arm of
St. Edmund is venerated. For more information visit their website at
www.endersisland.com. Saint Edmund's Retreat/Enders Island/P.O.
Box 399/Mystic, CT 06355-0399/USA Phone: 1 860 536-0565 Fax:1
860 572-7655 Email: programs@endersisland.com.

Taizé

Population 60

This tiny village is adjacent to the renowned Taizé Community, but has no overt relationship with it. In fact, they ask that you not to go into the village unless you have specific business there. When approaching the town of Taizé, follow the signs to "Communauté," which will lead you to the community welcome center (Accueil).

TAIZÉ COMMUNITY

"Whoever lives for God, chooses to love." Brother Roger

The Taizé Community is known worldwide as a haven of peace and a source of inspiration for millions of young Christians. Thousands of youthful souls find their way to Taizé each year to seek a personal experience of faith and love, and to embark on their own inner search for peace. At Taizé they find an environment that is accepting and non-judgmental—a place to open their hearts to love. Over a hundred Brothers from various Christian faiths live at the community and receive pilgrims year-round from all corners of the planet. Two orders of Sisters also live in the adjacent village of Taizé and serve in the welcome center.

The origins of the community began in 1940 when Brother Roger left his native Switzerland to find a place to start a community of love and reconciliation. At age twenty-five, he had long been interested in community living, and with the onset of WWII, he knew it was time

to start his mission in earnest. Having witnessed his fellow Christians spending all their energy justifying their conflicts with each other rather than sharing the love of Christ, Brother Roger longed to live where he could practice the teachings of Christ

Taizé Welcome Center

every day. For him, reconciliation is the experience of divine love that forgives all things.

Bicycling from Geneva, he arrived at the Burgundian village of Taizé, and was immediately welcomed by several elderly residents. There had been no priests in the tiny village since before the French Revolution, so the faithful were ready for this singular Brother. During this time of war, Taizé was on the border between occupied and unoccupied France, and refugees were often roaming the countryside searching for shelter. Brother Roger opened his humble home to anyone in need, especially the Jews escaping persecution, and his house became known as a safe haven. At one point, he actually had to flee the area for fear of being arrested by the Germans, but returned to Taizé when the conflict was over.

Over the years, other Brothers were attracted to Brother Roger's way of life, and joined the community. In 1949, seven Brothers made vows of commitment to a life of celibacy, simplicity and communal living. Initially, the Brothers were from Protestant backgrounds, but Catholic Brothers soon were attracted to the simple life, and today the Brothers hail from twenty-five differ-

Church of Reconcilation

ent countries and every continent of the world. All the Brothers live by the fruits of their own handy work, accepting neither donations nor gifts. They live simply, and share their life and love with all who come.

In the late 1950s, young people started to arrive at Taizé, like bees attracted to the honey of the hive. The Brothers did not understand the reason for the attraction, other than the openness and the love they shared with all. Since that time, Taizé has become a magnet for young people searching for spiritual guidance and inspiration. "For the young people above all, we would like to be people who listen, never spiritual masters," says Brother Roger. "We would like to go with them to the sources of the trusting of faith, especially through the irreplace-able prayer together which, through its beauty, touches the depths of the soul."

In the summer, Taizé welcomes as many as six thousand young people each week, who travel from Europe, Asia, Africa and the Americas. They live in a tent community on site, and attend weeklong programs while serving their fellow pilgrims. A typical day at Taizé includes scriptural study, service, and three periods of meditation and prayer. The Brothers gather together with the participants in the Church of the Reconciliation in the morning, noon and evening for these prayer services. Together they pray, sing songs of devotion, and meditate on the love of God. Brother Roger says, "The fullness of a prayer which is sung and also a moment of silence together can help everyone to take part personally. These are elements that can help to make Christ and the Holy Spirit accessible."

The goal of the community is to expose every-one to openness, love and prayer, and then send them back to their own com-munities to act as creators of peace and reconcilia-tion. At the end of each year,

Taizé Youth Group

young adults on each continent gather for a four-day conference where they share their experiences and goals, and support each other in their spiritual endeavors. Every year, Brother Roger writes an open letter to the greater community, which is translated into sixty languages, and serves as a basis for reflection in the meetings throughout the following year.

PROGRAMS

In the peak summer months, there can be as many as 6,000 people participating in the programs at Taizé. The Community offers programs for different age groups: 15 to 16 year olds; 17 to 29 years old; over thirty; and parents with children under 15. The weekly meetings go from Sunday to Sunday all through the year, but longer programs can be arranged. The Brothers of the community give Bible instruction every day, followed by reflection and discussion. Three times a day everyone gathers for prayer at the Church of Reconciliation, and everyone helps with chores for two hours each day. In the evening after prayer, silence is observed everywhere except in the café. There is also the option to spend the week in silence.

Register at least three weeks ahead of your visit. The website offers online registration. Even if you do not have an internet connection, an attempt should be made to refer to their website at a library or internet café. Everything you need to know about logistics is on their comprehensive website, including information about their history, prayer and Taizé-style meditation. The cost is nominal, ranging between 5 to 6.50 Euros a day, changing with the value of the exchange rate.

Where is Taizé?
Où est Taizé?

COMMUNITY INFORMATION

Shrine: The Taizé Community

Address: 71250 Taizé/France

Phone: 33 (0)3 85 50 30 02 (meetings & visiting), 33 (0)3 85 50 30 30 (community of Brothers).

Fax: 33 (0)3 85 50 30 16 (meetings & visiting), 33 (0)3 85 50 30 15 (community of Brothers).

E-mail: meetings@taize.fr (for taking part in the meetings or visiting Taizé); community@taize.fr (for contacting one of the Brothers).

Website: www.taize.fr — Official website in twenty-six languages, contains every detail you need to know about visiting Taizé with online registration.

Quiet areas for meditation: The Church of Reconciliation at different times of the day; the village church during the day, and St. Stephen's Spring.

English spoken: Typically

Hours: The "Casa" reception center is open 9AM–12PM, 2PM–5:30. Closed Sunday. Phone calls Mon-Fri 11AM–12PM & 6PM–7; Sat 11AM–12PM (Central European Time).

Prayer: Mon-Sat 8:30AM, 12:20PM, 8:30PM; Sat 8:30PM followed by a meeting with Brother Roger; Sun 10am, 8:30PM.

Feasts and festivities: The usual yearly Catholic celebrations.

Accessibility: There are several buildings equipped for wheelchairs: church, toilets & telephone booths.

Reception Center: The "Casa" or "Accueil/Welcome" center is open 9AM–12PM, 2PM–5:30. Closed Sunday.

Tours: When you arrive, a video is shown in your language that introduces visitors to the community.

Bookstore: The Exposition building contains books, CDs, and crafts made by the residents to support the Taizé community.

Recommended books: *The Story of Taizé*, by J.L. Gonzalez Balado; *Taizé: A Meaning to Life*, by Oliver Clément. These books and more are available in the community bookstore at the Exposition building.

Lodging: Dormitories and, in summer, camping in your own tent.

Directions: 60 miles north of Lyon. After turning off of D981 to Taizé, follow the signs "Communauté" to the Accueil/Welcome Center. If driving, turn left into the parking lots. The website has excellent detailed directions for every mode of transportation. Once you have arrived at Taizé, you can buy train tickets and make reservations for your departure at the "Espace-Voyages" in the "La Morada" building across from the "Casa" reception center.

COMING AND GOING

TAIZÉ

Car: From the north take A6 to exit 26—Chalon Sud. After the tollbooth, turn left onto N80/E607 towards Cluny for 5 miles (3 km). Exit

at 31 Taizé, follow D981 through Cormatin, 2.5 miles (1.5 km). After
Cormatin, turn right to Taizé. From the east or south: From A6
Lyon/Moulins, exit at 29 Mâcon-sud. After the tollbooth, follow the
roundabout for Montceau/Moulins/Nevers, followed by signs for
Cluny and Taizé on N79. Go for 10.5 miles (17 km), take D980 exit
4 to Cluny. Go for 3 miles (5 km), at roundabout turn onto D981
Taizé for 5 miles (8 km), turn left to Taizé.

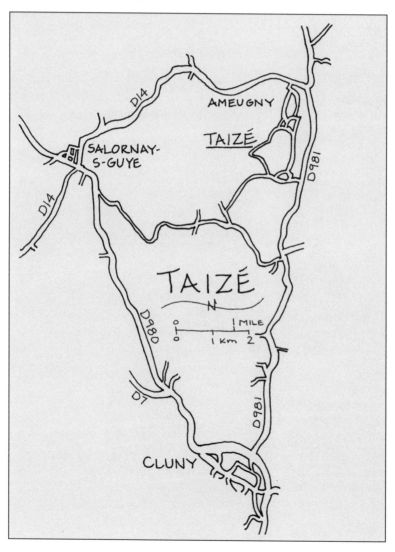

Train: Take a train to one of the following train stations: Mâcon-TGV, Mâcon-Ville or Chalon-sur-Saône. Then take the connecting SNCF bus to Taizé. If you buy your train ticket to Taizé it will be cheaper than buying two separate tickets. Not all trains have a connecting bus. If there is no bus, take a taxi or minibus.

Bus: On the Taizé website they have the SNCF timetable in English.

Air: The Taizé website has detailed information on flying from Paris, Lyon, Geneva, and Dijon.

Website

The Taizé Community www.taize.fr — Official website in twenty-six languages. This comprehensive site contains every detail you need to know about visiting Taizé, including online registration.

Farm near Taizé

PLACES OF INTEREST NEAR TAIZÉ

THE ANCIENT ABBEY OF CLUNY
Ancienne Abbaye de Cluny

The Benedictine Abbey of Cluny was founded in 910 in reaction to church corruption and, by the eleventh century, grew into a powerful center of monastic rule. At the height of its power, it commanded over 10,000 monks and 1,200 monasteries across Europe, and was the largest abbey church in Christendom until the sixteenth century. Closed in 1790, and sold as national property, it was used as a stone quarry and partially demolished. Some buildings remain today, and guided tours are available for the Holy Water Bell tower and the Musee d'Art. Cluny is more of a tourist stop than a spiritual destination. But, it is an easy stopover on the way to Taizé when coming from the south. Abbey Phone: 33 (0)3 85 59 12 79 Tourist Office: Tour des Fromages/6 rue Merciere/71.

Centre

 Often called the Loire Valley, along with the region of Pays-de-Loire, Centre is directly southwest of Paris and is known as the "Garden of France" for its beautiful vineyards, hillsides laced with flowers and the hundreds of medieval chateaux that adorn the countryside. An ancient capital at the time of the Gauls, Centre now features the major cities of Orleans, liberated from the British by Joan of Arc in 1429, and Tours, a bustling university town and once an important medieval pilgrimage destination. The city most famous to spiritual travelers and tourists alike is Chartres, in the northern part of this region, home to perhaps the world's most shining example of Gothic architecture. The Cathedral of Our Lady, more commonly known as Chartres Cathedral, is graced with soaring walls of stained glass and sculptured edifices that rival all others in Europe. In contrast, in the southern part of the region is the town of Pellevoisin where a small gem of a shrine is dedicated to the Virgin Mary. She appeared here fifteen times in the late nineteenth century.

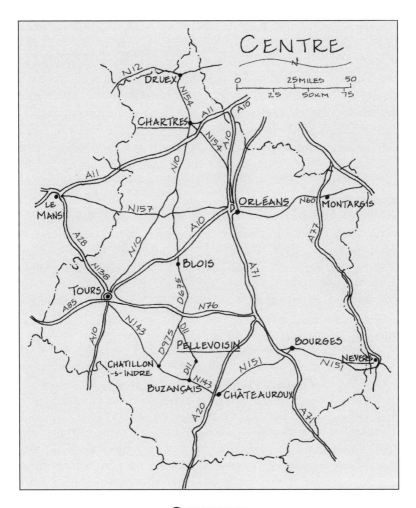

CHARTRES
Cathedral of Our Lady of Chartres

PELLEVOISIN
Our Lady of Pellevoisin

Chartres

Population 42,059

Chartres is a pleasant day trip from Paris, being only a one-hour train ride sixty miles southwest of the French capital. Built on the left bank of the Eure River in the department of Eure-et-Loir, this small city attracts 350,000 pilgrims each year to one of the largest and most beautiful Gothic cathedrals in Europe. The Cathedral of Our Lady houses the veil of the Virgin Mary, which miraculously survived a catastrophic fire in 1194, creating an upwelling of faith and support for the rebuilding of this magnificent edifice. Chartres Cathedral, called the "Acropolis of France" by Rodin, was built on a rocky outcrop that now overlooks the old restored districts of the city. Staircases, known as "Des Tertres," lead from the Cathedral down to quiet streets orna-mented with half-timbered houses, water mills, washhouses and a maze of humpback bridges. An hour walking tour that offers a beautiful view of the Cathedral can be taken with or without an audio guide provid-ed at the tourist office. For stained glass enthusiasts, two other small churches, St. Aignan's and St. Pierre's Abbey Church, can be visited easily, along with the International Stained Glass Centre. Behind the Cathedral are a park and the Musée des Beaux Arts, a former Episcopal palace. A day trip from Paris allows enough time to visit the Cathedral, but an overnight stay would be more relaxing, giving time to explore this charming city.

CHARTRES CATHEDRAL

Cathédrale de Chartres

The city of Chartres has always been an important site of Christendom, being a bishopric seat since the fourth century. The earliest Christian missionaries established churches venerating the Virgin Mary here, and the cult of Marian adoration was significant. In 876, King Charles the Bald presented the church with the relic of Mary's Veil, making Chartres a major pilgrimage destination.

The Cathedral of Chartres marks the highpoint of French Gothic art and architecture, soaring high above the other Gothic works of its day. But the construction of this architectural jewel had very rough beginnings. From 743 to 1020, three successive churches were built and destroyed by fire. After the third church was burned, Saint Fulbert, then Bishop of Chartres, began rebuilding again. Receiving financial support and generous gifts from all over Europe, the Bishop started with the construction of the crypt, followed by the structure of the upper church. But, fire swept through the town in 1134, destroying the front of the church and the bell tower. Undaunted, construction resumed on the east towers and the Royal Portal of the east façade, with the south tower rising to a glorious height of over 300 feet (105 meters). Chartres was by then one of the most popular pilgrimage sites in all of Europe, with thousands annually making their way to the shrine. Tragically, in 1194, fire once again ravished the town and almost entirely destroyed the church, with only the two towers and the east façade escaping damage. Even more dev-astating was the apparent loss of the sacred Veil of Mary. But four days later, the relic was miraculous-ly discovered amongst the ashes, and the people of Chartres rejoiced with an even greater determination to rebuild their church.

Cathédrale de Chartres

Over the next twenty-five years, the Cathedral was reconstructed in a uniform Gothic style that set a high standard for the churches that would soon follow, namely those at Reims and Amiens. The experimental use of flying buttresses on the exterior of the north and south aisles and walls allowed for a soaring structure with limited mass, giving way to large expanses of stained glass. This new structural concept led to an architectural evolution from the dark, heavy feeling of Romanesque churches to a light, lofty and airy-feeling Gothic cathedral. Everything concerning the interior architecture became lighter and more elegant, permitting large stained glass windows to be carried within a more refined and delicate tracery. All of these innovations originated at Chartres, and culminated in a church that rose to new heights, was filled with greater amounts of luminescent color flooding down from the elevated stained glass windows, and uplifted the hearts and souls of all who entered. These very same twelfth century stained glass windows have survived all the turmoil surrounding Chartres and are premier examples of medieval glass art.

The other remarkable part of the equation that makes Chartres a masterpiece is the incredible sculpture that is an integral part of the design. Each entrance and porch on the north, east and south edifices of the cathedral is encircled with exquisite stone carvings dating from the twelfth century. What is even more amazing is that they have survived these many centuries of war, fire and pollution. In fact, they are completely intact and continue to portray tales of devout lives and Christian lore.

For the pilgrim, the Holy Veil of the Blessed Virgin Mary (Sancta Camisia), Our Lady of the Pillar, and the Black Madonna of the crypt

Our Lady of the Pillar

are the primary objects of veneration. The Holy Veil was the relic that literally put Chartres on the map. After it was given to the church by King Charles the Bald, Chartres became extremely popular with pilgrims, similar to the modern day Lourdes. Pilgrims came from all over the continent for healings and were cared for in the crypt, usually for a period of nine days. They also slept in the Cathedral in great numbers, making the church a hostel of sorts. For this reason, the nave floor was sloped so it could be thoroughly washed, and some of the stained glass panels were removable to allow fresh air into the church. The Veil is now displayed in a side altar on the south isle, where a few chairs are set outside the iron grillwork. However, this is not a very contemplative space as tourists are constantly walking through the area.

Veneration of the Virgin Mother has long been part of the history of Chartres, and there are two statues of the Black Madonna within the Cathedral. Our Lady of the Pillar is located in its own shrine area along the north isle, and has an ample area for prayer and meditation. This original sixteenth century statue has survived the years and has always been an important pilgrimage icon. Our Lady of the Crypt has had a rougher time of it. During the French Revolution of 1593, the original statue was removed from the crypt and burned. The statue was replaced in 1857 after the cathedral was restored to a place of worship, then again in 1976 with the current statue, which closely resembles the original. The crypt itself dates back to the eleventh century and is the largest crypt in France. Only the crypts in St. Peter's in Rome and Canterbury Cathedral in England are larger. The well of Saints-Forts is a feature of the crypt, being part of the ancient history of this shrine. In Gallo-Roman times, Druid worship was centered around the well, and later, the first martyrs of Chartres were disposed of here.

In recent years, another aspect of Chartres has come to light with scientific energy studies conducted around the cathedral. Chartres is literally a spiritually magnetic site. Since the Druids performed ceremonies here in ancient times, the location of the church has been a focus of spiritual energy. Scientists have recently discovered that fourteen water channels travel under the Cathedral to merge at a single point under the choir. This convergence produces a measurable vibration level as elevated as those found in some Tibetan monasteries and Egyptian pyramids.

Another point of interest is the Labyrinth that is part of the stone floor design in the nave. The intertwined circular pattern is a metaphor for the pilgrim's journey and has been used since medieval times as a means of reaching one's "center." Following the guided path of the labyrinth from the exterior to the interior of the pattern, the pilgrim takes a contemplative journey to a place of peace and recon-ciliation at the origin. When examined in a scientific manner, the center of the labyrinth has an electromagnetic intensity similar to high states of consciousness and bliss.

All of the aspects of Chartres mentioned above make this one of the most interesting cathedrals to visit. A pilgrim can easily get lost in the splendor and majesty, for there are so many varied levels of complexity in the history, design and spiritual magnetism of this ancient holy shrine.

Where is Chartres Cathedral?
Où est la cathédrale de Chartres?

Where is the Holy Veil of the Blessed Virgin Mary?
Où est Sancta Camisia?

SHRINE INFORMATION

Shrine: Chartres Cathedral (La cathédrale de Chartres)

Address: 24, Cloître Notre-Dame/BP 131/28003 Chartres cedex/France

Phone: 33 (0)2 37 21 75 02 **Fax:** 33 (0)2 37 36 51 43

E-mail: visitecathedrale@diocesechartres.com

Website: www.diocesechartres.com/cathedrale — The website for the diocese of Chartres in French.

Quiet areas for meditation: At the Veil of the Blessed Virgin Mary and Our Lady of the Pillar there are chairs for prayer and meditation, though the Cathedral is not a quiet place. At the east end of the ambulatory is the chapel called "Adoration du Saint Sacrement," which is reserved for silent prayer.

English spoken: Typically at the tourist office.

Hours: Daily 8:30AM–7:30PM

Mass: Mon-Fri 11:45AM (crypt), 6:15PM; Sat 11:45AM (crypt), 6PM; Sun 9:15AM (Gregorian Mass in Latin), 11, 6PM (crypt).

Feasts and festivities: April 9–13 — Easter Festival (Festival de Pâques); August 15 — Feast of the Assumption with procession through town.

Accessibility: The main entrance (portal Royal) is accessible.

Cathedral Tours: Audio-guide tour rentals in the Cathedral Bookshop (on the left as you enter); guided lectures in English: Mon-Sat 12PM and 2:45PM during the season. Meet in front of the bookshop. Private tours by arrangement, contact Malcolm Miller Email: miller-chartres@aol.com. The Tourist Office also provides tours in English for a fee and by previous arrangement.

Crypt Tours: The Crypt is open at various times for guided visits in French. Arrange your visit to accommodate these tours. Check out the hours at: http://perso.wanadoo.fr/.diocese.chartres/cathedrale.

Bookstore: Inside the Cathedral, on the left.

Recommended books: *Chartres: Guide of the Cathedral* is available at the Cathedral Bookstore and the tourist office has a brochure for the Cathedral.

Lodging: None

Directions: One hour from Paris on the train. From the Chartres SNCF train station at Place Sémaud, walk down avenue Jehan de Beauce in front of the train station. Veer left on place Chatelet and from there to rue Sainte Meme (keep your eyes open for the cathedral's spires, which rise above the rooftops). Turn left on place Jean Moulin, which turns into rue de l'Etroit-Degré, and you will end up at the tourist office (pick up brochure here), which is in front of the Cathedral. It is only a five-minute walk from the station. By car, follow signs to "Cathédrale" and Cathedral parking with 256 spaces.

COMING AND GOING

CHARTRES

Car: Chartres is at the crossroads of many major highways of central France. From Paris (one hour) A6 direction Bordeaux-Nantes via Porte d'Orleans, then A10, A11 direction Nantes. From Tours, Orleans and the southwest of France, take RN10. From Brittany, RN23. From Rouen, RN 154 towards Orleans. In town, follow signs to "Cathédrale."

Train: ChartresTrainstation SNCF place Pierre-Sémard. 25 trains per day between Paris and Chartres. Phone: 33 (0)8 36 35 35 35 Taxi: 33 (0)2 37 36 00 00.

Bus: Filibus public transport Phone: 33 (0)2 37 36 26 98.

Plane: Airports of Paris: Orly 47 miles (75 km) and Roissy 75 miles (120 km) by A11.

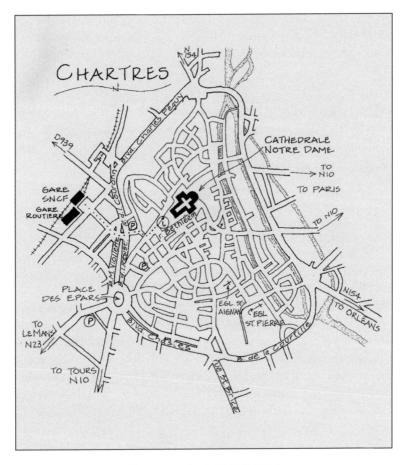

TOURIST INFORMATION

✤ Chartres Office de Tourisme/Place de la Cathédrale/BP 289/28005 Chartres cedex/France Phone: 33 (0)2 37 18 26 26 Fax: 33 (0)2 37 21 51 91 Email: info@otchartres.fr.

✤ Chartres.com www.chartres.com Email: info@chartres.com Detailed map of Chartres under "tourism," then "city."

✤ The Department of Eure-&-Loir Tourist Board Email: info@tourisme28.com www.tourisme28.com Phone: 33 (0)2 37 84 01 00 Fax: 33 (0)2 37 36 36 39

WEBSITES

Diocèse de Chartres www.diocesechartres.com/cathedrale — The website for the diocese of Chartres in French.

La Maison du Pèlerin www.lourdes-fr.com — Information about the major shrines in France and Europe, including Chartres Cathedral.

Lessons4living www.lessons4living.com/chartres_labyrinth.htm — Explanation of the Chartres labyrinth.

Sanctuaire du Monde www.chartres-csm.org/us.html — Descriptions of the Cathedral.

Villes Sanctuaries en France www.villes-sanctuaires.com — The Association of Shrine Towns in France with a suggested tour, and contact information.

Pellevoisin
Population 975

For the pilgrim seeking a tranquil setting of deep stillness, the shrine of Our Lady of Pellevoisin is made to order. This tiny rural town is off the beaten track, but is home to a chapel where the Blessed Virgin appeared fifteen times in the late nineteenth century to a devout young woman. Located fifty-seven miles southeast of Tours, Pellevoisin receives only 5,000 pilgrims each year, but this is an advantage to the pilgrim desiring a quiet place for prayer and meditation. The atmosphere is simple, sweet and inviting, with nine Brothers of St. John the Evangelist maintaining the shrine in association with twenty Sisters of Saint John. The religious community stresses contemplation, creating a peaceful atmosphere.

OUR LADY OF PELLEVOISIN
Notre Dame de Pellevoisin Feb 14 – Dec. 8, 1876

*"If you wish to serve me, be simple
and let your actions accord with your words."*

The Blessed Virgin Mary appeared many times in nineteenth century France—most notably at Lourdes and La Salette—but her appearance to Estelle Faguette at Pellevoisin is equally endearing and inspirational. Here is a unique pilgrim destination offering an atmosphere for deep contemplation and joyful communion with the Blessed Mother.

Estelle Faguette was born to a peasant family in rural France in 1843, but moved with her family to Paris when she was fourteen years of age. The family had hopes of a better life in the environs of Paris, but jobs were difficult to come by and they continued to struggle financially. Estelle's elder sister, Genevieve, would take her to Sunday services and the Sisters of St. Vincent de Paul received Estelle as a "Child of Mary." From this early age, Estelle was already consecrated to the Blessed Virgin.

Disease and illness were common in the poorer quarters of Paris and, at fifteen, Estelle became very ill, requiring two weeks of hospitalization. Experiencing the compassion and dedication of the Augustinian Sisters during her convalescence, Estelle inwardly made the commitment to a religious vocation. She spoke with her confessor concerning her desires and expressed doubt about beginning a religious life, for her family could not afford the trousseau, a dowry-like payment required to enter the monastic community. Shortly after this conversation, the required sum arrived at her home and Estelle was able to begin her novitiate, much to the distress and dismay of her mother and father.

Estelle Faguette

Estelle was eighteen when she began her religious training, but she was not well educated and found the required readings difficult. However, *The Imitation of Christ* greatly inspired her, and she strove to live her life accordingly. Her novitiate was positive in all spiritual aspects, but physically Estelle had many challenges. In her first year, she was hospitalized for a smallpox infection received while treating patients. Then, in her second year, she fell down a stairway and severely injured her knee. This proved to be a serious injury, possibly requiring amputation, and resulted in her returning home to mend.

Saddened by her departure from the religious community, Estelle prayed for guidance for a new direction. She began to work as a seamstress, as this was a sedentary occupation that allowed her to work while regaining her health. To the amazement of all, within a year Estelle was able to walk again and she began performing charitable acts in addition to her normal work. Visiting the poor, she would speak to them of God and distribute money, food and clothing. Her acts of kindness were welcomed and recognized by those she served, and Estelle became known as the "little sister."

Estelle's work as a seamstress proved to be fortuitous, as the Countess de La Rochefoucauld employed her, and soon came to like and respect the young woman. In the spring of 1865, Estelle was offered a permanent position as nursery maid to the children of the Countess, with the intention of her accompanying the family to their country residence at the Château de Poiriers, just outside Pellevoisin. But just before they were to leave Paris, one of the children fell ill and, at the child's request, Estelle stayed with her day and night for two weeks, nursing her back to health. Though the child recovered, Estelle was weakened. When she reached Poiriers, she became seriously ill with acute peritonitis. She was so sick that the local doctor was convinced she would soon perish and she was given the last sacraments. But Countess Rochefoucauld never gave up on Estelle. She applied eighty leeches to Estelle's body and had her placed in a healing bath. This severe treatment proved to be beneficial, and within a few weeks, Estelle was back to work, though the peritonitis would remain a chronic condition.

The next ten years were spent in the employ of the Countess, tending to the children in the family's homes in both Paris and Pellevoisin. "I read *The Imitation of Christ* a little; it was my only reading. I retained the habit of going to Mass as often as I could; it was my consolation."

Though she was well liked by the Countess, Estelle's fellow servants were disdainful of her piety and were often cruel and disrespectful to her, but she never complained. In June 1875, Estelle had a severe relapse of her ailment and was hospitalized. The doctor discovered an orange-sized tuberculin tumor on her left side and said she would not recover. Once again, the Countess cared for her servant and sent Estelle to Château de Poiriers to convalesce. Estelle's condition did not improve and she sank into a depression, crying frequently about her own state and for fear of her parents becoming destitute in her absence. It was at this time she petitioned the Blessed Virgin with a heart-felt letter. On the grounds of the château, the children in her care had built a small grotto dedicated to Our Lady of Lourdes, and Estelle arranged for her letter to be delivered to the miniature shrine. She sent out a desperate call for help, but it would be months before she received a response.

Montbel Grotto of the Virgin

These were lonely times for Estelle as no one would visit her in her contagious condition, and her fellow servants ignored her needs completely—often leaving her without food for entire days. Her condition became increasingly worse, and on a December night in 1875, she was once again given last rites by l'Abbé Salmon, the parish priest. She was only thirty-two years old. The housemaids prepared her death shroud, but Estelle held on to the barest of life's threads for the next two months. Her parents moved to Pellevoisin to be with their daughter and, in February, Estelle was moved to a small house in the center of Pellevoisin, near the cemetery. Growing progressively weaker, she was examined by a doctor on the evening of February 14th and given only hours to live. But God was not ready to take His servant, having greater things in store for her. It was now that Estelle's supplications to the Blessed Virgin were answered.

That same night, while in a restless sleep, Estelle suddenly awoke to the image of the devil at the foot of her bed. "Oh, I was afraid," she recalled. "He was horrible and pulled faces at me. I had only just caught sight of him when the Blessed Virgin appeared on the other side, at the corner of my bed. She had a veil of very white wool that fell in three folds. I couldn't describe her beauty! Her features were regular, her complexion pink and white, somewhat pale." The devil departed after being admonished by Our Lady, who then spoke to the terrified Estelle. "Fear nothing; you know well that you are my daughter." Estelle relaxed as the Lady continued, "Courage, be patient; my Son will be moved. You will suffer for another five days, in honor of the five wounds of my Son. On Saturday you will be dead or cured. If my Son restores your life, I want you to spread my glory." Estelle was at a loss to understand how someone as humble as she could spread such glory. She was then shown a white granite ex voto, a plaque used to express gratitude for answered prayers. When she asked if it should be placed in Paris or Pellevoisin, she was told, "At Pellevoisin, there is nothing there and they need some stimulus." The vision ended with Estelle promising to fulfill Our Lady's wish.

The next night, Estelle was again visited by the devil, and Mary quickly appeared to send him on his way. "Do not be afraid, I am here," she told Estelle. "This time my Son has been moved to pity. He spares your life; you will be cured on Saturday." Estelle told Our Lady that she was ready to die, but Mary reminded her that life is the most precious gift, and that her life was being restored for a specific purpose. The Blessed Virgin then invited Estelle to review her life and see her sins, then left, after giving Estelle a kindly look.

Once again the devil appeared on the third consecutive night, but remained distant. When Mary appeared, she comforted Estelle about her previous sins, saying, "All that is past: through your resignation, you have redeemed your faults. I am all merciful, and hold sway with my Son. Your few good deeds and fervent prayers to me have moved my maternal heart." The fourth night was similar, with Mary asking Estelle to "Publish my glory. Do all that you can."

Our Lady's appearance on the fifth night took on a different tone. As Mary appeared, she came much closer to Estelle, coming inside the curtains of the four-poster bed. Estelle was filled with exquisite joy in the presence of her radiant Blessed Mother. Once again Estelle was reminded of her promise and she saw a white marble ex voto, this time decorated with a golden heart in flames, with a crown of roses pierced by a sword, and with the inscription: "I invoked Mary in the depths of my wretchedness. She obtained for me from her Son my complete cure." Estelle assured Mary that she would do her best. "If you wish to serve me," Mary responded, "be simple and let your actions accord with your words." After more words of encouragement, and admonishment about "people who make a pretense of piety," Mary vanished into the ether. The gentle light that had surrounded her presence remained in the room for a while before likewise vanishing.

Estelle's suffering now became acute. Her heart pounded as if her chest would explode and the pain in her stomach became excruciating. She prayed with her rosary in her left hand and gave all her suffering to God. She soon became calm, and after a brief rest, awoke completely cured of her illness. She sat up in bed and later recalled desiring a drink of beer to refresh herself! Only her right arm remained paralyzed. But on the following morning, Saturday, Father Salmon came to give her Communion. After receiving the Eucharist, she regained complete use of her right arm. Estelle's cure was instant and complete, as she was able to take food and drink immediately after her recovery. She soon resumed working around the house and garden, showing no lingering effects of her illness.

The following July, Estelle experienced three more visits by the Blessed Virgin. On the night of July 1st, Estelle was praying in her room when she saw Mary. This time Mary was surrounded by roses and the fragrance permeated the room. From her outstretched hands fell droplets of crystal water, like blessings falling to earth. Estelle was told to remain calm and patient, and was reassured, "Courage. I shall return." Mary returned to Estelle's room the following two nights, again appearing as a vision with roses and crystal droplets.

After these visitations, Estelle greatly desired to see her beloved Mary, and was continually restless in hopes of another apparition. For several months, there were no visions, but on September 9th, Estelle once again felt the pounding of her heart, like that felt at the approach of a lover. She was working at the Château de Poiriers, and could not get permission to go to her room in the village until that afternoon.

There, after hours of prayer, Mary appeared to her, saying, "You deprived yourself of my visit on August 15th, for you were not sufficiently calm. You have the French character: they want to know everything before learning, and understand everything before knowing. I awaited an act of submission and obedience from you... The treasures of my Son have been available for

Chapel of the Apparitions

a long time: let them pray." Mary now lifted from her chest a small piece of cloth, similar to the plain ones Estelle had noticed previously, but this cloth bore the design of the Sacred Heart. Holding the scapular up for Estelle to clearly see, Mary said, "This devotion pleases me...It is here that I shall be honored." Estelle soon afterwards made copies of the scapular, and received approval and encouragement from Our Lady.

Over the next four months, Estelle was blessed on six different occasions with apparitions of Mary. The Blessed Mother always offered words of encouragement and thanked Estelle for her work and steadfastness. She also gave warnings to Estelle, the Church and all of France. "I will take note of your efforts to be calm," she said during one visit. "It is not only in your case that I request it, but also for the Church and for France. The Church is not as calm as I would like... There is something wrong... They should pray... And France! What I have not done for her! Such warnings and yet she will not listen! I can no longer restrain my Son...France will suffer. Take courage and have confidence."

The final visit to Estelle occurred on December 8th, 1876. Once again, Estelle was praying in her room when the vision of Mary and the roses appeared before her. Mary made it clear that this was the last of her visits, but that she would always be close to Estelle and speak to her in her heart. Mary invited her to kiss the Blessed Virgin's own scapular, and Estelle later described this embrace as an experience of incomparable joy. Mary then gave her specific instructions: "You will go yourself to the prelate and will present him with this copy (of the scapular) that you have made. Tell him to do everything within his power to help you, and that nothing would be more pleasing to me than to see this livery on each of my children…See the graces that will be poured forth on those who will wear it with confidence, and help you to spread this devotion." Estelle now felt complete confidence in her mission and in her Blessed Lady's constant presence in her life.

Estelle did as she was instructed and met with the Archbishop of Bourges. He listened to her stories and was convinced of their truthfulness, promising to help Estelle promote the veneration of Our Lady. In 1894, he authorized the establishment of an Archconfraternity to promote the scapular and devotion to Our Lady of Pellevoisin. The organization exists to this day, now known as L'Association Notre-Dame de Miséricorde. In 1900, Estelle appeared before Pope Leo XIII who approved the promotion of the Sacred Heart scapular.

Estelle continued to live in the house at Pellevoisin, and the Countess eventually gave the house and surrounding grounds to the Dominican Sisters. In 1893, the Sisters and the Countess co-founded a monastery for contemplative prayer. Both Estelle and the Countess lived on the grounds of the convent and took vows as Third Order Dominican tertiaries.

In September 1983, the Theological Commission of Enquiry gave a favorable judgment on the case of Estelle Faguette on two counts: the miraculous nature of her cure (inexplicable from a medical point of view), and the value of the cure as a sign. The judgment stated, "In granting a miraculous cure to Estelle, God wished to appeal to our faith and bring credibility to a message." Estelle Faguette died August 23, 1929 at eighty-six, living more than fifty years following her miraculous cure by her Blessed Mother.

SANCTUARY OF OUR LADY OF MERCY
Sanctuaire Notre-Dame de Miséricorde

The Sanctuary of Our Lady of Mercy is comprised of the Chapel of the Apparitions, an information/reception desk and boutique, pilgrim lodging, dining facility, and a cloistered monastery. This contemplative community of the Sisters of Saint John lives a secluded life in the adjacent monastery. The Sisters spend their time in continual contemplation of Jesus and Mary, and support themselves from the sales of beautiful pottery and crafts at the boutique. The sanctuary is currently managed by a new order of Brothers of Saint John who live outside of town and, in addition to running the shrine, work with the rehabilitation of drug addicts at another location in town.

The building where the Chapel of the Apparitions is located was donated by the Countess de La Rochefoucauld, Estelle Faguette's employer, and lay foundress of the monastery. After her husband died, the Countess lived as a Dominican tertiary in the guesthouse of the monastery, fol-

Sanctuaire Notre-Dame de Miséricorde

lowing a life of prayer and seclusion. The Chapel of the Apparitions was Estelle's bedroom—where she initially came to be closer to the cemetery. Here the Virgin Mary appeared to her fifteen times.

The gold leaf altar in the Chapel was a gift from the Count and Countess Arthur de La Rochefoucauld. The walls, covered with white marble ex votos, are testimony to prayers answered. Each prayer is marked with the Sacred Heart design, as revealed to Estelle by the Virgin Mary. The statue of Mary with outstretched arms is in the position that Estelle witnessed during the apparitions, with the graces pouring forth from the palms of her hands. The baskets are for notes and prayers written to the Virgin Mary as Estelle had done when deathly ill while living at the chateau.

This shrine is a particularly powerful place to meditate, and one of our favorites in France. First the Dominican Sisters, and now the Sisters and Brothers of St. John, have practiced contemplative prayer in this room for more than a century, and the deep inner stillness they bring to this place is very perceivable. If one just sits quietly with closed eyes, with a still mind and an open heart, one can readily feel the blessings of Our Lady.

Once a year, on the last Sunday in August, the Archbishop of Bourges presides over a pilgrimage to the shrine. The graves of Estelle Faguette and Father Salmon, her confessor, are very close to the shrine

(refer to map). As you walk into the cemetery, take an immediate left and then a right at the wall. On the left, near the end of the building, is the white marble slab with Estelle's name. Her father and mother are buried on either side of her grave.

Cemetery of Estelle Faguette

Where is the Sanctuary of Our Lady of Mercy?
Où est le Sanctuaire Notre-Dame de Miséricorde?

SHRINE INFORMATION

Shrine: Pilgrimage Center (Centre de Pèlerinages)

Address: 3B, rue Notre-Dame/36180 Pellevoisin/France

Phone: 33 (0)2 54 39 06 49 **Fax:** 33 (0)2 54 39 04 66

E-mail: sanctuaire@pellevoisin.net

Website: www.pellevoisin.net French

Quiet areas for meditation: The small Chapel of the Apparitions (Chapelle des Apparitions).

English spoken: Typically

Hours: Chapel of the Apparitions: Daily 6:30AM–9PM.

Mass: Daily 11:30AM Chapel of the Apparitions.

Feasts and festivities: February 19 — Celebration of the miraculous cure of Estelle in 1876; Second Sunday after Easter — Feast of Divine Mercy (Fête de la Miséricorde Divine); August 15 — Feast of the Assumption (Assomption de Marie); Last Weekend of August — Annual Pilgrimage (Grand Pèlerinage Annuel fin août); December 8 — Feast of the Immaculate Conception.

Accessibility: The Chapel of the Apparitions has a few small steps and the lodging is not accessible. There are future plans for a bigger chapel and more lodging, which will be accessible.

Information office: The "Accueil" and "Boutique" are in connected rooms. The volunteer staff might not speak English, but they may be able find someone who can, if necessary.

Tours: Tours of the Chapel of the Apparitions are available in English. Please arrange in advance. There is no information in English for a self-guided tour, but the booklet listed below tells the story of the shrine.

Bookstore: The Boutique has a booklet in English, and the nuns of the monastery make their living from the beautiful pottery for sale.

Recommended books: The booklet, *Pellevoisin: A Message of Mercy and a Mission of Prayer*, by Sr. Barbara Estelle Beaumont O.P. Only available at the Shrine Boutique.

Lodging: The shrine provides 80 beds, two single beds per room, with toilet/shower down the hall. Directions: Coming from the south on D11, the shrine is immediately on your left as you enter the small village. There are two signs on the black iron fence: "Sanctuaire Notre Dame de Míséricorde" and "Notre-Dame de Pellevoisin Sanctuaire / Monastère des Soeurs de Saint Jean." If the gate is open, drive through the gate and park to the left, otherwise, park on the road. On the building are two signs: "Chapelle des Apparitions," and "Accueil / Boutique."

COMING AND GOING

PELLEVOISIN

Car: Pellevoisin is located 57 miles (92 km) southeast of Tours; 186 miles (300 km) south of Paris; and 19 miles (30 km) west of Châteauroux. From Tours, take N143 toward Châteauroux. At Buzançais, exit at D11, taking it north into town, and following it about 8 miles (13 km) to Pellevoisin. Watch for the left turn in town after you cross the river. From Châteauroux on A20, exit on N143 towards Tours. At Buzançais, exit at D11 and follow the directions above to Pellevoisin.

Train: The nearest train stations are in Châteauroux and Tours. From the train station, take the bus to Buzançais, then take a taxi to Pellevoisin about 8 miles (13 km).

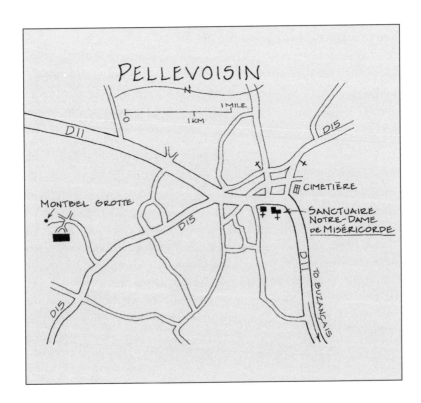

TOURIST INFORMATION

❋ The shrine operates as the only information center because it is such a small town.

❋ Comité Départemental de Tourisme de l'Indre/1 rue Saint Martin/ BP 141/36003 Châteauroux cedex/France Phone: 33 (0)2 54 07 36 36 Fax: 33 (0)2 54 22 31 21 Email: tourisme@cyberindre.org http://tourisme.cyberindre.org.

WEBSITE

Pèlerinage à Marie, Mère de Miséricorde www.pellevoisin.net — Official website about Our Lady of Pellevoisin shrine in French.

PLACES OF INTEREST NEAR PELLEVOISIN

MONTBEL GROTTO OF THE VIRGIN
Montbel Grotte de la Vierge

The Grotto of the Virgin is about five minutes out of town on the property of the chateau where the Count and Countess de La Rochefoucauld lived and where Estelle worked. The de La Rochefoucauld children built the grotto as a miniature version of the Lourdes grotto. From the Chapel of the Apparitions, go north on D11 to the north side of town. Turn left on D15 towards Villegouin. Turn right after two miles (3km) at Montbel, a sign will read "Montbel: Grotte de la Vierge." Drive about one mile until you see the carriage house and chateau on the left. Turn right and park on the dirt road: Do not block the driveway to the chateau. This is private property, so please stay on the path to the grotto. As long as visitors are respectful of the current resident's privacy, they will be allowed to visit the grotto. Walk toward the beautiful chateau, past the carriage house and turn right, following the blue signs on the path toward the grotto. Soon you will see the small grotto to the right. There is a basket to collect your prayer requests.

Ile de France

The Region of Ile de France is the number one tourist destination in the world, with over thirty-six million tourists flocking here each year. With Paris at its hub, there is no wondering why it is so popular, but there are also many sites to explore just outside of the French capital. Within an hour of Paris are the palaces of Versailles and Fontainebleau, and Monet's gardens at Giverny. As Paris is the international gateway to France, it is the logical place to start an adventure. The tourist can find many days worth of attractions and, for the spiritually inclined, there are many sites of inspiration as well. These include the Chapel of the Miraculous Medal, the shrine of St. Vincent de Paul, and the famous cathedrals of Notre Dame and Sacre Coeur. Within short distances of Paris are also the Gothic Cathedrals at Chartres and Reims. If one were planning a brief visit to France, Ile de France would be the "must see" region to explore.

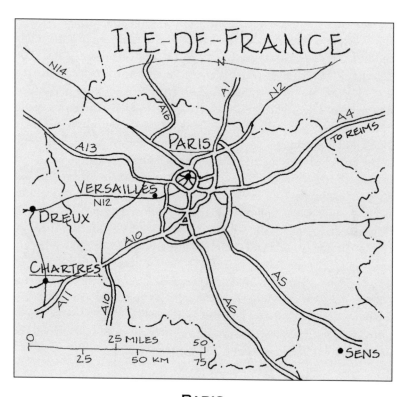

PARIS
St. Catherine Labouré
St. Louise de Marillac
St. Vincent de Paul
Bl. Frederic Ozanam
St. Genevieve

Paris

Population 2,125,000

One of the most popular tourist destinations in the world, Paris is known as the City of Light, with more than two hundred buildings lit up every evening to support that claim. Named after a Celtic tribe called "Parisii" that inhabited the area in 330 B.C., the city has been known since the thirteenth century as a cultural and artistic center of the Western world. Famous landmarks are in great supply, including the Eiffel Tower, Arc de Triomphe, and Notre Dame Cathedral. The Left Bank of the river Seine has drawn university students to the Sorbonne for over seven hundred years, creating a youthful, Bohemian atmosphere. The Right Bank, with the Champs Elysées and the Louvre museum, delivers a more upscale and cultured ambience. Notre Dame Cathedral is perched on the end of an island known as, île de la Cité, at the center of the city, and is a good place to start your pilgrimage. If visiting the Montmarte area, known for the Moulin Rouge and art scene, the Basilica of Sacre Coeur is a worthwhile stopping point. With so much to see and do in Paris, a visit to some small shrines will be a refreshing break. The Chapel of the Miraculous Medal is the site of Marian apparitions and contains the reliquaries of St. Catherine Labouré and St. Louise de Marillac. This is a lively shrine, located in a bustling area of the city, and just a few blocks away is the smaller and quieter shrine to St. Vincent de Paul. The sites and sounds of this dramatic city will always delight and stimulate the senses, while, fortunately for the spiritual seeker, these holy shrines create an oasis of peace, offering places of respite and contemplation.

ST. CATHERINE LABOURÉ

Sainte Catherine Labouré 1806–1876

"I tell Him everything that comes to my mind;
I tell Him my sorrows and my joys, and I listen."

Silence was a way of life for Catherine, as she kept within her heart sacred secrets of mystical experiences and visions of the Holy Mother. At the time it was created, no one knew who initiated the "Miraculous Medal," but millions of souls had been changed by the blessings imparted through its touch. After revealing her hidden identity in the final year of her life, the quiet Sister of Charity became known for her humble act of bringing the message and blessings of the Blessed Virgin to the world. But who was this enigmatic soul?

Born into the farming family of Madeleine and Pierre Labouré in the Burgundian village of Fain-les-Moutiers, Catherine was the ninth child to bless their ever-expanding household. May 2, 1806 was the day of her quiet arrival, and she was baptized the very next morning. The Labouré farmstead was a busy place, as the large family worked hard tending to the many fields and livestock. For the three girls of the family, education was of secondary concern, for feeding the workers and caring for the livestock

St. Catherine Labouré

was their primary purpose in life. It was not an easy life, and was particularly difficult for their mother, Madeleine. She had a total of seventeen pregnancies over twenty years, and died of exhaustion at the young age of 42, survived by ten of her children.

Catherine was nine at the time of her mother's passing. Though deeply saddened by her mother's departure, she quickly found solace in the Virgin Mary as her new Mother. Crying over her mother's lifeless body, the young girl looked up and saw a statue of Mary. She immediately rose and stood on a chair in front of the statue and pleaded for the all-embracing love of her Holy Mother. It was at this point that Catherine made her first commitment to the religious life by dedicating herself to Mary; "It is you that I choose as my Mother."

After spending the next two years in the home of her aunt at

Saint-Rémy, Catherine and her younger sister returned to work on the family farm. Their elder sister Marie wished to leave the farm for a religious vocation, which put their father Pierre in a quandary. Who would run the homestead? Catherine volunteered her services and quickly found herself as head of the household—before she was even twelve years old! Though the work was hard and tedious, Catherine always found time to attend Mass. She fasted on Fridays and Saturdays, as this practice helped her to keep the presence of Jesus and Mary foremost in her heart. During this time of her life she learned the art of silence. She would retreat to her tiny alcove off the dining room after serving meals to the workers. This routine established Catherine's dedication to duty and silence and would prove to be the hallmark of her life.

Catherine had her first mystical experience at age nineteen while still running her family household. In a dream, she saw herself praying in the church of Fain when an elderly priest entered and began performing Mass. At the conclusion of the rites, he motioned for Catherine to come near, but she ran away, and next found herself at the bedside of someone ill. As her dream continued, the elderly priest was again present, and told Catherine, "My daughter, it is good to care for the sick. You run away from me now, but one day you will be happy to come to me. God has designs on you! Do not forget it!"

With this dream, Catherine felt the calling to a religious life. However, her desire did not meet the approval of her father, and he decided to send her to Paris to work at the restaurant of her brother Charles. City life was not to Catherine's liking and she longed to become a nun. Charles was respectful of Catherine's plight and, after a year, sent her to Châtillon-sur-Seine to live in the household of her sister-in-law, Madame Hubert Labouré, who was the director of an aristocratic boarding school. Still desirous of a devout life, Catherine visited the nearby Daughters of Charity to communicate her yearnings to the superior there. When she was ushered into the parlor, she saw high on the wall a painting of an elderly man whom she immediately recognized as the priest in her dream. "He is our founder, Saint Vincent de Paul," said the young Sister accompanying her. Catherine remained silent, but her heart knew that she had found her true home. After much pleading, her father finally relented and allowed her to begin her postulancy in the house of Châtillon-sur-Seine in 1830, at the age of twenty-three. Three months later, she returned to Paris to serve at the Mother House of the Daughters of Charity, on rue du Bac.

On Catherine's return to the city, Paris was alive with a celebration of St. Vincent de Paul, as his relics were being moved from the Notre Dame Cathedral to the chapel of the Congregation of the Mission, just around the corner from rue du Bac. Catherine prayed there with her Sisters and felt an irresistible attraction to return each day. "I had the consolation of seeing his heart above the little reliquary in the Sisters' chapel...It appeared to me in three different ways, on three successive days: a white flesh color, which announced peace, calm, innocence and unity; and then fire red, which must inflame charity in hearts; and then, I saw it reddish-black, which makes the heart sad, this sadness implied a change in government." Within three months, King Charles X was overthrown, and France was once again thrown into the horrors of a revolution.

Catherine told her confessor of her inner visions, but he doubted their credibility and told her to keep her insights humbly to herself. She complied but continued to receive graces from the Lord. "I was favored with a great grace, that of seeing Our Lord in the Blessed Sacrament," she later wrote. " I saw him during the entire time of my seminary...except on the days I doubted." Though witness to many blessings, Catherine remained silent and held all her experiences safely in her heart.

In July of 1830, Catherine would have another extraordinary experience. On the night of the eighteenth, after celebrating the feast day of St. Vincent de Paul, Catherine retired to her room. Inspired by a devotional talk given by her Mother Superior, she longed to experience the presence of the Blessed Virgin. She went to sleep with the thought that St. Vincent would grant her this grace. She awoke at half past eleven to the sound of someone calling to her: "Sister, Sister." Gazing out from her bed, she saw a young child of four or five years, dressed in white and glowing with ethereal light. "Come to the chapel, the Blessed Virgin is waiting for you," said the child. Catherine dressed quickly, although with some trepidation, and followed the child to the chapel. Along the way, self-igniting candles lighted their path, and when they arrived at the chapel, all the candles were lit as if for midnight Mass. Catherine knelt in prayer until midnight when the child declared, "Look! The Blessed Virgin, She is here!" After first hearing a sound like the rustling of a silk robe, Catherine saw Our Lady seated on the director's chair at the altar. She stared in disbelief but, with coaxing from her young companion, she knelt before the beautiful Lady and placed her hands on her knees. "I don't know how long I stayed there," Catherine later wrote. "It was the sweetest moment of my life."

For two hours, Catherine was enraptured by the presence of Our Lady. Catherine was told many secrets—among them that she would be given a mission, that her order would reorganize, and that many evils would face France. "The times are evil. Misfortunes will befall France, the throne will be overthrown…the entire world will be overwhelmed by evils of all kinds… But," Our Lady continued, "come to the foot of this altar. There, graces will be poured out especially on those who ask Him for them. They will be poured out on the great and the humble." The vision faded soon thereafter, and Catherine returned to her room, once again led by her young angel guide. She laid in bed the remainder of the night, reverently contemplating the meaning of her vision.

At first light, Catherine sought her confessor, the young Father Aladel, and told him of her meeting with the Blessed Virgin. Catherine relayed to him the dire predictions, and also that one day he would found a new order called "The Children of Mary." Unmoved by Catherine's testimony, the Father told her to keep silent about her vision, and to continue in her normal life. Less than ten days later, the Revolution erupted again. The monarchy was overthrown, and blood flowed in the streets. Many churches and shrines were desecrated but, as the Blessed Mother had predicted, the Sisters of Charity were spared any harm. Father Aladel thought of Catherine's vision, but again dismissed its importance.

Four months passed, and Catherine longed for the reappearance of the Blessed Mother. This desire grew ever stronger in her heart, until she intuitively felt her prayer would be answered. On November 27th while seated among her Sisters, during the meditative silence of evening prayers, Catherine once again beheld a vision of Mary. "I seemed to hear some noise coming from the side of the tribune; looking to that side, I saw the Blessed Virgin. She was standing and was wearing a white silk robe, the color of dawn, her feet were resting on a globe, of which I could see only half; in her hands raised to the level of her breast, she held a globe effortlessly, her eyes were raised heaven-ward…her face was utterly beautiful, I could not describe it." Inwardly, Catherine heard a voice telling her that the globes represent the world, France, and each person in particular. Rays of light streamed from the image and Catherine heard, "This is the symbol of graces I pour out on the persons who ask me for them."

The vision now appeared as an oval framed picture before Catherine, and above the image were the golden letters: "O Mary, conceived without sin, pray for us who have recourse to you." The voice once again spoke inwardly to the young novitiate, saying, "Have a medal struck on this model. The persons who wear it will receive great graces; the graces will be inexhaustible for those who have confidence." The picture now rotated, exposing the reverse side, on which was the letter M surmounted with a cross. Beneath the letter

Reliquary of St. Catherine Labouré

M were two hearts, one circumscribed by a crown of thorns and the other pierced with a sword. The hearts were those of Jesus and Mary—united for the redemption of all souls.

When the apparition vanished, Catherine reveled in the joy of the mystical experience. She then sought out her confessor to relate the latest messages, but he ordered her to keep her "illusions" to herself. Catherine dutifully obeyed, though convinced of the validity of her visions. That December, the Virgin once again appeared to Catherine during evening prayers. Catherine understood her mission to be the founding of the medal and the spreading of the good news of

Mary's love and grace. But, this time Catherine refrained from confiding in her confessor, and kept her experience locked inside her heart.

The following January saw the end of Catherine's novitiate. Taking the habit as a Sister of Charity, she left rue du Bac to serve at the hospice of the community at Reuilly. Now twenty-four years old, Catherine found her final home and lived to serve this community for the remainder of her life.

But, what of the medal? The Virgin's words echoed in her mind and heart, and Catherine knew she must obey this inner guidance over the indifference of her confessor. She approached Father Aladel in the spring of 1831, and again in the fall of that year, telling him, "The Virgin is angry!" He listened politely to her pleas but again sent her off without consenting to her demands. However, he too was inwardly receiving a call to action. Speaking to a fellow priest and friend, Father Aladel was convinced to bring the subject before the Archbishop. Much to the Father's surprise, the Archbishop understood the grace of the project and ordered the medal struck. "There is no question here of prejudging the nature of the vision or its circumstances. We are simply going to distribute a medal. The tree will be judged by its fruits."

The judgment was not long in coming. Shortly after the medal was offered to the faithful, miracles were reported, healings witnessed and conversions made. The medal became known as "miraculous" and its fame spread throughout Europe. Within ten years, a million medals were produced, and by the end of Catherine's life, an astonishing one billion medals were gracing souls worldwide. Surely, Catherine's mission for the Virgin Mary was accomplished—but what of her?

For over forty years Catherine served at Reuilly, tending to the cows and chickens in her care and administering to the patients of the hospice, all without seeking recognition for her part in the creation of the medal. Rumors were constantly circulating about the mysterious visionary of the Miraculous Medal, but no one ever knew who was the recipient of the blessed apparitions. Catherine's secret remained hidden until the final chapter of her life. Nearing her death, Catherine inwardly felt the Virgin's permission to tell of her visions, so finally, she told her Superior about the events that took place at rue du Bac. Listening to the story with increasing awe, Sister Superior Dufés fell on her knees before the humble Sister and thanked the Blessed Mother for Her enduring grace.

Catherine peacefully passed away on December 31, 1876 at the age of seventy. By the time of her funeral procession on January 3rd, word had spread of her connection with the Miraculous Medal and thousands came to offer their gratitude. Catherine's body was buried at the chapel at Reuilly and was venerated there for fifty-six years, until 1933. In that year of Catherine's beatification, her body was exhumed and moved to rue du Bac, where it was interred in the Chapel of the Miraculous Medal. Canonized in 1947, Catherine was rightfully named "The Saint of Silence." Since then, her incorrupt body has remained in the chapel at rue du Bac as a constant reminder of the graces that come to us through our Blessed Mother.

ST. LOUISE DE MARILLAC
Sainte Louise de Marillac 1591–1660

"Love the poor, honor them, my children,
as you would honor Christ Himself."

While the name of St. Vincent de Paul is known throughout the world for the work of his charitable organizations, much of this work would not have been accomplished without the help of his friend and co-worker, Louise de Marillac. This little known saint was the co-founder of the Daughters of Charity and spearheaded that organization, which reshaped the entire philanthropic structure of seventeenth century France. Living in a time of great poverty and illness, Louise worked to reorganize how care was given in hospitals, orphanages, foundling homes, elderly hospices, foster homes, psychiatric facilities and relief centers. Her work, aided and guided by St. Vincent, has touched countless lives, but that is not what made her a saint. Louise's deep faith, strong will power, and devotion to God propelled her from an illegitimate birth to the role of sainthood.

Louise was born out of wedlock in 1591 to Louis de Marillac, a member of the prominent Marillac family. His brother was a major figure in the court of Queen Marie de Medici, and though Louis was not a member of the Queen's court, he lived and worked among the aristocrats. Louise grew up amidst this affluent society of Paris but without a stable home life. She did not know her mother and her loving father died when she was fifteen. Nevertheless, she was well cared for and received her education at the royal monastery of Poissy near Paris, where her aunt was a Dominican nun. Louise was educated among the country's elite and introduced to the arts and humanities as well as the spiritual life. She felt drawn to the cloistered life and made application to the Daughters of Passion in Paris, but was refused admission. It is not clear if her refusal was due to her continual poor health or other reasons, but her spiritual director's prophetic response to her application was that God had "other designs" for her.

St. Louise de Marillac

Devastated by this refusal, Louise was at a loss as to the next step in her spiritual development. Her family convinced her that marriage was the best alternative and an uncle arranged for her marriage to Antony Le Gras, an aspiring young man who seemed destined for great accomplishments. Louise took the marriage in stride and the couple had their only child in their first year of marriage, in 1613. Though devoted to her family, Louise still longed for a life of service to God and to fulfill her inner vow of dedication to Him. Soon after the birth of their child, Antony contracted a chronic illness and eventually became bedridden. Louise lovingly cared for her husband and child but always wondered if being a wife and mother was her true vocation.

Louise suffered for years with this internal doubt and prayed for resolution, which she finally received during an inner experience of divine communication with God. She wrote, "On the feast of the Pentecost (in 1623), during Holy Mass or while I was praying in the church, my mind was completely freed of all doubt. I was advised that I should remain with my husband and that the time would come when

I would be in the position to make vows of poverty, chastity, and obedience and that I would be in a small community where others would do the same." She also received insight that she would be guided to a new spiritual director (St. Vincent de Paul) and that this grace was coming to her from her recently deceased confessor, St. Frances de Sales.

Two years after this experience, Antony died and left Louise to fulfill her greater mission. Louise now took on the task of her own spiritual development. She turned her small home into her own personal monastery. Being a woman of great energy, intelligence, determination and devotion, Louise wrote her own "Rules of Life in the World" which detailed a rigid structure for her life, more rigid than most cloisters. Every minute of her day was accounted for, giving no room for spontaneity. Times were set aside for reciting the Offices of the Blessed Virgin, assisting at Mass, receiving Holy Communion, meditation, spiritual reading, fasting, penance, reciting the rosary, and special prayer. Still, Louise managed to find time to maintain her household, entertain guests and nourish her son, now thirteen years old. This great enthusiasm was a boon for Louise, but she also needed guidance and tempering of her energy. This came from her relationship with Vincent de Paul.

The two met around the time of Antony's passing in 1625. Vincent quickly recognized Louise's power and intelligence, and understood her need for spiritual direction. Over the next eight years, Vincent and Louise communicated often through letters and personal meetings, with Vincent guiding Louise to reach a more balanced life of moderation, peace and calm. In 1632, Louise took a reclusive retreat to seek inner guidance regarding her next step. Her deep intuition led her to understand that it was time to go into the world to help the poor and needy while still maintaining an inner spiritual life. Louise felt ready for her worldly mission and communicated these aspirations to Vincent. By the end of 1633, he too received the guidance for them to begin a work together, thus bringing the Daughters of Charity into existence.

The charitable care of the poor was completely disorganized in seventeenth century France. Many under-privileged people were victims of non-existent care or poor hospital conditions. The Ladies of Charity, founded by Vincent de Paul many years earlier, provided some care and monetary resources, but they were unorganized and inefficient. Starting in 1633, Louise took on the task of bringing order to the chaos. Though the wealthy Ladies of Charity had the funds to aid the poor, they did not have the time or temperament to work "in the trenches." Louise found her help in humble country girls who had the energy and the proper attitude to deal with the destitute and the suffering. With a group of four girls living in her home, Louise began training the young women to care for those in need and also taught them how to develop a deep spiritual life. "Love the poor, honor them, my children, as you would honor Christ Himself." This was the foundation of the Daughters of Charity.

Louise's work with the young women developed into a system of care at the Hotel-Dieu, the oldest and largest hospital in Paris. Their work became well known and the Daughters were invited to Angers to take over the organization of the hospital there. This was the first project outside Paris for the fledgling community, so Louise herself made the arduous journey to Angers in the company of three Sisters. After completing negotiations with the city and the hospital, Louise instituted collaboration among the doctors, nurses and others to form a comprehensive team. This model was highly successful and is still in use today by the Daughters of Charity. Under the guidance of Louise de Marillac the Daughters expanded their scope of service to include hospitals, orphanages, institutions for the elderly and mentally ill, prisons, schools and the battlefield.

In working with her charges, Louise emphasized a balanced life, as Vincent de Paul had taught her. It was the integration of contemplation and activity that made Louise's work so successful. The Sisters were encouraged to pray and work together, and to live every moment in the imitation of Christ by inwardly asking; "What would Jesus do in this situation?" The key for Louise was letting go of her personal ambitions and surrendering to God's will. She wrote near the end of her life, "Certainly it is the great secret of the spiritual life to abandon to God all that we love by abandoning ourselves to all that He wills."

Louise continued her work with the Daughters of Charity until she was almost seventy years old. It may be said that St. Vincent was the heart of the Daughters of Charity, while Louise was the head. This gives tribute to her strong intellect, organizational skills and the ability to get things accomplished. Louise was positive and exuberant in her energy, always urging her Sisters to do more and do it better. But along with the activity, she also preached love. Nearing her death, she wrote to her spiritual family, "Take good care of the service of the poor. Above all, live together in great union and cordiality, loving one another in imitation of the union and life of Our Lord. Pray earnestly to the Blessed Virgin, that she may be your only Mother." After a time of increasing weakness and ill health, Louise de Marillac left her body on March 15, 1660, six months before the passing of Vincent de Paul. Her legacy is the organization she left behind, and the inspira-

Reliquary of St. Louise de Marillac

tion of her active, God-centered life. Louise was canonized in 1934 and is the patron saint of social workers and caregivers.

CHAPEL OF OUR LADY OF THE MIRACULOUS MEDAL
Chapelle Notre-Dame de la Médaille Miraculeuse

The Chapel of Our Lady of the Miraculous Medal is the Motherhouse of the Daughters of Charity of St. Vincent de Paul, and houses one hundred and fifty Sisters. As you walk from the busy street into the entry courtyard, you will notice the information office on the right. The Sisters usually do not speak English, so unless you want to request to talk to an English-speaking Sister, keep on walking toward the rear of the courtyard. As you walk, notice the wall to your left that has a bas-relief of the story of the apparitions along with French text. On your right, past the bathrooms, is a room where Miraculous Medals are sold. At times, there is a priest in the hallway near the Chapel who

Chapelle Notre-Dame de la Médaille Miraculeuse

will bless the Medals for you. Continue on towards the Chapel at the end of the courtyard; the doors to the Chapel are on the right. Post-cards and a brochure in English are available on your left, across from the Chapel entrance.

Once inside this busy chapel, start at the right side altar, where the Saint Vincent de Paul shrine contains his incorrupt heart in a gold-plated reliquary below his statue. This relic was kept in Turin, Italy during the Revolution and brought to the Cathedral of Lyon in 1805. It was installed in its current location in 1947. This was the main and only altar of the Chapel from 1815-1856, and it was at this altar that the Blessed Virgin appeared to Catherine and told her: "Come to the foot of this altar. There, graces will be poured out on all those, small, or great, who ask for them with confidence and fervor." The chair thought to be the one that the Virgin Mary sat on during her first apparition to Catherine is also on display. To the left of this altar is the shrine of St. Catherine Labouré, under the statue that depicts her vision of the Virgin Mary as she appeared to Catherine on this spot on November 27, 1830. The Blessed Virgin is offering a golden globe of the world to God. Here she requested of Catherine, "Have a medal made on this model. Those who will wear it with confidence will receive great graces." St. Catherine's body was moved here in 1933 after fifty-seven years in the chapel of the House of Reuilly. At that time, her body was found to be completely incorrupt.

The main altar, installed in 1856, displays a white marble statue of

Mary standing on the globe. The rays falling from her hands represent the graces we receive when we pray to her. Although Catherine never directly approved of any of the statues embodying her vision, this statue attempts to replicate how the Virgin Mary asked to be represented on the Miraculous Medal. The golden silver tabernacle on the altar is the same one that the Blessed Virgin bowed before in 1815. The fresco above the altar recalls the first vision on the night of July 18, 1830.

To the left of the main altar is the St. Joseph Altar, installed in 1914. Further to the left is the shrine of St. Louise de Marillac, co-founder with St. Vincent de Paul of the Company of the Daughters of Charity (refer to her biography in this chapter).

Where is rue du Bac?
Où est la Rue du Bac?

Where is the Chapel of Our Lady of the Miraculous Medal?
Où est la Chapelle Notre-Dame de la Médaille Miraculeuse?

May we speak to an English-speaking sister?
Pouvons nous parler à une sœur qui parle anglais?

SHRINE INFORMATION

Shrine: Chapel of Our Lady of the Miraculous Medal (Chapelle Notre-Dame de la Médaille Miraculeuse)

Address: 140, rue du Bac/75340 Paris Cedex 07/France

Phone: 33 (0)1 49 54 78 88 **Fax:** 33 (0)1 49 54 78 89

E-mail: medaillle.miraculeuse@wanadoo.fr

Website: http://chapellenotredamedelamedaillemiraculeuse.com

Quiet areas for meditation: The chapel is the only place, and it is very busy, with sometimes two masses going on at the same time in different languages. Even so, it is a very devotional environment.

English spoken: You will need to request to speak with a Sister who speaks English for any questions.

Hours: Mon–Sat 9AM–12PM; 3PM-6; Sun 10AM–12PM. Closed annually from January 4–24.

Mass: Weekdays 8AM, 10:30, 12:30PM; Tuesdays 8AM, 10:30, 12:30PM, 4, 6:30; Sat 8AM, 10:30, 12:30PM; Mass of Anticipation: 5:15PM; Sun 7:30AM,10, 11:15.

Feasts and festivities: March 15 — St. Louise de Marillac's Feast Day; September 27 — St. Vincent de Paul's Feast Day; November 27 — Feast of the Miraculous Medal; November 28 — St. Catherine Labouré's Feast Day.

Accessibility: Everywhere except upstairs, where Mass is sometimes held for groups.

Information office: To the right, immediately as you enter.

Tours: For pilgrim tour groups, contact the Pilgrim Reception Office (Accueil des Pèlerins) at the numbers listed above to make arrangements ahead of time. Tours include a twenty-minute video in English. For individual pilgrims, there is usually an English-speaking Sister available.

Bookstore: Across from the chapel entrance, there are postcards and brochures for sale. The book in English on the life of St. Catherine Labouré is available at the reception office where you first enter the courtyard.

Recommended books: *The Life of Catherine Labouré* by René Laurentin, Collins Liturgical Publications/Sisters of Charity of St. Vincent de Paul, 1983, and a booklet *Catherine Labouré: The Saint of Silence*, both available at the shrine. *Saint Catherine Labouré of the Miraculous Medal* by Joseph Dirvin, Tan Books & Publishers, is available on the internet or from the publisher.

Lodging: None

Directions: The shrine is on the Left Bank in the Seventh Arrondissement. The nearest Metro is at Sèvre Babylone (not "rue du Bac") on Lines 12 and 10. From the platform, take the exit (sortie) "rue Velpeau" where you will see the department store Bon Marché. Walk towards rue de Sèvres and take a right along the Bon Marché and a right on rue du Bac, a narrow, one-way street in between rue de Babylone and rue de Sèvre. The Chapel is across from the department store at 140 rue du Bac. See Paris map, page 155.

Bus: 39, 63, 70, 84, 87, 94.

WEBSITES

Association of the Miraculous Medal www.amm.org/catherine.htm — Vincentians: Congregation of the Mission Midwest Province, St. Louis, Missouri, USA. Biography of St. Catherine Labouré and history of the Miraculous Medal.

Chapelle Notre Dame de la Médaille Miraculeuse http://chapellenotredamedelamedaillemiraculeuse.com — Official website for the Chapel of Our Lady of the Miraculous Medal in Paris.

The Company of the Daughters of Charity of St. Vincent de Paul www.filles-de-la-charite.org — Official international website for the Daughters of Charity.

Eternal Word Television Network www.ewtn.com/library/MARY/CATLABOU.HTM — Lengthy biography from the book by Fr. Joseph Dirvin.

THE GARDEN OF CATHERINE LABOURÉ
Jardin Catherine Labouré

Around the corner from the Chapel of the Miraculous Medal, at 29 rue de Babylone, is a garden once owned by the Daughters of Charity. It is now co-owned by the Sisters and the city and consists of a vegetable garden and children's playground. The garden is directly behind the convent, separated by a wall with the entrance on rue de Babylone. This is a good place for a picnic lunch and a rest while visiting the shrines in this area. See Paris map, page 155.

HOUSE OF CATHERINE LABOURÉ
Maison Catherine Labouré
Reuilly, Paris

Saint Catherine lived forty-six years in Reuilly. The building was torn down and the garden sold to build the current housing for seniors. St. Catherine was initially buried in a crypt here from 1876-1933, one floor below the chapel. This room is now a small museum with personal items and furniture used by the saint. Saint Catherine's incorrupt heart is in a reliquary over the old crypt. The chapel upstairs displays the saint's finger in a reliquary inside the altar.

Please be mindful that this is not a shrine, but operates as housing

Maison Catherine Labouré, Reuilly, Paris

for seniors. If you speak French, it will not be as difficult to find someone to show you around. They do not have staff to do this. One of the Sisters who live there is called to provide the tour, as the crypt/museum is locked. It is advisable to call ahead to see if you can arrange for someone to show you around. Be prepared to speak French.

Address: 77 rue de Reuilly/75012 Paris/France Twelfth Arrondissement Phone: 33 (0)1 44 75 45 45 Fax: 33 (0)1 43 46 54 26 Metro: Line 8 to Montgallet. Walk north about a half block and you will see an iron gate on the right side, with a chapel in front of a six-story building. Ring the bell and say you want to visit the chapel.

We would like to visit
St. Catherine Labouré's relics and chapel.
Nous voudrions visiter le reliquarie
et la chapelle de Sainte Catherine Labouré.

OTHER CATHERINE LABOURÉ SHRINES IN FRANCE

BIRTHPLACE OF ST. CATHERINE LABOURÉ
Maison St. Catherine Labouré
Fain-Les-Moutiers

The farm where Catherine Labouré was born is in Fain-les-Moutiers, 143 miles (230 km) southeast of Paris. The Sisters of Charity provide lodging, meals, and retreat facilities for groups, individuals and young people. Address: Maison Ste-Catherine Lavouré/21500 Fain-Les-Moutiers/France Phone: 33 (0)3 80 96 70 65 Fax: 33 (0)3 80 96 70 36. Be prepared to speak French.

PLACES OF INTEREST NEAR RUE DU BAC

ST. VINCENT DE PAUL

CHAPEL OF ST. VINCENT DE PAUL
La chapelle de Saint Vincent de Paul

The shrine of St. Vincent de Paul is within walking distance, a few blocks from rue du Bac, at 95 rue de Sèvres. As you exit the Chapel at rue du Bac, turn right and walk to rue de Sèvres. Cross the street, and then turn right. Walk about one block to the Chapel. Refer to St. Vincent de Paul's biography in this chapter.

SOCIETY OF FOREIGN MISSIONS IN PARIS
Missions Étrangères de Paris

The Society of Foreign Missions is one block from the Chapel of the Miraculous Medal, at 128 rue du Bac. Upon leaving the Chapel of the Medal at rue du Bac, turn left to go to the Missions. As you enter the courtyard, you will see the chapel up some side stairs, and the crypt located down the stairs directly in front of you. The upstairs chapel is a good place for quiet meditation and prayer. Downstairs is an extensive museum, relics of the martyrs and a chapel for Mass. In the eighteenth century, the Seminary of Foreign Missions, based here, sent new missionaries to countries in Asia. Since then more than two hundred priests have died as martyrs; twenty-three of them are officially recognized as saints. Their most famous missionary was St. Theophane Venard, to whom St. Therese of Lisieux prayed. The bookstore on the corner of rue du Bac and rue de Babylone is connected to the museum downstairs. See Paris map, page 155.

Address: Missions Étrangères de Paris/128, rue du Bac/75341 Paris/Cedex 07/France Phone: 33 (0)1 44 39 10 40 Website: www.mepasie.org French Hours: Chapel Daily 6:45AM–6PM; Crypt and Museum Tues–Sat 11AM–6:30PM. Directions: The Society of Foreign Missions is one block from the Chapel of the Miraculous Medal at 128 rue du Bac.

ST. VINCENT DE PAUL
Saint Vincent de Paul 1580–1660

"God is love and we must come to Him by love."

Seeking one's personal path to God is the basis of every spiritual life. Some find their path when they are young, while others wander through life for many years before finding their personal connection with God. Vincent de Paul's life is interesting in that he was forty-five years of age before he found his true mission and calling. Though a priest since the age of 20, it was twenty-five years later that he realized that his destiny was to serve God through the poor. He also discovered that the sacred life is a balance between activity and prayer, and that reaching this balance is the key to finding God. St. Vincent's journey is one of inspiration to all of us who seek our own path to the divine.

Little is known of Vincent's early life—only that he was born in 1580 or 1581 at Pouy, in Gascony, in the south of France. He was the third of six children born to a peasant family and his early goal was to earn a good pension to support his family. To reach this goal, Vincent looked to the priesthood, for in his day many priests lived a very comfortable life if they served in an affluent parish. Ordained by the age of twenty, Vincent soon sought to establish himself in a profitable situation—but to no avail. After two trips to Rome and unfulfilled promises of appointments to bishopric seats, the young priest found his hopes of an easy life diminishing. By the time he was twenty-eight, he still had no prospects, so he traveled to Paris to seek his future. Here he would find his heart's desire, but not in the way he initially intended.

The Paris of 1608 was in the midst of a spiritual revival. Many learned theologians made their homes here, most notably at the Sorbonne. Vincent made the acquaintance of Father (and later Cardinal) Bérulle and Father Duval. These men would be his spiritual mentors for decades to come and helped to shape his life. Father Duval introduced the young Vincent to the Rule of Perfection by an English Capuchin monk, and Vincent took the writing to heart. Through it he gained the understanding that to do God's will, one must be open and wait for God's lead. This would prove to be Vincent's motif operandi for his life's work.

In 1612, Vincent was named the parish priest for the rural community of Clichy, just northwest of Paris. This would prove to be a vital experience for Vincent, as he had his first real taste of working directly with the poor and serving their spiritual needs. This new form of service made him very joyful, and the normally dour priest told his superior that he was happier than the Bishop or the Pope! Certainly, he was starting to understand his calling. But in less than a year, he was called back to Paris to work as the tutor and chaplain to the wealthy Gondi family. Vincent was sad to leave the people of his parish, but unbeknownst to him, this next step in his life would lead him to his true calling.

Vincent served the Gondi family by tutoring their children, but also by acting as the family's personal priest and confessor. Madame Gondi was particularly taken by Vincent's spirit, and encouraged him to preach and serve all the people who worked on the family's many estates. On one such mission, Vincent heard the confession of a dying man who had not received a proper confession in years, and who felt sanctified by Vincent's indulgence. Madame Gondi was shocked to hear that such an absence of confessions was the common state of the peasants in the area and subsequently urged Vincent to serve all those in need. It was now that Vincent began to grasp his destined mission, and with great vigor, he began preaching and ministering to the poor.

During these years of service to the Gondi family, Vincent met a fellow priest who struggled with doubt about his faith. Vincent consoled the man, but as a result of this contact, fell into his own inner turmoil and experienced three years of agonizing doubts. This trial of

St. Vincent de Paul

darkness was difficult for Vincent, and he felt powerless to overcome his distress. At times, all he could do was clutch a copy of the Apostles' Creed he carried over his heart, and pray for redemption. Vincent gave his heart to God at the depths of his despair and realized that he could find peace only through serving the poor. He also knew that he could not continue to live in the wealthy confines of the Gondi's and rightly serve the needy, so he secretly left their home and moved to Châtillon-des-Dombes, near Lyon, where he began his new ministry.

In these environs, Vincent was again in his element. He, like his parishioners, was the poorest of the poor, but he thrived on the renewed feeling of an inner love for God. Vincent typically spent half of his day serving and teaching among the people, and the other half in contemplation and study. He encouraged the local priests to rejuvenate their own spiritual lives and they soon began to emulate his example. This balance between service and prayer was the foundation of Vincent's spiritual life and became a central theme in his teachings.

During his very first year at Châtillon-des-Dombes, Vincent began to organize the women of the community to help their destitute neighbors. One morning before Sunday service, Vincent was told of a needy family in the parish that could not make ends meet due to a severe illness. During the day's sermon, he preached of the need to serve one's fellow man and, by the end of the day, an overwhelming number of people had volunteered their time and resources to help the needy

Reliquary of St. Vincent de Paul

family. This was the seed of the first Confraternity of Charity, which later developed into the Ladies of Charity in Paris, and ultimately, into a worldwide service organization. Vincent's genius was his ability to create enthusiasm among his parishioners, lead them in organizing themselves, and then give them autonomy to continue their mission on their own terms. This act of empowerment was the successful cornerstone of Vincent's work, for it enabled his mission to expand at the grass roots level.

Vincent was in Châtillon-des-Dombes less than a year before Madame Gondi found him out, and demanded that he return to work in Paris. Seeing the opportunity to develop a wider mission, Vincent returned to Paris around Christmas, 1617. During the next seven years, Vincent's vocation came into complete focus as several experiences changed his life.

The first of these events occurred after Vincent had met Francis de Sales and Jane de Chantal. Vincent developed a close relationship with these two saints, and was especially inspired by Francis de Sales' great gentleness and overwhelming love for God. This love was so transforming that Vincent felt a deep longing to cleanse his own heart of its usual melancholy, and to awaken it in the joyous love of God. To this end, he went on an extended retreat in Soissons and prayed for his own transformation. Over time, his prayers were answered and his usually stern demeanor dissolved into a more loving and gentle one. His heart was opening to the grace and power of divine love.

A long unresolved aspect of Vincent's life was that of his relationship with his family. He had left them at the age of twenty and had not returned in twenty-three years. His first years away from home were spent in seeking a secure vocation to provide for his family's future, but he had failed in this endeavor. Though he had since abandoned this duty, he still felt an inward responsibility toward them. Finally, at the age of forty-three, Vincent returned home to Pouy to make amends. Vincent's parents had long since died, but the remainder of the family was doing well and welcomed the peasant priest. He spent ten days in their loving company and then told his kinfolk that he expected no inheritance from them and that they should expect nothing from him. Upon leaving Pouy, Vincent began to weep bitterly, for the feeling of responsibility for his family was still a heavy burden on his heart. For the next three months, Vincent wept often and tried to reconcile his internal conflict. He finally came to understand that the poor were his family now, and that his duty was to serve them with all his heart. Now inwardly feeling free of his former familial duties, Vincent began serving the needy with increased enthusiasm and energy.

The final step in Vincent's development involved the founding of the Congregation of the Mission. Vincent's benefactor, Madame Gondi, was nearing death and wished to finance a community of priests who would preach at all her estates. The Jesuits and other religious communities would not take on the mission, which left Vincent without a means to satisfy Madame Gondi's worthy desire. Vincent confided in his longtime mentor Father Duval, who immediately saw God's hand in the situation, and encouraged Vincent to begin his own organization. So, in April of 1625, Vincent de Paul founded the Congregation of the Mission to preach to the poor people in rural areas, which ultimately defined Vincent's life work.

The next thirty-five years of Vincent's life were spent in serving through the Congregation of the Mission and organizing its growth and direction. Though starting in 1625 with only three priests, by 1660 the Mission had chapters in France, Italy, Sardinia, Scotland, Ireland, Tunis, Algiers, Madagascar and Poland. The Mission's service to the poor included ministering to the convicts of the galleys, refugees from war-torn provinces and victims of epidemics. Several other organizations sprang from Vincent's work with the Mission, and these sister organizations fleshed out his greater work. These organizations and services included the Confraternity of Charity, the Ladies of Charity, the Daughters of Charity co-founded with St. Louise de Marillac (refer to her biography in this chapter), retreats for the laity and priests, and the Tuesday Conference of Priests. Vincent was also the spiritual director of Jane de Chantal and took on the direction of the Order of the Visitation.

When we look at the historical impact of Vincent de Paul's life, it is easy to see that he started his own French Revolution by organizing charity for the poor, developing proper hospital and elderly hospice care, establishing homes for foundlings and foster children, and finally, founding monastic orders to help run these institutions. It is difficult to imagine the energy required to accomplish all this in one lifetime!

Obviously, Vincent's life was one of intense activity, but in this activity he found God. "We have to sanctify our occupations by seeking

God in them," he wrote, "and by doing them to find God in them, rather than to get them done." The defining quality of his life was the balance between activity and prayer. It took him many years to finally achieve this balance, but it enabled him to work continually in God's grace and to carry out a mission of unimaginable scope. Another significant aspect of his life was Vincent's surrender to love. The early years of his priesthood were marked with stoic devotion and earthly goals. But over the years he softened and, especially after meeting St. Frances de Sales, opened his heart to accept all people as they are and to love them as children of God. These traits are those of a saint— ones we can strive to emulate.

True to his active life, Vincent died "with his boots on." In his eightieth year he was still completely engulfed in working for the poor through his multitude of organizations. The saint was growing progressively weaker, yet he unceasingly continued with his life's mission. Finally, on September 27, 1660, Vincent de Paul quietly left his body during the morning hour of prayer. How appropriate. A witness at his passing said, "At the moment of his death, he surrendered his beautiful soul into the hands of the Lord and, seated there, he was handsome, more majestic and venerable to look at then ever." St. Vincent de Paul was canonized in 1737 and was later proclaimed patron saint of all charitable societies—a fitting honor for this peasant priest.

THE CHAPEL OF ST. VINCENT DE PAUL
La chapelle de Saint Vincent de Paul

This Chapel, which houses the relics of St. Vincent, is discretely situated on the busy rue de Sèvres, near the Chapel of the Miraculous Metal. Upon entering the usually darkened chapel, you will see the wax figure of St. Vincent in a glass reliquary high above the main altar. There are stairs on either side of the altar that lead up to the reliquary, where there is some room to pray. The bones of St. Vincent are inside the wax figure, while his incorrupt heart is at the nearby Chapel of the Miraculous Medal.

On the left of the main altar is a small side chapel where local congregants are often found in prayer, and on either side of the main aisle are shrines containing the relics of St. John Gabriel Perboyere

(1802-1840) and Blessed Francis Regis Clet (1748-1820), both martyred in China. The chapel is usually very quiet. There is a small bookshop near the entrance on the left side.

SHRINE INFORMATION

La chapelle de Saint Vincent de Paul

Shrine: La chapelle des Lazaristes

Address: 95, rue de Sèvres/ 75006 Paris/France

Phone: 33 (0)1 45 49 84 84
Fax: 33 (0)1 45 49 84 85

E-mail: None

Website: None

Quiet areas for meditation: The church is not crowded and is quiet.

English spoken: Rarely

Hours: Open 6:45AM; closed 12PM-2.

Mass: Mon-Sat 7:15AM; Sun 10:30AM. Mass can be arranged with your own chaplain as part of a group with advanced notice, or with an English-speaking priest if available.

Feasts and festivities: September 27 — Feast Day of St. Vincent de Paul.

Accessibility: A side door has one step, then two inside the chapel.

Tours: If part of a church group, an English-speaking priest can give a tour, if available, and with advance notice.

Bookstore: Inside the chapel to the left is a small bookshop.

Recommended books: *Vincent de Paul and Louise de Marillac: Rules, Conferences, and Writings*, The Classics of Western Spirituality, Paulist Press, 1995.

Lodging: None

Directions: The Chapel is one block from the intersection of rue de Sèvres and rue du Bac, to the west, away from Bon Marché. Metro Lines 10 & 12, Sèvres Babylone station. See Paris map, page 155.

WEBSITES

Congregation of the Mission
www.cmvocation.org/html/links/links.html — Priests and Brothers of
St. Vincent with links to Vincentian organizations worldwide.

Daughters of Charity www.doc.org — Information on the mission of
the Daughters of Charity.

St. Vincent de Paul Society www.svdpusa.org — Information on the
society in the US.

Miraculous Medal Association www.amm.org — The history of the
Miraculous Medal.

Vincentian Family Worldwide www.famvin.org — Information on
the different branches and works of the Vincentian Family.

BLESSED FREDERIC OZANAM
Bienheureux Frédérique Ozanam 1813–1853

The Society of St. Vincent de Paul bears the saint's name, but it was
founded by Frederic Ozanam almost two centuries after the saint's
death. Born in Milan, Italy, on April 23, 1813, Antoine Fredrick
Ozanam was the fifth of fourteen children born to parents of French
and Jewish heritage. The family returned to France in 1815. Only
three of the children survived childhood and the Ozanam family felt
compelled to serve the poor out of their compassion for the unfortu-
nate. This compassion was handed down to their son Fredrick, who
would move to Paris to study literature and make his own mark in
service to the poor.

   At age twenty, this young student became involved in the founding
of the Conference of Charity, a fledgling organization seeking to serve
those in need. Based on the teachings of St. Vincent, the volunteers
worked with Sister Rosalie Rendu of the Daughters of Charity, and
began conducting charitable operations throughout Paris. The organization quickly grew, and with it, Fredrick's love of St. Vincent. Two
years later, in 1835, Frederic established the Society of St. Vincent de
Paul and oversaw its development. He graduated from the Sorbonne
with a degree in literature and later earned doctorates in law and
foreign literature. Married at the age of twenty-seven, Frederic had one
child with his wife Amélie while he taught and lived in the

Sorbonne. Serving the poor remained his passion and he saw the Society grow to 2,000 chapters worldwide by the year 1852.

Frederic experienced ill health most of his life, having survived typhoid fever at the age of six. He traveled often to Italy to regain his health. He died in 1853 while returning from such a voyage, and was buried in Paris. He was beatified in 1997 and is currently being reviewed for canonization. Frederic's relics can be found several blocks from the shrine of St. Vincent de Paul, in the crypt of the Church of St. Joseph des Carmes (Église St. Joseph des Carmes) at the Institute Catholique, in the sixth arrondissement. Address: 70, rue de Vaugirard/75006 Paris/France. Metro to Rennes line 12.

MORE CHURCHES TO VISIT IN PARIS

NOTRE DAME OF PARIS
Notre Dame de Paris 1163–1345

The site of Notre Dame has been a place of worship for nearly two thousand years. Excavations of the area have uncovered Gallic and Roman altars, as well as three Christian churches constructed prior to the current Cathedral that was built between 1163 and 1345. It replaced the French capital's sixth century cathedral and is considered to be a Gothic masterpiece. Twelve million visitors each year cross the threshold into the splendor of Notre Dame, but it has not always been so revered. During the Revolution many of its treasures were destroyed and the church was used as a warehouse for food. Fortunately, in 1845, a restoration project was initiated that lasted twenty-three years, and another ongoing program was begun in 1991. For all the details about the art and architecture of the Cathedral, purchase a guidebook in the bookstore.

The Treasury (Trésor) is in the center of the Cathedral, to the right across from the Choir and Pieta. Although pillaged several times, it contains what is believed to be the Crown of Thorns worn by Christ, and a fragment of the True Cross. The Crown of Thorns was originally brought from Jerusalem in 1239 by St. Louis, and kept in a shrine specifically built for it in Sainte Chapelle until the early 1800s. The relic is only exposed on Fridays during Lent, between 5-6PM. Other treasures are mementos of St. Louis, ancient liturgical books, and a photographic history of Notre Dame. Hours: 9:30AM-5:45PM. Closed

Sundays and Holidays. Phone: 33 (0)1 43 26 07 39.

The information desk is to the right as you enter the Cathedral. The north tower has 386 steps for a steep climb to view the city. Vespers are sung from Mon-Fri at 5:45PM followed by Mass at 6:15PM. Every Sunday after Vespers, which starts at 5:30PM, there is a free organ recital. There is a garden behind the Cathedral with benches for resting. The crypt under the square in front of the Cathedral (le parvis) displays ruins from the third to nineteenth centuries. Hours:

Notre Dame de Paris

10AM-6PM daily, except Mondays. A museum, le Musée Notre-Dame at 10, rue du Cloître, displays documents on the history of Notre-Dame. Hours: 2:30PM-6, Sun, Wed, Sat. In front of Notre Dame, at the opposite end of the square, is a geological marker from which all road distances in France are measured.

Address: Cathédrale Notre-Dame de Paris/Ile de la Cité/6, place du parvis de Notre Dame, 75004 Paris/France. Phone: 33 (0)1 42 34 56 10 Fax: 33 (0)1 40 51 70 98 Email: dti@dti.be Website: www.cathedraledeparis.com/EN Hours: 7:45AM–6:45PM Tours: Free English tours Wed and Thur at 12PM and Sat at 2:30PM.

Directions: Notre Dame Cathedral is located in the center of the city, fourth arrondissement, on an island in the Seine called "Ile de la Cité," on Place du Parvis or Viviani Square. Metro: Line 4: Cité. RER: Line B: Saint Michel-Notre Dame or Châtelet-Les Halles. Bus: 21, 24, 27, 38, 47, 85, 96.

BASILICA OF THE SACRED HEART
Basilique du Sacré Cœur 1875–1914

Sacre Coeur is a prominent fixture in the Paris skyline, resting atop the hill of Montmarte, north of the city center. Montmarte means Mount of the Martyrs and legend has it that St. Denis was beheaded here in 275, then picked up his head and carried it two miles to where the Abbey church of St. Denis now stands. This site is also believed to be where the first martyrs of Paris met their death and where a famous Benedictine abbey was built before being destroyed during the French Revolution. In 1870, when the Franco-Prussian War broke out between France and Germany, two Catholic men vowed to build a church dedicated to the reparation of sins on the site. The funds were raised in small amounts over the next forty-five years and the first stone of the Roman-Byzantine style basilica was laid in 1875.

Many obstacles beset construction of the Basilica. At the start, the soil was found to be inadequate to support the structure, so 83 piles, each, one hundred feet deep, were driven into the bedrock to support the foundation. Thus, all the original funds were spent before the structure was even above ground. Politicians tried to stop construction of the building, and then, World War I broke out in 1914. The church was finally consecrated in 1919, at the end of the war. During World War II, bombs destroyed stained glass windows and some surrounding buildings. In 1971, political protesters occupied and sacked the church. The last attack was in 1974, when a bomb exploded inside the church and disturbed one of the domes. But the church has survived all its detractors and would–be destroyers and is now one of Paris' most famous sights.

The name of the Basilica, Sacre Coeur, means Sacred Heart and refers to the heart of Christ. St. Margaret Mary of Paray-le-Monial popularized the adoration of the Sacred Heart of Jesus in the 1670s and this practice has survived many centuries among the faithful (refer to the chapter on St. Margaret Mary in the region of Burgundy). The two founders of the Basilica felt inspired by this adoration, and dedicated the church to the Sacred Heart of Christ.

Though more tourists than pilgrims currently visit the Basilica, there is still an air of sanctity within the cavernous church. Since 1885 and the first days of the Basilica, the lay people of Paris have maintained a perpetual prayer vigil here. Prayer is directed to the high altar where a monstrance containing consecrated Eucharistic bread has been exposed since 1885. Even during the German occupation of World War II, when they had to cross enemy lines to make their appointed times of prayer, and during the bombings of 1944 when the building shook and the stained glass fell, the people of Paris never ceased offering up prayers to the Sacred Heart of Jesus.

It is a long walk up the stairway to Sacre Coeur. If you don't want to walk, there is a funicular available at the bottom of the hill. For spectacular views of Paris from the dome, you can climb a steep spiral staircase, accessible from the western wing, to the left of the main entry. There is lodging for pilgrims at Maison d'Accueil Ephrem (see below for more information).

SHRINE INFORMATION

Address: Basilique du Sacre-Coeur de Montmarte/35, rue du Chevalier de la Barre/75018/Paris/France

Phone: 33 (0)1 53 41 89 00 **Fax:** 33 (0)1 53 41 89 09

Email: basilique@sacre-coeur-montmarte.com

Website: www.sacre-coeur-montmartre.com

Hours: Daily 6AM–11PM

Dome & Crypt access: Daily 9AM-7PM; 6PM winter.

Bookstore: Daily, except Mon, 9:15AM–5:45PM

Accessibility: There is an elevator at 35, rue du Chevalier de la Barre.

Lodging: Maison d'Accueil Ephrem/33, rue du Chevalier de la Barre/75018/Paris/France

Lodging phone: 33 (0)1 53 41 89 09

Lodging email: pax@sacre-coeur-montmarte.com

Directions: Metro Line 2: Anvers. Line 12: Abbesses or Lamarck-Caulaincourt. Line 4: Château-Rouge.

Bus: 30, 54, 80, 85. Montmartrobus Bus: 30, 31, 80, 85 (which arrive at the bottom of the hill).

ST. GENEVIEVE
Sainte Geneviève 422–512

St. Genevieve was born in Nanterre, just northwest of Paris, around 422 A.D. As with other early saints, there are stories about her life that cannot be validated. It is said that she was noticed as a saintly child at the age of seven by St. Germain of Auxerre, and that she dedicated her life to Christ at that time. After her parents died, she went to Paris to live with her godmother. Genevieve took the veil and served the poor, practicing severe austerities, including eating no meat and fasting. She was the target of many detractors and much persecution, but eventually was vindicated through her acts of courage, faith and charity. One such case was in 451, when Attila and the Huns were marching on Paris and the Parisians were ready to flee the city. Genevieve exhorted the fearful crowds to trust in God's mercy and perform acts of penance, and they would be saved. After the people followed Genevieve's lead, Attila diverted his army towards Orleans and spared Paris. She also distinguished herself years later when Merowig conquered the city but spared the citizens of Paris because of Genevieve's intercession.

It was Genevieve's idea to erect a church in Paris in honor of Saints Peter and Paul, which Clovis began shortly before his death in 511. Upon her death a year later, her body was interred in that church and following many miracles attributed to her, it was renamed St. Genevieve's. This Abbey Church of St. Genevieve was on the right of the current St. Stephen's Church, as you face it. St. Stephen's was built right next to St. Genevieve's in the thirteenth century, and rebuilt in stages between 1492 and 1626.

In the 1750s, King Louis XV vowed he would replace the decaying St. Genevieve's Abbey Church after he invoked the healing power of the saint and was spared from a serious illness. Accordingly, a large edifice was designed to house the remains of St. Genevieve, starting in 1758 and completed in 1789. This church was secularized during the Revolution in 1791, renamed the national Pantheon and dedicated to the men who died for French liberty. St. Genevieve's relics never resided in the Pantheon, but remained in St. Genevieve's Abbey Church.

On October 22, 1793, revolutionists desecrated the shrine of St. Genevieve in the old Abbey Church, burned her bones and threw her ashes into the Seine. The original tombstone was rescued from the old Abbey Church when it was torn down in 1802, and relics were brought from other abbeys to create a new shrine, dedicated within St. Stephen's Church in 1803. The Chapel of St. Genevieve is now in the church of St. Stephen in the middle of the right side aisle. A carved wooden shrine surrounds a gilded copper reliquary enclosing the tombstone and relics from the original tomb. The small altar has a copy of an old statue of St. Genevieve holding a key, designating her as the Patron Saint of Paris. The original statue is at the Louvre.

St. Etienne du Mont

St. Stephen's is in the fifth arrondissement on place Sainte-Geneviéve, behind the Pantheon, a few blocks from the Sorbonne. Take the RER Line B to Luxembourg, or Metro Line 10 to Cardinal-Lemoine/ Luxembourg. If you are visiting the Left Bank, St. Stephen's (St. Etienne du Mont) is a rewarding stop. It is a combination of Renaissance, Baroque and Gothic architecture, distinguished by natural light illuminating its richly carved white limestone interior. The roodscreen in the center of the church is the only one left in Paris and incorporates beautifully carved spiral staircases on each side. The nearby Pantheon contains the tombs of Voltaire, Rousseau, Victor Hugo and other important men of France.

Location address: Place Sainte-Geneviève, 75005 Paris/France. Fifth arrondissement. Postal Address: 30, rue Descartes, 75005, Paris/France Phone: 33 (0)1 43 54 11 79 Fax: 33 (0)1 43 25 38 49

COMING AND GOING

PARIS

Car: All French roads lead to Paris, so you can't miss it—but you also don't want to drive in the city! The streets are confusing, the traffic is merciless, and besides, the public transportation is much more convenient. Take a taxi, Metro or RER from the airport or train station and pick up a rental car when you are ready to leave the city for the countryside.

Train: There are six train stations that serve Paris: Gare du Nord, Gare Montparnasse, Gare de Lyon, Gare de l'Est, Gare St. Lazare and Gare d'Austerlitz. Each station serves a specific area of France and Europe.

Plane: Charles de Gaulle Airport is the largest serving Paris and is 14 miles (23km) north of the city. South of Paris is the Orly Airport which hosts intra-European flights. From either airport, take the RER or a taxi to the city.

Bus: The main bus station is Gare Routiere Paris-Galliene located in the suburb of Bagnolet. There are connections to all parts of Europe, but the trains are faster and more convenient.

TOURIST INFORMATION

✻ The Paris Convention and Visitors Bureau Carrousel du Louvre/ place de la Pyramide Inversée/99, rue di Rivoli/Paris/France Phone: 33 (0)8 92 68 30 00 www.paris-touristoffice.com There is not one main office anymore. There are six tourist offices located around the city (listed is the one at the Louvre museum). Check out their website, call or write for information packets.

✻ Paris Ile-de-France www.pidf.com Official Paris tourist website.

WEBSITES

Basilique du Sacré Couer de Montmartre
www.sacre-coeur-montmartre.com — Official website of The Sacred Heart Basilica of Montmarte.

Chapelle Notre Dame de la Médaille Miraculeuse http://chapellenotredamedelamedaillemiraculeuse.com — Official website for the Chapel of Our Lady of the Miraculous Medal in Paris.

Missions Étrangères de Paris www.mepasie.org French — Official website for the Society of Foreign Missions.

Notre Dame Cathedral www.cathedraledeparis.com/EN — Official website for the Notre Dame Cathedral in Paris.

Paroisses et services diocésains Paroisses en ligne http://catholique-paris.cef.fr/paroisses/paroisses.htm — Catholic churches in Paris, in French.

The Paris Pages www.paris.org — Comprehensive information about the major sites in Paris. See the Metro pages for maps of the metro and RER.

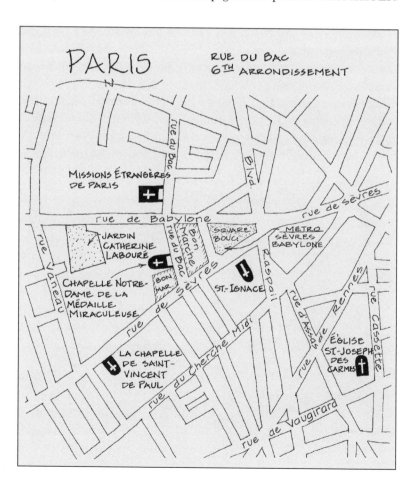

PLACES TO VISIT OUTSIDE OF PARIS

CHARTRES

Located in the Centre region, Chartres is a pleasant day trip from Paris, being only an hour train ride and sixty miles southwest of the French capital. Refer to the chapter on the region of Centre for complete information.

Reims

Population 192,000

Reims is located in the Champagne-Ardenne region, only an hour-and-a-half northeast of Paris and is noted for two churches: Notre Dame Cathedral and St. Remi Basilica. Associated with the Cathedral is the Tau Palace and the Abbey of St. Remi—museums that house tapestries and artifacts from the French Kings' coronations. The Germans surrendered to the Allies in Reims on May 7, 1945, in the Collège Moderne, and St. John Baptist de la Salle was born here in 1651. Champagne tasting is among the other tourist attractions in this cosmopolitan city and a night's stay would be advisable. Reims is difficult to pronounce. If you think of it like the word "France" pronounced with a British accent, "Rawnce," you might come close!

NOTRE DAME CATHEDRAL OF REIMS
Cathédrale Notre-Dame de Reims

Cathédrale Notre-Dame de Reims

Since Saint Remi baptized Clovis, the first king of the Franks, in 496 A.D., most of the French monarchs have been crowned in Notre Dame Cathedral. In 1429, Joan of Arc witnessed the coronation of King Charles VII here. This beautiful Gothic cathedral was built between 1211-1311 and has survived serious damage from modifications, the French Revolution and the two World Wars. Twenty years of major restoration took place prior to 1938, and it continues to this day. This is one of the most splendid cathedrals in all of Europe and a place to get lost in sheer beauty. Some of the architectural treasures include the thirteenth century stained glass windows that coexist beautifully with the Marc Chagall windows in the apse. Be sure to notice the famous smiling angel statue on the front left portal outside the Cathedral.

Address: (Rectory) 1, rue Guillaume de Machault (facing the Tourism Office)/51100 Reims/France Phone: 33 (0)3 26 47 55 34 Fax: 33 (0)3 26 77 94 64 Email: cathedrale.reims@wanadoo.fr French. Website: www.cathedrale-reims.com French. Tourist Center Website: www.tourisme.fr/reims. Hours: Daily 7:30AM–7:30PM Tours: See tourist information below. Directions: The Cathedral is at the end of rue Libergier, in the heart of the city. Follow signs to Cathédrale.

ST. REMI BASILICA
Basilique de Saint Remi

St. Remi lived from 437-533 A.D. and is the patron saint of Reims; St. Remi's Basilica was built to house the saint's relics. Recognized for his intellect and sanctity, he was elected as Archbishop of Reims at the age of twenty-two. He is best known for baptizing King Clovis and bringing Catholicism into acceptance in the area. In the 570s, after several moves, his remains arrived in this final resting place on October 1st, the date that became his feast day.

The recorded history of St. Remi's Basilica began with Gregory of Tours writing of it in the sixth century, and continued with records of the coronation of three kings. This tradition ended in 1027 when the coronation ceremony was transferred to the main Cathedral of Reims. In the early eleventh century, a larger church was built, and many modifications were made through the years, some as a result of ransacking during the

Basilique de Saint Remi

Revolution and damage from the conflict of World War I. Major restoration was completed in 1958. The church is Romanesque in style while the apse an example of early Gothic architecture.

There is a legend about the Holy Ampulla (a small crystal vial filled with oil and balsam) used for anointing in religious ceremonies. Supposedly a dove brought the vial to St. Remi when he was crowning Clovis, and it was thereafter kept at St. Remi abbey. During the Revolution, in 1793, the church was desecrated and the original vial broken, but just a few days before, a parish priest had removed some of the balm for safe keeping. This balm is still kept in the tomb with St. Remi's relics, and is exhibited each year in a procession around the Basilica on the first Sunday of October, in celebration of the feast day of the saint.

When you enter the building through the side entrance, on your left is a token machine for lighting up the Basilica. For two Euros you can enjoy the splendor of this space for ten minutes. This immense church is rarely crowded and most often peaceful. With the sounds of organ music wafting through the space creating a serene atmosphere, the side chapel next to St. Remi's reliquary is a place where the pilgrim can spend some meaningful time in meditation and prayer.

Address: Basilique de Saint Remi/place du Chanoine Ladame/51100 Reims/France. Phone: 33 (0)3 26 85 31 20

Directions: The Basilica is about a mile southeast of the cathedral, between rue Simon and rue du Grand-Cerf.

Cathédrale Notre-Dame de Reims

COMING AND GOING

REIMS

Car: Reims is 84 miles (134km) northeast of Paris, on A4-E50. When approaching the city by car, follow signs to Centre-ville and Cathédrale. Park in the Parking Cathédrale garage or on the streets surrounding the Cathedral.

Train: SNCF railway station. Reims is at the intersection of the Lille-Dijon-Mediterranean and the Paris-Charleville-Sedan lines. There are twelve daily connections with Paris.

Shuttle bus: Several companies offer shuttle services to Orly or Charles de Gaulle Airports.

Airport: Reims-Champagne Airport

TOURIST INFORMATION

✤ Office de Tourisme/2, rue Guillaume de Machault/F - 51100 Reims/France Audio guided and person guided tours of the city and Cathedral. Phone: 33 (0)3 26 77 45 25 Fax: 33 (0)3 26 77 45 27 website: www.tourisme.fr/reims/ Email: tourismreims@netvia.com.

Loire Valley
Pays de Loire

As the Loire River winds its way to the sea, it leaves behind valleys rich with luscious vineyards, beautiful chateaux and royal history. The western extent of the Loire valley begins with the fairytale Chateau de Saumur, continues through the city of Angers, and finally reaches the sea west of Nantes, the region's capital. The Loire has always had a connection with the royalty of France, as the various monarchs built their elegant "homes" up and down this picturesque river. In the thirteenth century, St. Louis IX built a formidable chateau at Angers and today we can see the exquisite Tapestry of the Apocalypse on display here. The Troglodyte Caves and the rugged Atlantic coastline offer unusual natural sites, while Le Mans is home to some of the world's most prestigious automobile races. Off the beaten path are many small villages with old Romanesque churches awash with frescoes and splendid architectural detail. Among these are the villages of Pontmain, where the Blessed Virgin appeared to several children of the town, and Saint-Laurent-sur-Sèvre where the relics of St. Louis de Montfort are enshrined. (It should be noted that the Loire Valley is sometimes grouped together with the region of Centre).

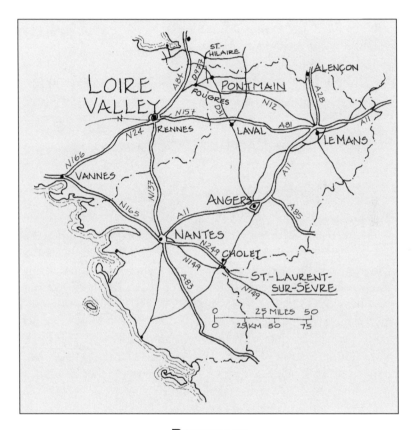

PONTMAIN
Our Lady of Pontmain

SAINT-LAURENT-SUR-SÈVRE
St. Louis de Montfort

Pontmain

Population 825

Pontmain is only thirty miles southeast of Mont Saint Michel. This tiny village would be easily overlooked except for the apparitions of the Virgin Mary that occurred here in 1871. She appeared to four small children and signaled the end of the Franco-Prussian War, bringing some notoriety to the small farming community. Though still relatively unknown, Pontmain welcomes 300,000 pilgrims each year. The town is not much more than a country crossroad flanked by the Basilica, the Parish Church and the barn associated with the apparitions. Still, it is worth the time to stop, open to the presence of the Blessed Virgin, and experience the place where she wrote a page into the history of France.

OUR LADY OF PONTMAIN

Notre Dame de Pontmain 1871

"But oh! do pray my children. God will very soon answer you."

The Marian apparitions of France are numerous and her message has usually been one of hope and redemption. But her appearance at Pontmain related directly to the circumstances of the day and ushered in an era of peace. At the time, western France was under attack by the Prussians, who had besieged Paris in the fall of 1870, and were now marching west. In January of 1871, Le Mans fell, then Laval—a town only 32 miles south of the small village of Pontmain—and the foreign troops were advancing without significant resistance. Thirtyeight youths from the parish of Pontmain were drafted for the war and were on the front lines, fighting to protect this remote corner of France. On the evening of January 17th, all this would change.

At six in the evening, the Barbedette family was finishing up chores before the evening meal. Victoire, the mother of the clan, was inside preparing the meal, while her husband Cesar and their two sons were working in the barn. Joseph and Eugene, ages ten and twelve, completed their chores and Eugene walked to the barn door and gazed out into the gathering darkness. The moonless sky was afire with dazzling stars and the young boy took in the exquisite view. Suddenly, his attention was drawn to the sky above a nearby house. There he saw the smiling image of a beautiful lady gowned in a blue robe laced with golden stars. On her head was a black veil topped by a crown of gold.

His brother and father, who wondered what he was staring at, soon joined Eugene. Joseph also saw the Lady and the two boys told their father of her presence. A neighbor and the boy's mother also looked into the sky, but no one could see the image except the children. Victoire suggested that it could be the Blessed Virgin Mary and asked everyone to say five Our Fathers and five Hail Marys in her honor. It was now time for dinner and the boys were told

Our Lady of Pontmain

to go inside to eat. After a hurried meal, the boys ventured outside again and could still see the image clearly. After falling to the their knees and saying their prayers again, they returned inside to tell their parents, "It's just the same. The Lady's as big as Sister Vitaline." The reference was to their schoolteacher, who was promptly summoned to solve the mystery.

The Sister could not see the glorified image and sent for some other school children to collaborate what the Barbedette boys were still witnessing. Three girls could also see the Lady and their descriptions matched those of Joseph and Eugene. By now, a small crowd was gathering, including the local priest. More than sixty people were staring skyward to catch a glimpse of the vision, but alas, only the four children could see the Blessed Lady. As the priest, Father Guérin, led the crowd in saying the rosary, the children began telling of the changing scene before them.

They described a dark blue oval frame surrounding the Lady, along with four unlit candles, two at shoulder height and two by her knees. Over her heart appeared a short red cross, the size of a finger. The apparent size of the Lady was increasing as the rosary was recited, and now she appeared twice her previous size and many more stars adorned her dress. The Lady smiled continually, offering support and encouragement to the children.

The children continued to describe the evolving vision as the crowd began to sing the Magnificat. Before the end of the first verse, the four children cried out, "Something else is happening!" A white scroll appeared below the feet of the Lady and began slowly unrolling, exposing a message. One by one, the children recited the letters of the message, which finally read, "But do pray, my children."

It was now seven o'clock, and the Lady had been visible for an hour. Father Guerin encouraged the crowd to sing the Litany of the Blessed Virgin. As they began singing, the children called out, "Look, there's something more happening. Look, some more letters…" Another message appeared on the banner; this time it read, "God will answer your prayers very soon." Shortly thereafter, a final line appeared, which said, "My Son lets his heart be touched." Now the people were certain that the vision was truly of the Blessed Virgin. Hymns were sung in her honor and the townspeople were overjoyed.

La Grange Barbadette

The image of Mary was also joyful, but then

her countenance turned to one of sadness as a larger red cross appeared in front of her, and on the cross was a deep red figure of Jesus. One of the children later wrote of the sight, "Her face was marked with a deep sorrow… The trembling of her lips at the corners of her mouth showed deep feeling…No tears ran down her cheeks." Soon after this sorrowful scene was described to the crowd, a star began to move within the vision and lit the four candles which surrounded the image of Mary. The red crucifix vanished as Mary spread her arms open and, with a glorious smile, seemed to offer blessing to the world. On each shoulder appeared a small white cross. A white veil appeared at her feet, which began rising slowly, obscuring her from the children's view. By nine o'clock, the apparition was over. Everyone returned home to reflect on what had just occurred and to absorb the blessings of the event.

Not too far away, Prussian soldiers also saw a mysterious vision in the sky that night. Some reported that they saw a Madonna hovering over a distant town. Many soldiers fled in fright, deserting their posts. For unknown reasons, the Prussian army advanced no more into western France and, on the 28th of January, an armistice was signed, bringing to an end the brief but bloody war. Within days, the thirty-eight conscripted young men from the Pontmain parish returned to their homes with great celebration. The prayers of the people of Pontmain had surely been answered.

Stories of the apparitions were reviewed by the bishop and several inquires were made of the children. They were separated for interrogation and asked many questions, but they all held firm to what they witnessed that cold January night. On February 2, 1872, the bishop declared the validity of the appearance of the Blessed Virgin. In 1900, a large basilica was built and consecrated in Pontmain.

The children who witnessed the apparitions went on to dedicate themselves to a life of devotion to the Blessed Virgin. Joseph Barbadette became a priest of the Congregation of the Oblates of Mary Immaculate, while his brother Eugene was ordained a parish priest. One of the girls became a nun while the other assisted in the house of Eugene. Their lives were obviously touched by the vision of the Virgin Mary, and they dedicated the rest of their lives to sharing er love.

SANCTUARY OF PONTMAIN
Sanctuaire de Pontmain

Sanctuaire de Pontmain

The Basilica was built immediately after the apparitions in 1873 and is of a modern Gothic style with twin bell towers flanking the facade. The central column of the entry portico is faced with a carved statue of Mary with her hands raised in blessing. Above her, the tympanum is filled with an abstract splash of bright colors. Tall, stained glass windows bring much light into the sanctuary, bathing the interior in a heavenly blue light. These windows tell the story of the apparitions of Lourdes, La Salette and Pontmain. The main altar is encircled with abstract design and a red crucifix in the center. To the left of this altar is a side chapel dedicated to the Virgin Mary, which is a quiet place to sit and reflect on Our Lady's appearance in Pontmain. The Basilica has both a modern and an historic feeling due to the juxtaposition of the conservative architecture and the abstract motifs. In front of the Basilica is The Statue of theApparition, which shows Our Lady gowned in a blue robe covered in gold stars and holding a red crucifix. This statue marks the location of the apparitions.

PARISH CHURCH
L'église paroissiale

Across the street from the Basilica is the original Parish Church, dedicated to St. Simon and St. Jude in the fourteenth century. Statues of these saints are on either side of the altar. This simple church has been remodeled many times over the years and was completely restored in 1984. The arched vault of the nave, together with its blue sky and stars painted in 1860, gives a charming, intimate feeling to the building.

BARBEDETTE BARN
La Grange Barbedette

The barn is located diagonally across the street from the Parish Church and is easily recognized by the large thatched roof with an image of Mary cut into the straw. This is where the children first saw the apparition while they were standing in the doorway and looking in the direction of the Basilica. The townspeople gathered here to gaze into the night sky and hear the children tell of their vision. Today, the barn contains a series of statues and paintings that relate the story of that night in 1871.

Where is the Sanctuary of Pontmain?
Où est le Sanctuaire de Pontmain?

SHRINE INFORMATION
Shrine: Pastoral Center of the Sanctuary (Centre Pastoral du Sanctuaire)

Address: 3, rue Notre-Dame/53220 Pontmain/France

Phone: 33 (0)2 43 05 07 26 **Fax:** 33 (0)2 43 05 08 25

E-mail: contact@sanctuaire-pontmain.com

Website: www.sanctuaire-pontmain.com, French

Quiet areas for meditation: The parish church can be busy, but it is quiet.

English spoken: Occasionally

Hours: Summer 7AM–7PM; Winter 7AM–6PM

Mass: Sun/Hol: 9AM, Pilgrims' Mass 10:30AM, 5PM: Weekdays 7:30AM, Pilgrims' Mass 11AM

Feasts and festivities: January 17 — Anniversary of the Apparitions; The Ascension; August 15 — The Assumption

Accessibility: The Basilica is accessible.

Tours: Tours in English can be arranged ahead of time.

Bookstore: There is a small bookstore (Boutique du Sanctuaire) at the "Centre Pastoral du Sanctuaire."

Recommended book: *Pontmain: The Apparition*, by René Laurentin, a booklet in English available at the sanctuary bookstore.s

Lodging: Contact Pastoral Center of the Sanctuary above.

Directions: Look for the tall towers of the Basilica appearing above the rooftops when approaching Pontmain from any direction. The Basilica, Parish Church and Barbadette Barn are all within a block of each other in the center of the tiny village.

COMING AND GOING

PONTMAIN

Car: Pontmain is 32 miles (52km) north of Laval and 29 miles (46 km) from Mont Saint Michel. From A81 at Laval, take D31 north to Ernee then St. Mars (in the direction of St. Hilaire-du-Harcouët). At St. Mars, take D290 west to Pontmain. From Rennes, take N12 north to Fougères, then continue north on D177 to Landéan, then take D19 east to Pontmain (four miles). From the north and Mont Saint Michel and A84, exit at N176 for St. Hilaire-du-Harcouët. At St. Hilaire, head south to Landivy on D977, then D999 and D31. At Landivy, take D122 to Pontmain.

Train: The closest train station is in Laval, about 30 miles from Pontmain. From there take a taxi to Pontmain.

Bus: No bus lines serve Pontmain. The closest cities served by buses are Ernée and Fougères.

TOURIST INFORMATION

✳ Office de Tourisme/5 rue de la Grange/53220 Pontmain/France Phone: 33 (0)2 43 05 07 74 Closed Monday. Winter months, call the town hall. Phone: 33 (0)2 43 05 06 45.

✳ Conseil général de la Mayenne/39, rue Mazagran/BP 1429/53014 Laval cedex. Phone: 33 (0)2 43 66 53 36 Fax: 33 (0)2 43 66 52 59 E-mail : doc@cg53.fr www.cg53.fr/Fr/ French.

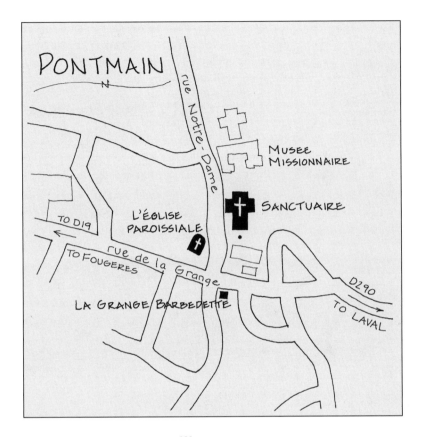

WEBSITES

Sanctuaire de Notre Dame de Pontmain
www.sanctuaire-pontmain.com — Official website of the sanctuary in French. An English version is in process.

PLACES OF INTEREST NEAR PONTMAIN

MONT SAINT MICHEL

Mount Saint Michel is only thirty miles northwest of Pontmain. See Brittany for the chapter on Mont Saint Michel.

Saint-Laurent sur Sèvres

Population 4,563

The town of Saint-Laurent-sur-Sèvre straddles the meandering Sèvre Nantaise River about seven miles south of Cholet, and is known as the resting place of St. Louis de Montfort. The saint died here in 1716 while on his last mission, and the town has since become the home to three congregations dedicated to him. The first of these congregations was established in 1720 when Mother Marie Louise Trichet, co-founder with St. Louis of the Daughters of Wisdom, took up residence here. The religious facilities of St. Laurent are the focal point of this rural town and everything is within easy walking distance. For the pilgrim, visiting the sites of St. Louis de Montfort will take a half-day.

ST. LOUIS DE MONTFORT
Saint Louis de Montfort 1673-1716

*"This devotion consists in doing all our actions with Mary,
in Mary, through Mary and for Mary."*

The life of St. Louis de Montfort is interesting to view in retrospect, for he was clearly a saint in his lifetime, yet he received much abuse and misunderstanding. His motives were always of the highest caliber, yet he was ridiculed, physically threatened and run out of town on many occasions. His life seems to be an allegory for the inner life, for we all have our saintly side that is whispering sage advice to us, yet we also have the inner voices that tempt us away from what is best. We "run out of town" our own good intentions when we convince our-selves that the right way is too difficult or self-effacing. St. Louis de Montfort lived his life on his own terms, or actually on God's terms, for his motto was "Dieu Seul" (God Alone). His every action was a re-flection of this understanding.

The theological importance of St. Louis is found in his writings on the Virgin Mary and the path to God through devotion to Her. His books, *True Devotion to the Blessed Virgin Mary*, and *The Secret of the Rosary*, are among several manuscripts he wrote to instruct truth seekers in the ways of bringing Mary, Jesus, and God directly into their lives. These profound works have touched millions and are some of the defining writings on Marian devotion. The life of St. Louis was a testament to his devotion, perseverance, and love for God in all His manifestations.

Louis Marie Grignion was born on January 31, 1673, in the small town of Montfort-sur-Meu, near Rennes in Brittany. The eldest surviving child of a large family, Louis worked on the family farm until he was twelve, when he began his studies at the Jesuit College in Rennes. During the course of his education, he made the inner commitment to become a priest and, at the age of twenty, was ready to leave home to seek his vocation. Louis's family did not have the financial means to send their son to the seminary, but a Parisian benefactor came forward with the funds for Louis's theological education in Paris.

St. Louis de Montfort

When Louis left home, he made a complete commitment to the spiritual life, and immediately demonstrated his austere and determined nature. As Louis was preparing to leave, his parents gave him new clothes, money, and the offer of a horse for the 100-mile trip to Paris. Louis refused the horse and set out on foot for his new life. As soon as he left his family behind, he spotted a beggar on the side of the road and exchanged his new clothes for the beggar's rags. He also gave away all his money and relied on begging alms to make his way to Paris.

He arrived in Paris with holes in his shoes and his rags in tatters, yet he was delighted to begin his service to God. The only problem was that his benefactor did not come through with the required funds for him to attend the seminary at Saint-Sulpice, so he had to attend lesser institutions to receive his training. Louis lived in various hovels with other poor students and, after a while, became extremely ill and was hospitalized. But upon his recovery, he was given the opportunity to attend Saint-Sulpice, where he completed his education at the top of his class. The reward for his superior academic skills was a pilgrimage to Our Lady of Chartres. His deeper reward was the opportunity to pray in the sacred crypt of the Cathedral, where he spent all his time in prayer and meditation, making a heart-felt connection with his Holy Mother.

After being ordained a priest in 1700 at the age of twenty-seven, Louis left Paris for his first appointment in Nantes, in western France. Louis inwardly felt that his personal mission was to serve the poor and spread the gospel. He also had dreams of serving in Canada as a missionary in the wilderness. But this assignment was not to be his.

Crypts of St. Louis de Montfort and Bl. Marie Louise

Within months of arriving in Nantes, he was offered a position in Poitiers as chaplain for the inmates of a hospital for the destitute. Louis jumped at this new opportunity. With great passion he served the needs of the patients and worked at reorganizing the hospital itself. He made tremendous improvements by utilizing his intelligence, compassion and enthusiasm, but also made many enemies. Those in power were intimidated by the changes brought about by the proactive priest, and he was soon dismissed.

Louis returned to Paris for the next year and lived in poor circumstances while serving as best he could. The poor of Poitiers never forgot Louis, and through their wishes, he was asked to return to his post as hospital chaplain. He again worked on reforming the stodgy institution and, this time, he found support in the form of two young women, Marie Louise Trichet and Catherine Brunet. This was the beginning of a long relationship between Louis and these women, who later became the founding members of the community of Sisters called the Daughters of Wisdom. But Louis's work at the hospital of Poitiers was again rejected and he was asked to leave a second time.

Dismayed but not broken, the austere priest remained in Poitiers and ministered to the poorest of the poor, in neighborhoods were no one else would serve. His enthusiastic preaching, lively processions, and humanistic caring touched the hearts of the common people and made him a great success in the community. However, the Bishop of Poitiers did not approve of Louis and, in 1706, he forbade him to preach in the diocese. Was he to forsake his inner calling to serve the poor? What was his mission? To consult with the highest earthly authority, Louis decided to walk to Rome to see the Pope and get his answers straight from the top!

Louis and a companion walked the thousand miles to Rome and sought out Pope Clement XI, who received the men and listened to their story. The Holy Father appreciated Louis' sincerity and sent him to continue his work in western France, giving him the title of Apostolic Missionary. His only concession was that Louis had to work under the approval of the local Bishops. Recharged with vigor and purpose, Louis returned to France, and after retreating to Mont Saint Michel for fifteen days, he resumed his missionary work throughout Brittany.

The next years were spent in various communities in Brittany, spreading the Gospel, preaching to the masses, resurrecting dilapidated churches, and always serving the poor. Louis walked everywhere he went and occupied the most meager housing, choosing to live in austerity along side his flock. Exuberant in his expression of faith, Louis would often lead joyous processions through the towns and, at other times, conduct book burnings where lewd books were set afire. The people appreciated his energy and called him "the good Father from Montfort," but he often had to move on when Church authorities grew weary of his behavior. Louis was always very demonstrative of his faith, and maybe that's what made people uncomfortable.

Two events, at this time in his life, give some insight into Louis's character. On one occasion, while taking a ferry across the river in

Rouen, the passengers of the boat were singing raucous and vulgar songs. Louis began reciting his rosary aloud. The crowd taunted him, but he continued his vocal prayers. After some further jeers, some passengers began to join him, and by journey's end, they were all reciting the rosary and had listened to his eloquent homily. This was a common occurrence for the ragged priest, for he continually walked in the presence of Mary, Jesus, and God, and would seek to uplift the spirits of those around him.

Another event happened in the rural community of Pontchateau, near Nantes. Louis was fond of building models of the scene at Calvary, and would place large crosses and monuments on country hilltops. In Pontchateau, he organized the local peasants to build such a memorial, and for over a year, two hundred volunteers worked on the project, creating a beautiful monument to Christ. People came from all over western France to witness the construction and offer support. Just before the dedication, the King caught wind of the project. After hearing advice from his overzealous advisors, who thought the English could use it as an observation point, the monument was ordered destroyed. Pleas were made to the Bishop and King, but to no avail. The hilltop tribute was removed over the next few months as the people mourned its destruction. But, for Louis, it was just another instance of living for God alone. When speaking of the monument's demise he said, "If the thing depended on me, it would endure as long as the world; but as it depends immediately on God, may His will be done and not mine."

Louis was now invited to preach in the region around La Rochelle, south of Nantes. The next five years were spent in exhaustive service and missions. The vagabond Father continually traveled through the area spreading his lively message, but he also took the time to write *True Devotion to Mary* and *The Secret of Mary*, two books that would, in time, inspire great Marian devotion. Music and singing were another important part of Louis's service. He wrote many hymns and songs of praise, often set to popular melodies, to help involve people in his services. During this period, he wrote the rules for the Daughters of Wisdom. He also founded the fledgling community of Sisters with the help of Marie Louise Trichet and Catherine Brunet, who had waited ten years for their chance to serve with Father Louis. For the priests serving his mission, Louis founded the Company of Mary and wrote their rules of conduct.

After years of service, Louis was weakened and ill—some say as a result of poison secretly administered to him in an assassination attempt. Still, he continued serving. In April of 1716, Louis traveled to Saint-Laurent-sur-Sèvre to celebrate a new mission. With the Bishop in attendance, the ailing priest led the congregation in a procession and devotional songs. After a halting sermon, Louis retired to the neighboring monastery where he lingered for four days. Three times he allowed his room to be filled with well-wishers, and he gave them his blessing.

Finally, on April 28th, as he was nearing the end, Louis weakly sang a few lines from a favorite hymn, "Dear Friends, let us go. Let us go to Paradise. Nothing we may gain from here below is worth more than Paradise." How St. Francis-like was this monk from Brittany—after living a life of complete poverty and service, he departed with songs of praise on his lips! After this short incantation, Louis's face reflected an internal battle with the devil. But, he resolutely said, "It is in vain that you

La Sagesse and L'Oratoire

attack me, I am in between Jesus and Mary! I am at the end my life, I shall not sin any more." With that, he passed into God's hands.

Louis de Montfort received little notoriety outside of Brittany after his death. Though many miracles were reported to have occurred around his tomb, scarce attention was paid to the wandering Father. But a century later, the manuscripts for his books were discovered in a trunk and posthumously published. His inspired writings on devotion to Mary have circulated around the globe, being translated into many languages and read by peasants and popes alike. His message was one of utter surrender and devotion to Mary as a means of reaching God.

"You must make the sacrifice of yourself to the Blessed Mother," he wrote. "You must disappear in Her, so that you may find God alone." With the publication of his writings, Louis finally gained acceptance and appreciation. He was beatified in 1888 and was canonized in 1947. The congregations of the Company of Mary, the Daughters of Wisdom and the Brothers of Gabriel, a lay order started years later, have survived, and continue to spread his message.

The cause for his declaration as a Doctor of the Church is underway.

THE BASILICA OF
ST. LOUIS MARIE DE MONTFORT
Basilique Saint Louis Marie de Montfort

The Basilica of St. Louis Marie de Montfort was begun in 1889, replacing the original eleventh century church on this site. The Romanesque-Byzantine style basilica was built in stages and not completed until 1949. The sanctuary was designated a Basilica in 1963 but remains also the parish church. The interior has a light and airy feeling, with white limestone columns and a white vaulted ceiling. The stained glass windows of the church record the life of the saint and the mysteries of the Rosary. The crypts of St. Louis de Montfort and Blessed Marie Louise of Jesus (Marie Louise Trichet) are located in the left transept and are a focal point of devotion. Side by side in a single granite encasement, the crypts rest under a sculptured canopy while a portrait of the two saints hangs on the wall to the left. On the wall behind the canopy is an early tombstone of St. Louis.

Basilique Saint Louis Marie de Montfort

Down rue Jean-Paul II, one block from the Basilica, is "La Sagesse" with the oratory (L'Oratoire) where St. Louis died of exhaustion at age forty-three. When you walk in the entrance at 3, rue Jean-Paul II, check in with a Sister in the room on the right. You will need to speak in French and ask to see "L'Oratoire" where the saint died. The oratory is on the left as you walk into the courtyard. This room contains a glass reliquary with a wax figure of St. Louis; in his hand is the crucifix blessed by Pope Clement XI, which St. Louis received on his pilgrimage to Rome in 1706. On the wall behind the reliquary is written his motto, "Dieu Seul" (God Alone). As you enter the Oratory, on the left is a one-page description of the shrine and an audio presentation in various languages, including English. The Oratory is a very quiet place for contemplation.

At La Sagesse you can also ask to visit the Founders' Chapel (Chapelle des Fondateurs) built in the nineteenth century, and the Daughters of Wisdom Chapel (Chapelle des Filles de la Sagesse) which is usually open. Across from La Sagesse is the Saint-Esprit (Le Saint-Esprit), home to the Montfortian Missionaries, at 2, rue Jean-Paul II. The Chapel of the Montfortians (Chapelle des Montfortians) is open to the public. It was built before the French Revolution in Romanesque style, and contains a statue possibly carved by St Louis. In the garden behind the Chapel is a monument to three Brothers killed on the grounds during the Revolution.

The three orders that trace their foundation to St. Louis de Montfort are: The Daughters of Wisdom (Les Filles de la Sagesse), the Company of Mary or Montfort Missionaries (Les Missionnaires Montfortians), and the Montfort Brothers of St. Gabriel (les Frères de saint Gabriel).

Where is the Basilica of St. Louis de Montfort?
Où est la Basilique Saint Louis de Montfort?

Where is the Oratory of St. Louis de Montfort?
Où est l'oratoire de Saint Louis de Montfort?

SHRINE INFORMATION

Shrine: The Basilica of St. Louis Marie de Montfort (La Basilique Saint Louis Marie de Montfort)

Address: 2, place Grignion de Montfort/85290 Saint-Laurent-sur-Sèvre/France

Phone: 33 (0)2 51 67 81 34 **Fax:** 33 (0)2 51 67 70 46

E-mail: Fr. Jean Hémery, hemery.j@wandadoo.fr

Website: No official website for the Basilica, but there are English-speaking websites under "Websites" below that describe a Montfortian pilgrimage in France.

Quiet areas for meditation: The Oratory (L'Oratoire) at La Sagesse, 3, rue Jean-Paul II, or any of the chapels mentioned. It is a small town with few visitors.

English spoken: Occasionally. There are a few people who speak English if needed.

Mass: Basilica: Sat 10:30AM; summer 8:30PM, winter 8PM; Weekdays 9:30AM; Chapelle de la Sagesse 10:30AM; Chapelle du Saint-Esprit 6PM, except Sat.

Feasts and festivities: October 12 — Annual pilgrimage for St. Louis de Montfort and Blessed Marie Louise.

Accessibility: Entrance for wheelchairs to the right of the Basilica.

Tours: If contacted ahead of time, there are a few people who can conduct a tour of the Basilica in English. During the months of July and August, tours are available between10AM-12PM and 3PM-7; for English, arrange before your visit.

Bookstore: The bookstore, Mediathèque Familiale et Religieuse, is on the corner to the right of the Basilica and is closed on Monday. They do not have the book below, but they have a children's book in English and French, *Saint Louis-Marie* by Jean Marie Onfroy. They also have a music CD, Cantiques de St. Louis-Marie de Montfort, with beautiful canticles written by the saint.

Recommended book: *God Alone: The Collected Writings of St. Louis Marie de Montfort* by Montfort Publications, available in the US. Phone: 1 631 665-0726 Fax: 1 631 665-4349 Email: info@montfort-missionaries.com. In the UK, Montfort Press. Phone: 44 (0)151 287 6862 Fax: 44 (0)151 287 0410.

Lodging: Missionnaires Montfortains/4 rue Jean Paul II /85292 St Laurent sur Sèvre cedex/France. Rooms available only in the months of July and August.

Directions: The Basilica is south of the main highway N149. Follow signs to "Basilique Tombeau de Père Montfort." In the town center, turn left to reach the Basilica. It is on place Grignion de Montfort, and there is parking in front of the church. Up the street to the right are La Sagesse and Le Saint-Esprit.

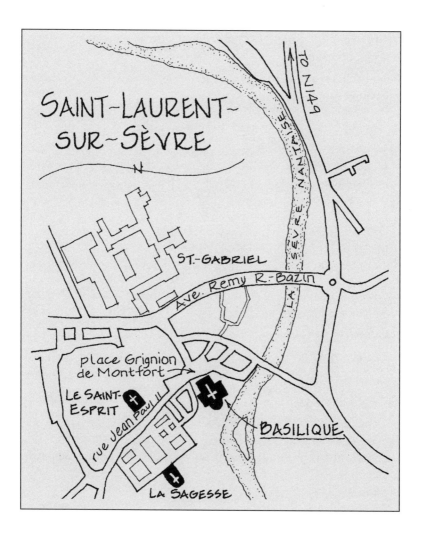

COMING AND GOING

SAINT-LAURENT-SUR-SÈVRE

Car: Saint-Laurent is between Nantes and Poitiers, 7 miles (11 km) south of Cholet. From Nantes, take N249-E62 to Cholet (direction Poitiers). Exit at N160, drive south towards Les Herbiers. At N149, turn east towards Poitiers. After 3 miles (5 km), at La Trique, there is a traffic light and signs to Saint-Laurent. From Poitiers, take N149-E62 towards Nantes for 74 miles (119 km). Saint Laurent is (20 km) past Mauléon. Turn left at the stoplight at La Trique.

Train: There is a station in Saint-Laurent with connections to Cholet, Angers and Nantes.

Plane: Closest international airports are Nantes-Atlantique and La Rochelle.

TOURIST INFORMATION

✳ L'Office de Tourisme du canton de Mortagne-sur-Sèvre/La Gare, avenue de la Gare/85290 Mortagne-sur-Sèvre/France Phone: 33 (0)2 51 65 11 32 Fax: 33 (0)2 41 71 17 24 Open September 15 to May 15.

✳ Office du Tourisme du Pays des Herbiers/2 grande rue Saint-Blaise/85500 Les Herviers/France Phone: 33 (0)2 51 92 92 92 Fax: 33 (0)2 51 92 93 70 Email: contact@ot-lesherviers.fr.

✳ Town Hall/Saint-Laurent-sur-Sèvre/Place de la Mairie/BP 36/85290 Saint-Laurent-sur-Sèvre/France Phone: 33 (0)2 51 67 81 44 Fax: 33 (0)2 51 67 81 41.

✳ Vendée Conseil Général www.vendee.fr Virtual tour of two abbeys in the area in French. Go to "Culture & Patrimone," "Site Thématiques," "Abbayes de Nieul-sur-l'Autise et de Maillezais."

✳ Vendée Tourist Board/8 place Napoléon/85000 La Roche sur Yon/France Phone: 33 (0)2 51 47 88 20 Fax: 33 (0)2 51 05 37 01 Email: info@venee-tourisme.com www.vendee-tourisme.com French.

WEBSITES

Company of Mary www.montfort.org.uk — Montfort Missionaries in Great Britain and Ireland. For a detailed description on places in France related to St. Louis de Montfort, click on "A Montfortian Pilgrimage." Home of Montfort Press in the UK.

The Missionaries of the Company of Mary United States Province www.montfortmissionaries.com — Home of Montfort Publications in the US.

The Montfortian Religious Family
www.montfort.org/English/LifeLM.htm — Comprehensive website maintained by the Montfort Missionaries in Rome, with detailed information on St. Louis de Montfort.

Basilique Saint Louis Marie de Montfort

Midi-Pyrenees

Midi-Pyrénées

The region of the Midi-Pyrenees exhibits some of the most beautiful scenery in the southwestern area of France, sharing a snow-capped mountain range with Spain and boasting the last remaining wilderness in this area of France. The mountains give way to the rolling foothills and plains of the central area of the region and culminate in the serene and picturesque valleys of the Dordogne. The pilgrimage mecca of Lourdes nestles in the foothills of the Pyrenees and the cosmopolitan city of Toulouse is found in the central plains, while Rocamadour hangs from the cliffs above a tributary of the Dordogne River in the north. The area offers not only geographical variety but architectural diversity as well. The quaint town of Conques, with its tiny medieval streets and petite basilica, stands in contrast to the modern city of Albi, home of the imposing brick edifice of Sainte-Cecile Cathedral. For the spiritual traveler, the Midi-Pyrenees offers many treasures to choose from, but the jewel not to be missed is Lourdes and the Grotto of Massabielle.

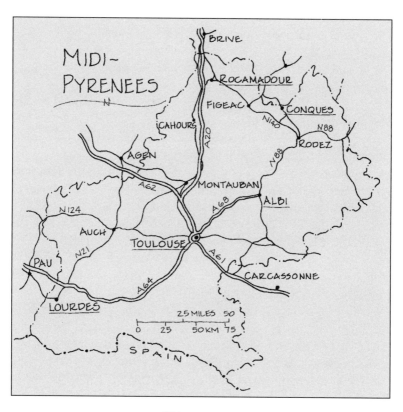

CONQUES
St. Foy

LOURDES
Sanctuary of Our Lady of Lourdes

ROCAMADOUR
St. Amadour

Conques
Population 300

As you drive along the Dourdou River, the charming rural countryside greets you at every turn. At the end of the scenic Gorge de Dourdou you come to the remote village of Conques, a pilgrimage destination for more than a thousand years. This picturesque hillside town is perched on a sunny slope surrounded by woods, overlooking the valley that leads to the Dourdou River. The village has a rich history revolving around an unlikely trio of personages: a hermit, the son of a king, and a twelve-year-old Christian martyr.

The word "Conques" is derived from the Latin, meaning "shell," and describes the shape of the valley in which the town is situated. A hermit originally chose the site for his secluded retreat. Over time, others joined him in his spiritual mission and the Abbey of Conques was founded. The Abbey-church was later endowed with both land and money by the son of King Charlemagne. The village developed into a medieval pilgrimage destination only after the relics of St. Foy were brought to the Abbey and, subsequently, pilgrims traveling the road to Santiago de Compostella in Spain made this a ritual stopping point. The village has maintained its medieval charm and the Romanesque Abbey-church of St. Foy continues to be a highlight along the still-traveled pilgrims' road.

While in Conques, you are apt to see pilgrims—with conch shells hanging from their necks, brandishing walking sticks and hefting full backpacks—walking alongside you as you traverse this lovely ancient town. Between the Abbey-church, its cloister, the relics of St. Foy and the enchanting atmosphere of the village, there is enough to see in Conques for a full day's visit, so take your time to explore and relax.

ST. FOY
Sainte Foy 290–303 A.D.

The details of the life of St. Foy are few, yet the legacy of this saint was the driving force behind the development of Conques into a major pilgrimage destination. Her life was short—a mere twelve years—but kings, saints and pilgrims have traveled here from all corners of the earth to venerate her relics, and experience her blessings.

St. Foy did not live in Conques, but in the city of Agen, in what is now western France. She was born near the end of the third century, when Agen was under Roman rule and its citizens were expected to follow Roman traditions. The wealthy family of young Foy was prominent in the community and they willingly participated in the pagan rituals. Even though her father ordered her to perform these rites, Foy had recently been converted to the new teaching of Christianity, which prohibited her from making sacrifices to idols.

St. Foy Reliquary

Bands of Christians were beginning to practice their faith in secrecy throughout the Roman Empire because their religion was unlawful. In Gaul, the Roman governor Dacien was notorious for his persecution and execution of Christians. It was before him that Foy was brought when she refused to take part in the pagan rituals. Even after severe questioning and threats of death, the girl of twelve was steadfast in her profession of faith in Christ and would not recant. Finally, as an example to the other Christians in Gaul, Foy was tortured and then beheaded. But instead of suppressing the Christians of Gaul, Foy's martyrdom aroused great passion among the people, and as a result, many more followed in her footsteps of martyrdom, and were persecuted under the orders of Dacien.

Shortly after her death, Foy's remains were secreted away by her comrades and hidden from the authorities. The members of the Christian community met annually to venerate the relics of the young martyr, and rumors of miracles spread throughout the area. After Christianity was made the state religion by Constantine in 324 A.D., Foy's relics were openly enshrined in Agen, where they remained for over five hundred years. Her remains were placed in a small golden statue and she became well known as St. Foy.

In 866, the monks of the Abbey of Conques were actively seeking to obtain the relics of a saint to grace their church, for a church without relics did not attract pilgrims or prosperity. After failing in an attempt to negotiate with St. Foy's church in Agen, the monks took it upon themselves to make a "discreet transfer" of her relics, and St. Foy was secretly stolen from Agen and delivered to Conques.

The "Little Saint" was welcomed with great celebration. Conques quickly became a major pilgrimage site and, for three centuries, the Abbey flourished and enjoyed continual expansion. In 1000, a book entitled *St. Foy Book of Miracles* detailed stories of miracles attributed to the saint. Sixty years later, a popular song related the story of her faith and martyrdom, and her popularity continued to blossom. Her fame peaked in the eleventh century with the onset of the Santiago de Compostela pilgrimage to Spain. The road starting at Le Puy ran through Conques and made it a primary stopping point, bringing countless pilgrims to venerate the relics of the little one from Agen.

THE ABBEY OF ST. FOY
Abbatiale Sainte Foy

The original basilica dedicated to St. Foy was built in the tenth century. It was later razed to make room for the Romanesque Abbey-church we see today. Construction of the Abbey of St. Foy began in the eleventh century under the direction of Abbot Odolric, and was finally completed in the late twelfth century. The vast influx of pilgrims making their way to Santiago de Compostella in Spain brought great wealth to Conques, allowing for the construction of the new abbey, its cloister and monastery. The eastern façade, with its two towers and grand tympanum, were the last elements to be finished.

Over the years, notable changes have been made to the church, starting in the fifteenth century with the replacement of the cupola over the transept. The original Romanesque dome had collapsed and a new one was built using the newer techniques of Gothic stone vault construction. The biggest change occurred in 1568, when the Huguenots overran Conques and attempted to burn the church to the ground. The roof, the spires of the eastern façade, and the top floor of the central bell tower were all destroyed but eventually repaired. Following the French Revolution, the church was abandoned and fell into catastrophic disrepair. Fortunately, in 1837, Prosper Merimee became General Inspector of Historical Buildings and inaugurated a restoration project to save the ancient structure. The Bishop of Rodez installed the Premonstrant Friars to be in charge of the church in 1873, and two years later, they discovered the reliquary chest of St. Foy in the church choir. The relics had been hidden since the Religious Wars of the fourteenth century, and this discovery inspired a renewed interest in Conques and St. Foy. (The relics of St. Foy are now displayed in the museum adjacent to the cloister.) The restoration process continued throughout the rest of the nineteenth century, and the cloister area was renovated in the 1970s. The church, as it now stands, is a beautiful testament to eleventh century architecture and fine stone sculpture.

The tympanum on the eastern façade is the highlight of the Abbey-church. This immense piece of sculptured stone details the Last Judgment of Christ, with a total of 124 characters making up the graphic scene. With Christ in the center, there are two sides to the story. On one hand, there are saints and angels ascending to heaven, enjoying the fruits of their faith. On the other, souls are damned to hell and depicted in pain and agony. Satan is holding court and demons are devouring those who have lost their souls to the darkness. This fascinating piece is in excellent condition, having survived

Abbatiale Sainte Foy

Tympanum Abbey of St. Foy

for almost 900 years, and is a stirring example of medieval art and religious thought.

The church itself has little decoration, simple lines, and modern stained glass installed in 1995. Circling the choir is an ambulatory with several small chapels dedicated to various saints, including St. Foy and St. James. There are chairs for prayer and meditation in these chapels and the area is quiet. As a whole, the church is more of a museum than a holy site, so it attracts more tourists than pilgrims, yet it is still a place of devotion. The church, along with the cloister and reliquary of St. Foy, gives this charming town the authentic feeling of Medieval France.

Where is the Abbey of St. Foy?
Où est l'abbatiale Sainte Foy?

SHRINE INFORMATION

Shrine: Prieure et Accueil Sainte Foy (Priory and Reception St. Foy)

Address: 12320 Conques/France

Phone: 33 (0)5 65 69 85 12 **Fax:** 33 (0)5 65 69 89 48

E-mail: conques@mondaye.com

Website: www.mondaye.com The website for the Premonstratensian Order, or Sons of St. Norbert, who administer the Basilica in Conques. This website does not have any information about the Basilica in Conques, but there are two others under "websites" below that do.

Quiet areas for meditation: Side chapels in the Abbey of St. Foy.

English spoken: Rarely

Hours: Daily 7AM–10PM

Mass: Weekly 8AM; Sun/Hol 11AM

Feasts and festivities: The Sunday that follows October 6 — Feast of St. Foy (Fête de la sainte Foy).

Accessibility: The Abbey of St. Foy is accessible. Inquire to the address above for more details.

Information office: Inquire to the Priory and Reception St. Foy above.

Tours: Guided tours in English can be arranged ahead of time. Inquire to the address/phone above.

Bookstore: None connected to the Basilica. There are tourist guides in the local shops.

Recommended books: *Visiting Conques* by Jean-Claude Fau, available in the local tourist shops.

Lodging: There are 20 rooms and dormitory spaces that are given first to pilgrims. If they are not full, it is possible to reserve space for non-pilgrims. Use Phone/Fax/email above.

Directions: Parking is available directly outside the village, for a fee. It is a short walk into the town.

OTHER PLACES OF INTEREST IN CONQUES

THE CLOISTER OF ABBOT BÉGON
Cloître Abbot Bégon

A great monastery and cloister, built in the twelfth century by Abbot Bégon, originally stood on the southern and western sides of the abbey. Though mostly destroyed during the protestant raids and the French Revolution, what remains was saved during the first renovation in the nineteenth century, though not completely restored until the 1970s. The current cloister consists of remnants of the original foundations and a central fountain—a green serpentine basin restored in 1973. A series of archways adorn the eastern side of the cloister and lead to what was the monk's refectory. The ornately carved column capitals are very interesting, composed of figures of knights, masons, and pilgrims.

THE TREASURY OF ST. FOY
Trésor Sainte Foy

Cloister column

The Treasury of St. Foy is entered from the cloister refectory, and requires paid admission. If you are interested in stunning gold craftsmanship and ancient relics, it is worth the time and money. The relics of St. Foy are housed in a bejeweled, gold statue depicting the martyr. The statue was made in the ninth and tenth centuries and is covered in gems and cameos given by pilgrims. The other relics include a piece of the true cross, presented to Conques by Pope Pascall II in 1110, and a reliquary containing the arm of St. George. This is strictly a museum and not a place of devotion, but the pieces are exquisite and the level of craftsmanship is very high.

COMING AND GOING

CONQUES

Car: Conques is remotely located, 375 miles (605 km) south of Paris, 106 miles (170 km) northeast of Toulouse. From the south or east, drive to Rodez, then take N140 northwest towards Figeac. After 15 miles (24 km), turn right on D22 and go 5 miles (8 km) to D901. Turn left and travel 6 miles (9 km) to Conques. From the north, go to Aurillac, and head south towards Figeac on N122. At Maurs, take D663 for 9 miles (14 km) south and turn left on D42, and follow it along the river for 9 miles (14 km). At D901, turn right and drive 1 mile (2 km) to Conques.

Train: The nearest train station is located in St. Christophe Vallon 13 miles (20 km) from Conques on N140. Phone: 33 (0)5 65 72 71 55. It connects to the Rodez station that has several trains a day from Paris, Toulouse and Montpellier. Phone: 33 (0)5 65 42 50 50.

Taxi: Conques 33 (0)5 65 72 84 76.

Airport: The Rodez-Marcillac airport is 21 miles (33 km) from Conques. Phone: 33 (0)5 65 76 02 00 or 33 (0)5 65 42 20 30. Take a taxi from the airport.

TOURIST INFORMATION

❋ Office de Tourisme Phone: 33 (0)8 20 82 08 03 Fax: 33 (0)5 65 72 87 03 Email: tourisme@conques.fr www.tourisme.fr/office-de-tourisme /conques.htm French.

❋ The Department of Aveyron www.aveyron.com Email: redaction@aveyron.com

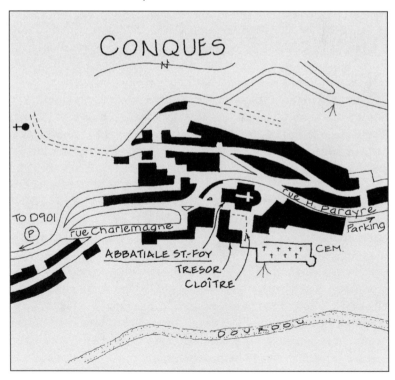

WEBSITES

Official Website for the Town of Conques www.conques.fr French — Comprehensive information on Conques.

Regional Council of Aveyron www.conques.com/index1.htm — Comprehensive website about St. Foy Abbey–church and town of Conques. After you leave the home page, the English buttons will work. Email: conques@conques.com.

Lourdes
Population 15,000

In the foothills of the Pyrenees, situated on a tributary of the Gave de Pau River, Lourdes rests in the shadow of the ancient castle that towers high above the town. The castle dates back to Charlemagne and was a crucial pawn in the war with the Moors attacking from Spain. The Virgin Mary has long been venerated here, and as early as the eleventh century was declared mistress of the region. In 1858 Lourdes was a sleepy town of 4,000 villagers when the Virgin Mary appeared to the shepherdess Bernadette and transformed the town forever. Lourdes is now one of the most visited pilgrimage sites in the world, attracting seekers of all faiths. This once small town now hosts 6 million visitors a year at its 400 hotels (second in France only to Paris) and a profusion of tourist shops lining the streets that lead to the Basilica and grotto. However, don't let the large numbers of pilgrims deter you from visiting this great spiritual center, for the multitudes actually add a tangible grace through the sheer force of their prayers and devotion.

OUR LADY OF LOURDES
Notre-Dame de Lourdes

"I am the Immaculate Conception."

The Blessed Virgin Mary has appeared to many souls in France, but the best known of these apparitions occurred in 1858 in the small Pyrenean village of Lourdes, as witnessed by the young girl Bernadette Soubirous. In our day, millions of pilgrims travel to Lourdes each year just to bathe in the blessings that flow from the sacred grotto and miraculous spring, but in Bernadette's time, the remote village was unknown to the world. It was simply a quiet place for a small girl to grow up among the mountains, fields and pastures of the Pyrenees. All this would change forever when Our Lady of Lourdes began appearing to this child, attracting the attention of the world's faithful and renewing their belief in the loving presence of their Holy Mother. There are two parts to this miraculous story, that of the apparitions and that of Bernadette herself. In this chapter,

Bernadette Soubirous 1844-1879

we will tell of the apparitions and the blessings received at the grotto of Lourdes. We will portray the saintly life of Bernadette in the chapter on Burgundy, where she spent the later years of her life in a monastery in Nevers.

Bernadette was not unlike the other girls her age at fourteen as she attended school, helped with household chores and, when time allowed, played in the beautiful hills around Lourdes. Time for play was often scarce for Bernadette as she was the first-born child of a poor family and had to help care for her siblings. This was not an easy task, for she was a slight and sickly child as a result of a bout with cholera at the age of two, followed by a fight to survive tuberculosis. Bernadette overcame those tests, but was thereafter permanently afflicted by asthma.

The winter of 1858 was like many others in Lourdes, as it was cold and blustery and the Soubirous family needed a good supply of wood to keep their meager one-room home warm. On February 11th, Bernadette, her sister Antoinette, and a friend set out to scrounge for firewood around the outskirts of the village. South of town, along the Gave River, the children gathered bits of firewood and followed the river past the inactive Savy Mill to the area of the Massabielle massif, a rocky area where they were told they would find more wood. The small canal leading from the mill was nearly empty that day, and Bernadette's companions waded knee deep through the frigid water to collect more branches on the other side. Bernadette was careful not to aggravate her sickly condition, and chose to walk upstream towards the rocky grotto, where she could walk across the waterway in shallow water and not risk a chilly bath. Near the grotto, she bent down to remove her stockings, then heard the sound of a strong wind. She looked over the river to her right, and saw that the trees there were perfectly still. Perplexed, she continued to remove her stockings, and began to step across the brook when the sound of the wind returned. She saw before her the branches in a small niche above the grotto swaying in the breeze.

Our Lady of Lourdes Grotto

Suddenly, a glowing light appeared and a smiling figure emerged and gazed into Bernadette's eyes. The image of a young girl her own size, in a white veil and dress with a sash of blue, was shrouded in dazzling light. A rosary with a yellow chain and white beads hung on her right arm, and her toes were visible beneath the hem of her dress, where a yellow rose rested atop each foot. Bernadette was initially startled by the apparition and rubbed her eyes repeatedly to make certain they were not deceiving her. She tried to call to her friends, but she could not speak. The figure remained in the niche, smiling continually, and beaming love and light to the child. Bernadette's next reaction was to pray, and taking her rosary from her pocket, she tried to cross herself but was unable to lift her arm in reverence. Turning and stepping towards Bernadette, the vision of light made the sign of the cross. Bernadette was then able to repeat the sign and, upon doing so, all her fears departed. Kneeling, she said her rosary with her gaze fixed on the beautiful girl before her. As Bernadette whispered her prayers and slipped the smooth beads through her fingers, the figure did the same, but did not move her lips. Finally, as Bernadette finished her round of prayers, the figure of light bowed to her and disappeared into the niche. When describing the beauty of the vision, Bernadette said the girl was "so lovely that, when you have seen her once, you would willingly die to see her again."

This was the first of eighteen apparitions during a five-month period that were experienced by young Bernadette. She visited the grotto frequently over the next several months, returning whenever she received an inner calling to do so. The visions she beheld varied in their substance and message—sometimes she would simply pray before the angelic presence, while at other times she would receive special instructions or blessings. (Here we have included descriptions of the most important apparitions of Bernadette, but a full reading of her experience is very inspiring. Please see the bibliography for references.) It is interesting to note that Bernadette definitively described the vision as a young girl of her age and size, and that she communicated with her in the local dialect, not formal French. Although we refer to her as the Lady, or Our Lady of Lourdes, it is delightful to imagine her as a young girl, as she appeared before Bernadette.

Among the eighteen apparitions, the third apparition was significant in two ways. First, Bernadette promised her Lady that she would return in a fortnight to be with her. Secondly, she received a prophetic promise from the Lady: "I do not promise you happiness in this world, but in the next." This was to become Bernadette's mantra, for she experienced great suffering in this material world, but always lived in the blissful expectation of her next life in God. She endured much pain, doing penance for many souls, but always while living in the presence of God. In this way, Bernadette lived a saintly life; not because of her visions, but because of her response to them.

Four other apparitions were also very significant in the unfolding of this heavenly drama. In the seventh vision, three secrets were revealed to Bernadette—secrets for her ears only. She never revealed

The Spring at Massabielle Grotto

the content of these secrets to anyone. During the ninth apparition, on the 25th of February, the Lady told Bernadette to drink from a spring, and pointed to an area of the grotto. Bernadette found only muddy ground there, but at the insistence of the vision, dug up the earth to reveal murky water, which she drank as requested. She was also instructed to eat some grass growing near the grotto. This became a day of mocking for the gathering crowds, as they laughed at the obedient girl and ridiculed her silly behavior. But all were astonished the following day when the area exposed up by Bernadette was transformed into an abundant spring, bubbling with blessed water. This water would soon become known worldwide as the famous healing elixir of Lourdes. The spring runs strong almost a century and a half later and remains a source of countless blessings and miracles.

During the thirteenth apparition, Bernadette was instructed to tell the local priests to build a chapel at the grotto. When confronted with this news, the parish priest demanded to know the name of the Lady of Bernadette's visions. On what authority could they build a chapel if they did not even know who was making the request? Bernadette returned to the grotto the next day, but received no answer, just sublime smiles and gracious love. At the insistence of the priests, she asked again on the following day and finally received her answer: "I am the Immaculate Conception." Although confused by the answer, Bernadette repeated it over and over to herself so as not to forget it—for the meaning of the words made no sense to her. When she repeated the words to the parish priest, he was amazed at the reply, but knew it was the truth, for the simple child before him obviously did not comprehend the expression or its implications. The church had just introduced the dogma of the Immaculate Conception two years prior to this event. This doctrine maintains that the Blessed Virgin was conceived and born without sin, a concept unknown to Bernadette.

This was the last time the Blessed Virgin of Lourdes spoke to Bernadette, although she witnessed the Lady's presence twice more. The grotto was soon fenced-off by the local authorities, and two years would pass before the truth of the visions was confirmed through the authority of the church. But for Bernadette there was never any doubt, for she always held the truth of the experience in her heart.

During the time of the apparitions, the news of the miraculous visions quickly spread throughout the countryside, and crowds started gathering at the grotto to witness the young maid in ecstasy. As the crowds grew in size from hundreds to thousands, the local authorities, both secular and religious, became nervous about all the attention. On several occasions Bernadette was detained by the Commissioner of Police and questioned about her behavior and the meaning of the visions. Though threatened with imprisonment for disturbing the peace, she never changed her story or attitude. She was always forth-right and calm in the inner knowledge of the righteousness of her visions. The clergy questioned her too, anxious to discover the source of her ecstasies. She was a quiet, simple girl—why would God use her as a tool of inspiration? What was in it for her? In time, Bernadette would win over all her opponents through her sincerity and joyous spirit. They would come to respect her and even support her story, for they could feel the truth of her conviction.

Bernadette continued to live in Lourdes for the next eight years, two years with her parents then six years as a boarder at the Hospice of Lourdes. She finally left the secular life behind in 1866 to become a novice at the convent of the Sisters of Charity of Nevers. Here, she would spend the final thirteen years of her life serving her fellow Sisters, fighting against continual bouts of illness, and blessing many souls through her prayers and penitence. Though she never saw the construction of the Basilica at Lourdes, or witnessed the growth in popularity of the grotto, she lived always in the memory and presence of her Blessed Lady. As for her secrets—she took them with her to her next life in God.

SANCTUARIES OF OUR LADY OF LOURDES

Sanctuaires Notre-Dame de Lourdes

Sanctuaires Notre-Dame de Lourdes

The Sanctuaries consist of a complex of buildings built above and around the Grotto of Massabielle, where the visions occurred. The three primary buildings are the Basilica of the Immaculate Conception, the Crypt, and the Rosary Basilica, all built atop or adjacent to the stone Grotto of Massabielle. The other buildings of the complex are located around the enormous central Rosary Square and along the banks of the River Gave. There are two entrances to the complex: St. Michael's Gate enters from Blvd. de la Grotte and faces the front of the Basilicas; and St. Joseph's Gate leads from Place Mgr. Laurence at the left side of Rosary Square, directly to the front of the Rosary Basilica.

To accommodate the six million pilgrims who visit Lourdes each year, many facilities with a variety of uses have been constructed. These include 22 places of worship, where an average of 52 masses are celebrated each day. To avoid confusion, it is best to go straight to the Forum Information (see map) for a map and guides in English or, better yet, request information before you leave on your trip. There is an excellent website, www.lourdes-france.org, which has all the information required for an inspiring visit.

If you have only a single day to experience Lourdes, visit the Grotto and the Basilicas built around it. If you have the time and energy, add a dip in the water at the baths and walk in the torchlight Marian procession at 9PM. If you have more than a day, there are many other options to consider. Among the many points of interest in the Sanctuary grounds, check out the Museum of St. Bernadette, the Museum of

Precious Objects, and the 30-minute video of Bernadette's life. In town, you can visit the birthplace of Bernadette at the Boly Mill, and the room at the Cachot where her family lived at the time of the apparitions. There is also a walking path to Bartrès, 2.5 miles (4 km) from Lourdes. Leave time to collect the healing water from the miraculous spring. You may want to collect it in a large bottle, and later pour it into smaller bottles available at the multitude of tourist shops.

The Sanctuaries are open all year, but the official pilgrimage season is from April through October. During the season more services and activities are offered than during the winter months. Mass in English is held at 9:00AM in the Chapel of St. Cosmos and St. Damian every day during the season. Once on site, see the daily program for other Masses in English.

Eight thousand volunteers offer their services each year at Lourdes, and donations account for 70% of the 19.8 million Euro annual budget. This is evidence of the staggering amount of faith and service that supports this shrine. The volunteers are the members of the Hospitality and Youth Services, which consists of lay people from all nationalities, and each one pays his or her own way to Lourdes to help welcome pilgrims and accompany the disabled and sick. The tradition of welcoming the sick and disabled started in 1887 when Mademoiselle de Saint-Frai and Father Ribes, founders of the Daughters of Our Lady of Dolours (Filles des Notre-Dame des Douleurs), built a hospice near the Sanctuary.

THE GROTTO OF MASSABIELLE
Grotte de Massabielle

The swiftly flowing Gave de Pau winds its way past the Grotto where the Blessed Virgin appeared to Bernadette. This is to the right of the Rosary Basilica. The statue of Our Lady stands in the same little hollow in the cliff where she appeared to Bernadette. Pilgrims enter the Grotto from behind barricades on the left side of the Grotto. Lined-up next to them are pilgrims with disabilities in carriages. As you step into the cave you will see the miraculous spring through a hole in the floor covered in glass. You may touch or kiss the rock as you pass under the statue of Our Lady that is inscribed in the local dialect, "I am the Immaculate Conception." Prayer requests are collected in baskets placed along the path. In front of the Grotto,

Sanctuaries and Grotto of Massabielle

Masses are performed throughout the day in different languages. Every afternoon at the Grotto there is a blessing for children at 4PM, then at 5PM there is a blessing of the sick, and in the evening, a torchlight procession leaves from the Grotto at 9PM.

The Baths are to the right of the Grotto. If you wish to be immersed in the water of the spring, volunteers will assist you in the ritual. Once you pass through the lines, a dip in the bath takes only a few minutes. There are separate lines for women and men, and 17 baths in all: 11 for women, 6 for men, including 2 for children. The water is changed twice every day. The Virgin said to Bernadette, "Go and drink at the spring and wash yourself there." Bathing in the water is believed to cleanse sins and heal the sick.

THE BASILICA OF THE IMMACULATE CONCEPTION
Basilique de l'Immaculée Conception

The Gothic style Basilica of the Immaculate Conception, or Upper Basilica, was built on top of the rock of the Grotto between 1866 and 1872. The Basilica creates an inspiring image with its spires rising towards the heavens. Two sloping pedestrian pathways reach out on each side to encompass the open plaza below, inviting the multitudes of pilgrims to come pray in this holy place. Inside, the stained glass windows tell the story of the Blessed Virgin Mary from her birth until the Apparitions of Lourdes in 1858.

THE CRYPT
Crypte

The Crypt is below the Basilica of the Immaculate Conception and above and behind the Rosary Basilica. By following either of the long descending ramps on each side of the Basilica or climbing the stairs outside the Rosary Basilica, you will arrive at the level of the Crypt. This was the first chapel to be built at the site, and it was opened in May of 1866 with Bernadette attending. Built into the rock, the small, intimate crypt is very calm and peaceful, often filled with people praying with deep devotion. It is the best place for quiet contemplation in this busy sanctuary.

THE ROSARY BASILICA
Basilique Notre-Dame du Rosaire

The Basilica of Our Lady of the Rosary was begun in 1883 and finished in 1889. It is on ground level, in front of the Crypt and the Basilica of the Immaculate Conception. It can seat up to 1500 people and has ongoing services for different pilgrim groups. The Blessing of the Sick is held outside every afternoon in front of the Basilica.

THE BASILICA OF SAINT PIUS X
Basilique Saint Pius X

This cavernous underground Basilica was consecrated in 1958 to celebrate the centenary of the apparitions. It is a large concrete structure with little atmosphere, but it accommodates 25,000 worshipers and is used continuously for gatherings of large groups of pilgrims. After you enter the gate of St. Michael (Porte St. Michel), entrance to the Basilica is on the left at the bottom of the ramp, before you reach the Forum Information and the Crowned Virgin statue.

THE CHURCH SAINT BERNADETTE
Eglise Sainte Bernadette

Across the bridge from the Grotto, the most recent church, inaugurated in 1988, was built on the spot where Bernadette saw her last apparition of Our Lady. Unable to reach the Grotto because of police barricades, she crossed the river to this location and proceeded to experience the Blessed Virgin at the Grotto. The church holds 5,000 people and also contains meeting rooms. In addition, it has an Adoration Chapel that is a quiet place to pray and meditate.

Where is the Forum Information?
Où est le Forum Information?

Where is the grotto?
Où est la grotte?

SHRINE INFORMATION

Shrine: Forum Information/Sanctuaries of Lourdes (Sanctuaries de Lourdes)

Address: 2, avenue Mgr. Théas/65108 Lourdes Cedex/France

Phone: 33 (0)5 62 42 78 78 **Fax:** 33 (0)5 62 42 89 54

E-mail: saccueil@lourdes-france.com

Website: www.lourdes-france.com/bonjour.htm — Official website for the Sanctuary.

Quiet areas for meditation: The Crypt under the Basilica of the Immaculate Conception; across the river, in the Adoration Chapel in the Church of St. Bernadette; and the Tent of Adoration in the meadow.

English spoken: Typically

Daily Hours: Forum Information: 7AM–7PM; Main entrances: 5:30AM to midnight; Grotto and the grounds are accessible at all times through a smaller gate behind the Upper Basilica and opposite the Chaplains' Residence. Follow a winding path that leads directly to the grotto.

Mass: Mass in English is held at 9:00AM daily at St. Cosmos and St. Damian chapels in the Accueil Jean-Paul II. Get a copy of the list of all the Masses at the Forum Information.

Feasts and festivities: February 11 — First Apparition; February 18 — Feast St. Bernadette.

Accessibility: Lourdes prides itself on being at the forefront for providing accessibility. There are many accommodations for the sick and disabled called "Accueils" and many of the hotels in town are equipped also. The Accueil Notre-Dame is on the grounds of the sanctuaries. Phone: 33 (0)5 62 42 80 61 Email: and-lourdesl@lourdes-france.com. The Accueil Marie Saint-Frai is in town. Phone: 33 (0)5 62 42 80 00 Email: contact@marie-saint-frai.org. More details are on their website at www.lourdes-france.com/bonjour.htm. All the churches are accessible. Inquire about details before you go.

Volunteer: If you are interested in volunteering, contact: Hospitality of Our Lady of Lourdes/Phone: 33 (0)5 62 42 80 80 Fax: 33 (0)5 62 42 80 81 E-mail: hospitalite@lourdes-france.com.

Information office: Facing the Basilicas from St. Michael's gate (Porte St. Michel), to the left of the Crowned Virgin statue on the ground floor of the convention center, is the Pilgrimage office (Abri du pèlerin or Forum Information). Maps, hours of Mass, and information regarding all the sites are provided in English. Ask for everything they have in English.

Tours: A free tour in English is provided every day from July 1st to September 30th. It meets at 8:30AM at the Statue of the Crowned Virgin near the Forum Information. It consists of Mass, the Message of Lourdes, Way of the Cross, visits to the places associated with St. Bernadette and the two Processions. There are also audio guides and personal guided tours. Inquire at the Forum Information.

Groups: If traveling in a group, it is advised to contact the group offices a few months in advance so that a guide may be provided. Phone: 33 (0)5 62 42 79 11 or Email: reservation@lourdes-france.com.

Bookstore: The Pastoral Administration Centre contains the bookstore and is part of the small cluster of buildings that make up the Forum Information.

Recommended books: *The Official Guide of the Sanctuary* has everything you want to know about the sanctuaries, with brief descriptions of the apparitions and St. Bernadette. For more depth (393 pages), read *Saint Bernadette Soubirous* by Abbé François Trochu, and *The Song of Bernadette*, by Franz Werfel.

Lodging: Lodging for the sick and handicapped is provided in the "Accueil's" mentioned above under Accessibility. There is no lack of lodging, with 400 hotels in Lourdes and many close to the Sanctuary.

Directions: www.lourdes-france.org/gb/gbvb0003.htm — A map of Lourdes using Adobe Acrobat and directions by all modes of transportation. Once in town, just ask directions. Everyone is either going to the shrine or knows where it is.

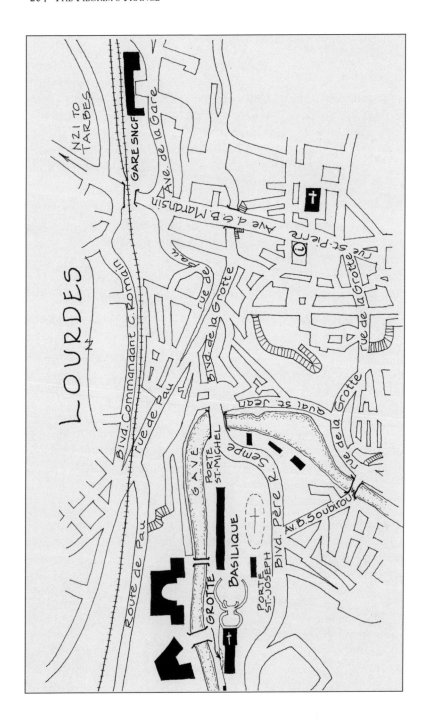

OTHER PLACES OF INTEREST IN LOURDES

THE BOLY MILL
Moulin de Boly

The Boly Mill is near the Sanctuary exit of porte St. Michel and across the bridge Pont St. Michel on rue Bernadette Soubirous. This is the birthplace of Bernadette (La Maison Natale de Bernadette) and where she lived for ten years, from 1844–1854. In 1854, her family was evicted because of financial difficulties, and they moved into the Cachot. Open daily 9AM–12PM, 2PM–6:30.

THE CACHOT BERNADETTE
Cachot Bernadette

Located near place Peyramale on rue des Petits Fossés, this single room dwelling had once been used as a prison cell before it was offered to Bernadette's family for free. They stayed here less than a year, but it is important because Bernadette lived here while she experienced the eighteen apparitions at the Grotto. Open daily 9AM–12PM, 2PM–7.

There are other places to visit if you have the time: The Presbytery—the Parish Church where Bernadette was baptized; the Hospice—where she was educated; and the village of Bartrès—where Bernadette was raised as a baby and later labored as a shepherdess. All these places are described in your guide and on the maps you will receive from the Forum Information.

COMING AND GOING

LOURDES

Car: From Toulouse, take A64 Toulouse-Bayonne to Tarbes, exit #12 Tarbes-Ouest ou Soumoulou. Then take N21 south to Lourdes. From Bayonne, take A64 past Pau to exit #11, then take N177 to Soumoulou, and D940 to Lourdes. Call the tourist information office 33 (0)5 62 42 77 40 about free car parks. There are also car parks for a fee close to the Sanctuaries. Some hotels provide parking.

Train: TGV Paris-Lourdes-Tarbes takes 5 hours 30 minutes: 4 daily return departures from April to October, 3 daily return departures from November to March. Direct rail links from Bordeaux, Toulouse, Montpellier, Marseilles, Nice, Lyon, Vintmille, Geneva, Hendaye, Irun.

For further info contact: GARE SNCF de Lourdes at 33 (0)8 36 35 35 35 or www.sncf.com. For a taxi, call Taxi Lourdais: (0)5 62 94 31 30.

Bus: Most buses arrive at the train station. Pau and Tarbes have local bus service to Lourdes.

Plane: Tarbes-Lourdes-Pyrenees International Airport (TLP) Phone: 33 (0)5 62 32 92 22 Email: aeroport@tarbes.cci.fr www.tarbes-lourdes. aeroport.fr www.tarbes.cci.fr/aeroport/AeroportG.htm

TOURIST INFORMATION

❋ Office de Tourisme de Lourdes/Place Peyramale/BP 17/65101 Lourdes cedex/France; Phone: 33 (0)5 62 42 77 40 Fax: 33 (0)5 62 94 60 95 E-mail: Lourdes@sudfr.com www.lourdes-infotourisme.com.

❋ Hautes-Pyrérées Regional Council www.cg65.fr

WEBSITES

Official website of Lourdes www.lourdes-france.com — Comprehensive website with information about all aspects of your pilgrimage.

Villes Sanctuaries en France www.villes-sanctuaires.com — The Association of Shrine Towns in France with a suggested tour and contact information.

MORE ST. BERNADETTE SHRINES IN FRANCE

NEVERS
Espace Bernadette Soubirous Nevers

Bernadette chose to join the Congregation of the Sisters of Charity of Nevers in 1864 but, due to her bad health, she did not leave for Nevers until July 4, 1866. She would never return to Lourdes. She spent her final thirteen years at the Convent Saint-Gildard and, on April 16, 1879, died at the age of 35. The Convent at Nevers is a special place to visit. St. Bernadette's incorrupt body is on view in the chapel, and you can visit the grounds where she walked and prayed. It is an excellent place for retreat, with lodging available in the Convent. To read more about St. Bernadette and her time in Nevers, refer to the chapter on Burgundy.

Rocamadour

Population 614

The small medieval village of Rocamadour clings to limestone cliffs overlooking the valley of the Alzou River. The dramatic location and the ancient pilgrimage site make this a popular destination, attracting one million tourists each year. Just south of the Dordogne Valley, the area is filled with picturesque landscape, quaint towns and primordial caves. In the middle ages, Rocamadour was a major pilgrimage destination dedicated to the Virgin Mary and has received saints, kings and popes within its walls. The hamlet L'Hospitalet, above Rocamadour, was built in the eleventh century for pilgrims hiking to Compostela, Spain, and exhibits a majestic overview of the valley. This village has survived by providing pilgrims' lodgings and includes a chateau that looms over the cliff-side structures of Rocamadour. Immediately below the chateau is a complex of sanctuaries, known as the Religious or Holy City, which houses the Black Virgin in the Notre Dame Chapel and the original crypt of St. Amadour. The village of Rocamadour itself is just below the sanctuaries, and is bursting with lodging, shops and restaurants. Being pedestrian friendly, the medieval town is charming and quaint. It is lit up at night from Palm Sunday to November 11th, and can be viewed from many vantage points around the rim of the valley and from the motorized-trains that traverse the town.

The ancient cliff town of Rocamadour

ST. AMADOUR
Saint Amadour

The cave of St. Amadour

In the eleventh century, many pilgrims made their way to this remote village to see a small chapel built into the cliffs of Rocamadour, that contained a statue of the Black Virgin. In 1166, an incorrupt body was discovered buried in a cave just outside the chapel and thus began the legend of St. Amadour. The identity of the body was unknown, but it was assumed he was a hermit who had lived in the area. For his apparent devotion to God, he was given the name Amator or "the lover," and from this evolved the name of the town, Roc-Amadour, the rock of the lover.

Reports of the newly discovered "saint" rapidly spread and several legends began to unfold. One legend proposed that he was the servant of the Holy Family and married to St. Veronica. After being driven from Palestine, he made his home in Gaul. He became a hermit in the hills after the death of Veronica and built the chapel of the Black Virgin. The other story is that he was St. Zaccheus from the gospel of St. Luke, and made his way to Gaul after the death of Christ.

There were no facts to support either legend, but the stories aroused the interest of the medieval pilgrims and Rocamadour became an important site. The hermit was initially buried in a niche cut into the cliff at the entrance to the Notre Dame chapel, but later entombed in the floor of St. Amadour chapel. Unfortunately, during the religious wars of the sixteenth century the relics were destroyed. In present day Rocamadour, you can see the cave where his body was discovered (in the cliff adjacent to the church square) and the crypt of St. Amadour where his relics were buried for many centuries (guided tour).

THE SANCTUARIES
Les Sanctuaries

There are seven small sanctuaries that make up the spiritual heart of Rocamadour. The sanctuaries encircle a church square (Le parvis des Eglises) that is 216 steps above the village street level, atop the Great Stairway. In times past, pilgrims traditionally climbed these stairs on their knees as a means of penance. The sanctuaries include: The Basilica of St. Sauveur; the Chapel of Notre-Dame; the crypt of St. Amadour; the St. Michel Chapel; and three small chapels dedicated to St. Anne, St. Blaise, and St. John the Baptist. The basilica of St. Sauveur and the chapel of Notre-Dame are open to the public and are inter-connected, and the statue of the Black Virgin is enshrined in Notre-Dame (see the description below). The crypt of St. Amadour and St. Michael chapel are adorned with twelfth century frescoes and are open for viewing when you take a guided tour, but the three small chapels are inaccessible to the public. There are also a museum and a bookshop within the courtyard, as well as a kiosk for signing up for tours. Lastly, there is a short tunnel with a sign over it reading "Chemin de Croix – Remparts – Ascenseurs," that leads to the Way of the Cross, the ramparts and the elevators, which all take you to the plateau above.

The sacred shrines of Rocamadour were well known in the middle ages, especially after a monk from the village published the *Book of Miracles* in 1172. The book detailed 126 miracles that occurred after pilgrims prayed for intercession

Les Sanctuaries

to the Black Virgin or St. Amadour. To commemorate the miracles, grateful people left their crutches, prisoners' chains, paintings and models of boats as testimony to their salvation. You can still see a model of a boat hanging from the ceiling in the Chapel of the Black Virgin presented by a sailor saved at sea. There is also a bell from the ninth century that would reportedly ring of its own accord when a sailor at sea would pray to the Black Virgin and be saved. As the shrine grew in popularity, many famous pilgrims found their way to this remote area including popes, saints and kings. St. Bernard, St. Dominic, St. Anthony of Padua and King Louis XI all made pilgrimages here, and the pope gave special dispensation to anyone making the arduous journey.

In 1317, a Chapter of Canons replaced the resident Benedictine monks of Rocamadour. By 1425, their numbers had dwindled to fifteen. In 1562 the churches were pillaged and burnt by the Protestants, and the body of St. Amadour was destroyed, along with the city's archives. Neglect and time took their toll on Rocamadour until the mid-1800s when two priests began gathering funds for the restoration of the sanctuaries. One of these priests had been miraculously cured by the Virgin of Rocamadour, and had consequently dedicated his life to restoring the glory of the shrine. Luckily for us, they were successful in their mission and we can today still experience the sacred sanctuaries and mingle with the ancient blessings of this site.

OUR LADY OF ROCAMADOUR–
THE BLACK VIRGIN
Notre Dame de Rocamadour – Vierge Noire

You can enter the chapel of Our Lady up either staircase off the church square, or through the Basilica of St. Sauveur. Follow the sign: "Chapelle Miraculeuse—Vierge Noire." Some of the twelfth century frescoes that decorated the walls of the landing of the chapel are still visible. The empty tomb of St. Amadour is in the side of the cliff to the left of the entry. If you look up above, you can see the legendary sword of Roland, nephew of Charlemagne, sticking out of the rock.

The first recorded mention of the Black Virgin was in 1105, and in 1112, Rocamadour was mentioned as a place of pilgrimage. The statue of the Black Virgin was carved from walnut in the eleventh century and rests on an altar built over a Druid stone. The current

Chapel of Our Lady (Chapelle Notre Dame) has been rebuilt several times over the centuries: after a rock fall in 1479, after it was pillaged by the Huguenots in 1562 and, finally, complete reconstruction occurred in the 1800s. Through it all, the Black Virgin has remained unharmed. The darkly lit chapel and its legendary icon are still the main pilgrimage attraction at Rocamadour, and the devotion is embedded in the ancient stone walls.

Our Lady of Rocamadour

THE CHATEAU AND THE RAMPARTS
Le Château et les Remparts

On the plateau overlooking the village of Rocamadour rests the Chateau and its ramparts. The Chateau was built to protect the sanctuaries below and now houses a religious community that offers pilgrim lodging. This is a more secluded place to stay than the lodging in town, which is amidst all the activity. The Ramparts (Les remparts) were built in the fourteenth century and provide a fantastic view over the town below. It is well worth the effort to walk the Ramparts and experience the views.

There are three ways to travel on foot from the sanctuaries to the Chateau and Ramparts. The first and most direct route is the Way of the Cross (Chemin de Croix) that begins just outside the Porte St. Martial. This walk is fine for anybody in moderately good shape and there are many resting points along the way. The second pathway begins further down from the Porte St. Martial and also meanders up the hill, giving many spectacular views of the valley. It arrives at the plateau midway between the Chateau and L'Hospitalet, the ancient pilgrim's hostel. The third way is the elevator. There are two stages of the elevator, the first rises from the main street of Rocamadour to the plaza outside the sanctuaries at Porte St. Martial. The second stage begins at this same plaza, but several hundred yards from the gate, and rises up to the plateau by the Chateau parking area. There is also a motorized train that traverses the village and travels to the plateau above.

Where is the Black Virgin?
Où est la Vierge Noire?

SHRINE INFORMATION

Shrine: Director of Pilgrimages (Directeur du Pèlerinage)

Address: 46500 Rocamadour/France

Phone: 33 (0)5 65 33 23 23 **Fax:** 33 (0)5 65 33 23 24

E-mail: None

Website: None

Quiet areas for meditation: The Chapel of Our Lady, before closing.

English spoken: Typically at the tourist offices, rarely by the locals.

Hours: Daily 8AM-8PM

Mass: Daily 11AM, 11:45

Feasts and festivities: May 1 — St. Amadour's feast day; August 14 & September 8 —Torchlight processions from L'Hospitalet to the sanctuary; Week of September 8 — Annual Pilgrimage.

Accessibility: The elevators provide access between the castle and the sanctuaries and the sanctuaries and the city.

Lodging for persons with disabilities only: Le Pech de Gourbière/46500 Rocamadour/France Phone: 33 (0)5 65 33 62 74 Fax: 33 (0)5 65 33 68 44 Email: pechdegourbiere@rocamadour.com

Information office: None for the sanctuaries. Use the tourist offices for any questions.

Tours: Tours in French are available at a counter set up on the square in front of the sanctuaries from May 1 to November 11. For tours in

English call ahead to arrange. A one-day pilgrim tour is arranged with the sanctuary. Phone: 33 (0)5 65 33 23 23 Fax: 33 (0)5 65 33 23 24. Contact the tourist office for group tours and night tours. Phone: 33 (0)5 65 33 22 00 Fax: 33 (0)5 65 33 22 01 Email:rocamadour@wanadoo.fr.

Bookstore: On the square in front of the churches. Tourist books are also sold at the tourist office and at the tourist shops.

Museum of Sacred Art (Musée d'art sacré): Phone: 33 (0)5 65 33 23 30 Fax: 33 (0)5 65 33 23 24 Open all year.

Recommended books: Any of the tourist guides on Rocamadour sold at the tourist office or at tourist shops.

Lodging: For pilgrims and for youth groups, Le Relais des Remparts/Le Chateau/46500 Rocamadour/France Phone: 33 (0)5 65 33 23 23 Fax: 33 (0)5 65 33 23 24 Email: relais.des.ramparts@wanadoo.fr Website: http://pro.wanadoo.fr/relaisdesremparts/index.htm French.

Directions: The first town you come to is L'Hospitalet, above Rocamadour. There is parking here, or you can park down in the valley below. The first gate you come to driving into Rocamadour is "Porte du Fignier," with a sign to parking in the valley to the left: "Parking de la Vallée."

COMING AND GOING

ROCAMADOUR

Car: 110 miles (177 km) north of Toulouse, 120 miles (194 km)south of Limoges. Heading south on A20 from Limoges, take exit 54 at N140. After 18 miles (29 km), turn right on D673, drive 3 miles (4 km) to Rocamadour. From Toulouse or Cahors, take N20 north to Payrac, turn right on D673, drive 20 miles (32 km) to Rocamadour.

Train: Gare Rocamadour 2.5 miles (4 km) from the village and Gramat station, 6 miles (10 km). Direct links with the Paris-Toulouse express. Taxi: 33 (0)5 65 33 70 50.

Bus: Accessible from local towns.

Airport: Closest is Toulouse–Blagnac with national and international flights.

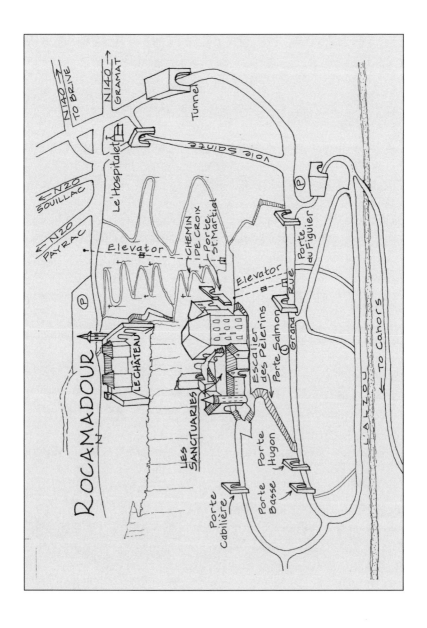

TOURIST INFORMATION

❋ Office du Tourisme/46500 Rocamadour/France Phone: 33 (0)5 65 33 22 00 Fax: 33 (0)5 65 33 22 01 Email: rocamadour@wanadoo.fr www.rocamadour.com. One tourist office is in l'Hospitalet and one at the Hôtel de Ville in the village of Rocamadour.

❋ Le Lot http://monolith.tourisme-lot.com/annuaire/lotcrawler/FR French. Official site for the department of Lot. Email: info@tourisme-lot.com.

WEBSITES

La Maison du Pèlerin www.lourdes-fr.comn — Information about the major shrines in France and Europe including Rocamadour.

Office de Tourisme www.rocamadour.com — Tourism Office for Rocamadour.

Villes Sanctuaries en France www.villes-sanctuaires.com — The Association of Shrine Towns in France with a suggested tour and contact information.

PLACES OF INTEREST NEAR ROCAMADOUR AND CONQUES

ALBI

THE CATHEDRAL OF ST. CECILE
La Basilique Sainte Cécile

The Cathedral of St. Cecilia of Albi (1282-1512) is a unique fortress style church—a masterpiece of Southern Gothic style. The imposing solid brick exterior is uninviting, but once you enter through the richly carved portico, the interior explodes with delightful architectural detail. The radiant blue and gold ceiling hovers over the delicate stone tracery of the rood screen and a huge mural of the Last Judgment from the Flemish School. This painting once covered the entire width of the choir, but in 1693, an archway to the tower's lower chapel was built through the center of the immense piece. The side chapel dedicated to St. Cecile contains a vivid sculptural piece of her martyrdom and some of her relics brought from Rome in 1466. Website Albi Town Hall: www.mairie-albi.fr English version upper-left rotating ball.

TOULOUSE

THE BASILICA OF ST. SERNIN
La Basilique de Saint Sernin

Built in the eleventh and twelfth centuries for the pilgrims walking to Santiago de Compostela in Spain, the Basilica of Saint Sernin is the largest Romanesque church in France. Its namesake was the first bishop and martyr of Toulouse, Saturnin or Saturnius. In 250 A.D., he refused to sacrifice to the pagan gods and was subsequently tied to a bull and dragged through the streets to his death. His remains are in the "Reliquaire de Saint Saturnin," and are housed along with the relics of 128 other saints, including Saints Peter and Paul and a thorn from the crown of thorns. It is worth paying the small fee to enter the ambulatory to see what pilgrims of old called the "holy bodies circuit." Don't miss the two crypts below that contain more beautiful reliquaries, liturgical objects and sculpture. Hours: July-Sept: Weekly 8:30AM-6PM; Sunday 12:30PM-6. Oct-June: Weekly 8:30AM-11:45, 2PM-5:45; Sunday 8:30AM-12:30PM, 2PM-7:30. La Basilque de Saint Sernin/ place St. Sernin/31000 Toulouse/France. Phone: 33 (0)5 61 21 80 45.

La Basilique de Saint Sernin

THE CHURCH OF THE JACOBINS
Eglise des Jacobins

The Church of the Jacobins was constructed between 1230 and 1235, and used by the Dominicans to fight Catharism in Toulouse. The fortress-like exterior expresses the embattled feelings of the time, but gives way to an interior of vaulted ceilings supported by columns resembling palm trees. These are known as "Palmier des Jacobins" and the church is considered a masterpiece of Gothic construction. The columns march down the center of the Church, so there is no central nave with side isles, but only the single space. This makes the altar

Cloister of Eglise des Jacobins

on the side seem almost like an afterthought, and that is where the relics of the great theologian St. Thomas Aquinas are enshrined. The church is run as a museum and concert hall, so St. Thomas does not receive the attention he deserves. Even if the setting doesn't feel appropriate for prayer and contemplation, if you take the time, his blessings are tangible. There is no entry fee to the church, but paid admission of €2.20 is required to see the cloister. Open daily 9AM-7PM.

Ensemble conventuel des Jacobins/69, rue Pargaminières/31000 Toulouse/France www.jacobins.mairie-toulouse.fr/accueil.htm Email: jacobins@mairie-toulouse.fr Phone: 33 (0)5 61 22 21 92 Fax: 33 (0)5 61 22 22 09 Email: jacobins@mairie-toulouse.fr. Directions: Jacobins Square (Parvis de Jacobins) off rue Lakanal. Tourist Information: Official site of Toulouse www.mairie-toulouse.fr — For churches go to "culture," then "monuments." The web°site has the hours of the church and good maps.

Normandy

Normandie

Normandy is actually two regions, Upper Normandy (Haute-Normandie) and Lower Normandy (Basse-Normandie). This mostly rural area, in the northwestern part of France, is popular with natives as well as tourists. History buffs can relive the Allied invasion of France on June 6, 1944 at the D-Day beaches, visit the great eleventh century abbey churches and castle in Caen which tell the story of William the Conqueror, and travel to Bayeux to see the 230 foot long tapestry that documents William's invasion of England. The general sightseer can take pleasure in the beautiful countryside with rolling hills and grazing cows, apple orchards that are the source of a local apple brandy called Calvados, half-timbered houses, Monet's colorful garden at Giverny, and dramatic granite cliffs and charming villages along many miles of coastline. The spiritual seeker has many opportunities for prayer and devotion, including the town where St. Therese of Lisieux grew up, the majestic island abbey of Mont Saint Michel, and two sites in the modern city of Rouen—the heavenly Gothic Cathedral Notre-Dame made famous by Monet, and the Old Market Square where St. Joan of Arc was martyred.

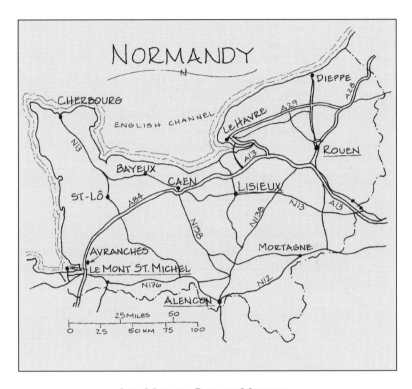

LE MONT SAINT-MICHEL
The Abbey of Mont Saint Michel

LISIEUX
St. Therese of Lisieux

ROUEN
St. Joan of Arc

Le Mont Saint-Michel

Population 46

The Abbey of Mont Saint-Michel is one of the most photographed icons of France, second only to the Eiffel Tower. As one approaches the site, the Abbey rises on the horizon, majestically floating above the sea, as if a mirage. It sits atop the island of Mont-Tombe, which is situated at the mouth of the Couesnon River in the bay of Mont Saint-Michel. A pilgrimage destination for more than a millennium, this famous Abbey now attracts 3 million tourists a year. The village at the foot of the Abbey consists of houses dating from the fifteenth and sixteenth centuries, while the Grande Rue or Main Street, is clogged with tourist shops, restaurants and wax museums. The island is connected to shore by a two-mile causeway built in 1879, which has unfortunately, resulted in silting of the bay and the spread of marsh grass. Construction of a bridge to replace the causeway will begin in the near future. The bay has some of the strongest tides in Europe and becomes a mud flat in low tide. If you take any hikes along the water, consult a tide table and the locals to avoid getting caught in high tide, quicksand or fog.

Le Mont Saint-Michel

THE ABBEY OF MONT SAINT MICHEL
Abbaye du Mont Saint-Michel

The Abbey of Mont Saint-Michel is an architectural marvel, constructed on a tiny granite island surrounded by dangerous tides and treacherous quicksand. It is the result of many centuries of building evolution, beginning in 709 A.D., when St. Aubert built the initial church dedicated to the Archangel Michael.

A new church was constructed in the tenth century. At about the same time, the site was turned over to the Benedictine Order. In the eleventh century, a larger, Romanesque abbey church was built over the top of this structure.

In 1204, troops loyal to King Phillipe Auguste took the island by force, damaging many of the buildings during the conquest. To make amends, the King ordered the construction of the famous Marvel (la Merveille) on the north side of the Abbey. This three-story

Abbaye du Mont Saint-Michel

structure, with its buildings perched on the steep rocky slopes rising up to the Abbey church, is considered a jewel of Gothic architecture. It includes the cloister, refectory, knights' and guests' chambers, and undercroft. Despite this physical expansion of the Abbey, and its recognition as a pilgrimage destination, by the end of the thirteenth century, the number of Benedictine monks had so diminished that they merged with the congregation of St. Maur.

During the wars with England in the fifteenth century, massive ramparts were built around the base of the island. Though frequently attacked, the island was never captured, and it soon became a symbol of French valor, with Archangel Michael as the protector. At the end of the fifteenth century, the flamboyant gothic choir was built, ending the major construction on the site.

The structures began to fall into disrepair in the late sixteenth century, coinciding with the decline of the monastic life. During the French Revolution the few Maurist monks that were left were expelled and the Abbey church became a prison until 1863. After being designated an historical monument in 1874, the French Government undertook its restoration and it is now administered by the National Center of Historic Monuments (Caisse nationale des Monuments Historiques). In 1922, Mass was once again celebrated in the Abbey church, but it wasn't until 1969 that the Benedictine monks returned. Since 2001, the Monastic Fraternities of Jerusalem, a community of monks and nuns, have lived in the Abbey and they ensure that the church is a source of perpetual prayer.

In the early days of the Abbey, the monks recorded many stories of miracles attributed to Michael the Archangel, and the site became a major pilgrimage destination in the thirteenth century. Pilgrims traveled here on roads called "paths to paradise" and brought with them funds that supported the Abbey. It is thought that the symbols of the pilgrim—the cockleshell, horn, and staff—originated at Mont Saint-Michel. The staff was used to check for quicksand, the horn to summon aid, and the cockleshell was a souvenir signifying the pilgrim's journey to the water's edge.

For a modern day tour, follow the Grande Rue around the base of the Mont, which leads to the Grand staircase that climbs up to the Abbey entrance. We recommend renting the audio guide to lead you through this conglomeration of buildings. On the north side, there are three levels, all of which are very interesting, but if you are short on time, go directly to the top to see the Abbey Church and the cloister with its magnificent view.

Mass is celebrated every day at 12:15PM, accompanied by the beautiful live chanting of the monks and nuns. Entry into the Abbey Church is free for the fifteen minutes preceding the Mass, but this does not give you a free pass to visit the rest of the structure. No one is allowed to enter the Church once the service has begun.

There are volunteers at The Pilgrim's House (Maison du Pèlerin) who will help you organize your pilgrimage. It is located in the lower town, the last house on the right going up the Grand Rue. The Pilgrim's House operates as the sanctuary's secretarial office and includes a shop where one can buy religious articles. St. Peter's Church across the street celebrates Mass in July and August every day at 11AM and on Saturdays at 6:30PM. The other months of the year, Mass is celebrated on Thursday and Sunday at 11AM.

Abbaye du Mont Saint-Michel

If you want to bypass the tourist shops and head straight for the Abbey, you will find a steeper climb up the first stairs to the right after passing the drawbridge. Either way, there is a lot of uphill walking, so be prepared.

Where is the Abbey of Mont St. Michel?
Où est l'abbaye du Mont Saint Michel?

SHRINE INFORMATION

Shrine: Sanctuary (Sanctuaire) or House of the Pilgrims (Maison du Pèlerin)

Address: BP 1/50170 Le Mont St. Michel/France

Phone: 33 (0)2 33 60 14 05 **Fax:** 33 (0)2 33 60 14 26

Email: abbayemichel@wanadoo.fr

Website: www.abbaye-montsaintmichel.com French

Quiet areas for meditation: Everywhere on the island is very crowded, but the two places for prayer and meditation would be St. Peter's (St. Pierre), a small church on the Grande Rue across from the Pilgrim's House, and the Abbey church at the top.

English spoken: Occasionally

Hours for the Abbey: May 2-August 30: 9AM-7PM; October 1-April 30: 9:30AM-6PM; Closed Jan 1, May 1, Nov 1 & 11, Dec 25.

Mass in the Abbey: 12:15PM, every day except Monday.

Mass in the church of St. Pierre: Daily 11AM; Sat 6:30PM; Sun in July & Aug 5:30PM.

Feasts and festivities: One Sunday in May — St. Michel Spring Feast Day; Second half of July — Pilgrimage across the sand (4.5 miles); Nearest Sunday to September 29 — St. Michael's Autumn Feast Day; October 16 — Consecration Feast Day.

Accessibility: Contact: contact@monum.fr for detailed information.

Information office: You can pick up a map and a brochure at the Tourist Office, to the left as you enter the island. The Pilgrim's House (Maison du Pèlerin), where volunteers will help you organize your pilgrimage, is the last house on the right walking up Grand Rue.

Tours: Reserve two weeks in advance at the Tourist Office for guided one-hour tours in English. Audio guide for a seventy-minute tour is available at the entrance to the Abbey. The audio guide took us two hours, stopping and starting.

Bookstore: The Abbey has a big bookstore.

Recommended books: At the entrance to the Abbey they give you a brochure in English. For more detail purchase *Wonderful Mont Saint-Michel*, by Lucien Bély, in the tourist shops.

Lodging: Lodging is available for persons wanting to retreat. Contact the Abbey for more information (see above). You must speak and write in French.

Directions: If you drive onto the causeway you will have to pay for parking. If you park in the parking lots on the lower sides of the causeway, be aware that during high tide your car will be submerged. Note the signs that tell the times of high tide. There is also parking on the mainland and a short walk to the island.

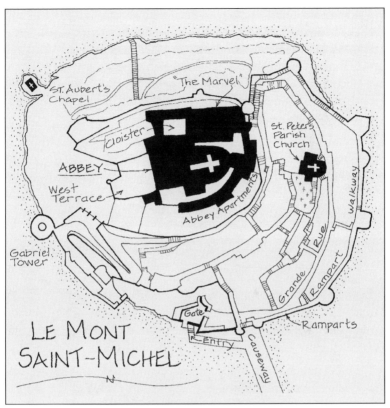

LE MONT SAINT-MICHEL

COMING AND GOING

MONT SAINT MICHEL

Car: Exit A84 south of Avrances in the direction of Saint-Malo. Mont Saint-Michel is 6 miles (9 km) north of Pontorson on D976. After exiting A84, you can also take secondary roads: D 43, D 75 and D 275 to Mont Saint-Michel.

Train: Take the Paris-Brest train from Montparnasse station in Paris to Rennes, then take the connecting Caen train to Pontorson. Then take the STN bus or a taxi to Mont Saint Michel.

TOURIST INFORMATION

❋ Administrative Office for the Center of National Monuments (Centre des Monuments nationaux)/Abbaye du Mont Saint-Michel/

50116 Le Mont-Saint-Michel/France Phone: 33 (0)2 33 89 80 00
Fax: 33 (0)2 33 70 83 08 E-mail: contact@monum.fr www.monum.fr
— Official website for historic monuments in France.

❋ Maison du Département/50008 Sain-Lô cedex/France
Phone: 33 (0)2 33 05 98 70 Fax: 33 (0)2 33 05 99 55 Email:
mtr@cg50.fr www.manchetourisme.com.

❋ Office du Tourisme/BP4/50170 Mont Saint-Michel/France
Phone 33 (0)2 33 60 14 30 Fax: 33 (0)2 33 60 06 75 Email:
ot.mont.saint.michel@wanadoo.fr.

WEBSITES

Abbaye de Mont Saint-Michel www.abbaye-montsaintmichel.com —
Official website for the Monastic Fraternities of Jerusalem at the
Abbey of Mont Saint-Michel.

Centre des monuments nationaux www.monum.fr — The National
Center of Monuments.

La Maison du Pèlerin www.lourdes-fr.com — Information about the
major shrines in France and Europe, including Mont Saint-Michel.

Villes Sanctuaries en France www.villes-sanctuaires.com — The
Association of Shrine Towns in France with a suggested tour and
contact information.

Lisieux
Population 27,639

At the turn of the twentieth century, Lisieux was the hub of the
French textile industry, producing almost a third of the country's
fabrics. Now, the town is mostly known as the home of St. Therese of
the Child Jesus and the Holy Face, and tourism has become one of the
primary industries of this two thousand year old city. The history of
Lisieux is reflected in the many timber-framed houses, the old
chateaux in the surrounding countryside such as the sixteenth century
Le Château de Saint-Germain, and the eleventh century St. Pierre
Cathedral in the heart of the city. As the capital of the Pays d'Auge,
Lisieux invites more than 700,000 pilgrims a year to follow in the
footsteps of St. Therese, the town's patron saint. Saint Therese moved

to Lisieux when she was four years old, and lived here until her passing at age twenty-four. Her life was spent at her childhood home and at the Carmelite monastery, where she lived a cloistered life starting shortly after her fifteenth birthday. There are many places to see in Lisieux that related to the life of this little saint including her home— Les Buissonnets, St. Pierre Cathedral—the church of her youth, Carmel—the Carmelite monastery where she lived and died, and the immense Basilica of St. Therese, built in her memory. The town is easy to negotiate, and is a great place to use as a hub for travel around Normandy to see Caen, Bayeux and the Normandy Beaches.

ST. THERESE OF LISIEUX
Sainte Thérèse de Lisieux 1873–1897

*"I have never given the good God aught but love,
and it is with love that He will repay."*

The "Little Flower" of Lisieux has made a broad impact on modern spirituality through the example of her simple devout life and especially through her writings. Though she lived for only twenty-four years, Therese blazed the trail of a modern day saint by following her self-described "little way" to God and left behind a litany of prose and poems that give us a profound understanding of her inner life. Her autobiography, *The Story of a Soul*, has been printed for more than a century in almost every language, with a

St. Therese of Lisieux

total publication of many millions of copies. Countless souls have received guidance from this "little one" and she has lived up to her prophetic promise, "After my death I will let fall a shower of roses," by continuing to shower her blessings on all those who invoke her intercession.

The story of Therese actually begins with her parents, for Louis and Azelie-Marie Martin created a household filled with love and religious fervor. Both had individually sought to enter religious orders in their youth, but upon being refused admittance, decided to dedicate their lives to raising children for God. Azelie prayed, "I beseech Thee to make me mother of many children, and to grant that all of them may be consecrated to Thee."

Southern transept of the Basilica of St. Therese

The couple met and was married in 1858 in the town of Alençon, where they began their life together, Louis as a watchmaker and Azelie as a very successful entrepreneur producing lace. The young couple attended Mass daily and raised their family in a loving and devotional environment. Therese was the last of nine children born to the couple, but four of their children died in infancy. All of the surviving children were girls and the entire family fawned over young Therese, showering her with love and affection. "My earliest memories are of smiles and tender caresses," she later wrote of this first stage of her life. A testament to the devout nature of the Martin family is the fact that both parents were proclaimed Venerable by the Church, and all five daughters made perpetual religious vows.

Therese's idyllic life was shattered at the age of four and a half when her mother died. "With Mamma's death...began the second period of my life, the most sorrowful of all," Therese wrote in her autobiography. "If Our Lord had not lavished His sunshine upon His Little Flower, she never would have become acclimatized to this earth. Still too weak to bear either rain or snow, she needed warmth, refreshing dew, and gentle breezes—gifts never denied her, even in the wintry season of trials." The two youngest girls of the family clung to their older sisters for support and Pauline, the second oldest, became Therese's "new" mother. Louis also became more motherly in his love and the family stuck together in their faith.

The family moved to Lisieux so the children could be nurtured under the watchful eye of their aunt and uncle, who loved the children dearly. Therese attended school and displayed a keen intelligence, although she remained somewhat withdrawn and shy, often giving way to tears of sadness. The height of her sorrow occurred when her sister Pauline left home in October of 1882 to enter the Carmelite monastery in Lisieux, known as Carmel. She later wrote to Pauline of this episode, "I shall never forget how tenderly you tried to console me, my little Mother (Pauline). You explained to your child the nature of the religious life, and one evening, while pondering all alone on the picture you had drawn for me, I felt that Carmel was the desert where God wished me also to hide. I felt it so strongly that there was no room for doubt. It was not the dream of an impressionable child, but the certainty of a divine call, and this sensation, which I am unable to describe, brought with it a wonderful peace." Therese was nine years old. Pauline, now Sister Agnes of Jesus, took Therese for an interview with the Mother Superior at Carmel. But, Therese was told she would have to wait until she was sixteen to seek admittance to the order. Undeterred, Therese bided her time.

The next year marked another turning point for Therese, as she began to experience severe headaches and was often ill. These episodes increased in intensity and frequency to the point where her family feared for her life. In May of 1883, Therese's illness appeared fatal and Louis asked for a novena to be prayed for her recovery at Our Lady of Victory in Paris. One morning in May, three of Therese's sisters huddled about her bed, and together they prayed fervently for the Blessed Virgin's healing. Therese was so ill she could not recognize her sisters, yet fell into a prayerful ecstasy while gazing at the family statue of Our Lady. " Suddenly the statue became animated and

St. Therese's miraculous statue of Our Lady

radiantly beautiful — with a divine beauty that no words of mine can ever convey," she later recalled. "The look upon Our Lady's face was unspeakably kind and sweet and compassionate, but what penetrated to the very depths of my soul was her gracious smile. Instantly all my pain vanished, my eyes filled, and big tears fell silently, tears of the purest heavenly joy." Therese was cured and soon returned to good health.

The inner life of Therese progressed quickly from this point forward. She loved to read about the saints, especially St. Joan of Arc, and aspired to achieve their greatness. This was not a childish whim, but a firm desire growing in her heart. The young Therese was spiritually mature for her age and was able to perceive inner guidance and accept its truth. "Our Lord made me understand that the only true glory is the glory that lasts for ever," she wrote at a later date. "Then, as I reflected that I was born for great things, and sought the means to attain them, it was made known to me interiorly that my personal glory would never reveal itself before the eyes of men, but would consist in becoming a Saint...I still feel the same daring confidence that one day I shall become a great Saint."

A year following her miraculous recovery, Therese received her first communion, "the most beautiful day of all the days of my life." Gowned in white and crowned with roses, the girl of ten made her first betrothal to Jesus. "How sweet was the first embrace of Jesus! It was indeed an embrace of love," she wrote. "I felt that I was loved, and I said: 'I love Thee, and I give myself to Thee for ever.' That day our meeting was more than simple recognition, it was perfect union. We were no longer two. Therese had disappeared like a drop of water lost in the immensity of the ocean; Jesus alone remained...And then my joy became so intense, so deep, that it could not be restrained; tears of happiness welled up and overflowed...all the joy of heaven had come down into one heart."

An amazing aspect of Therese's life is that she experienced all the stages typical of the spiritual life, but condensed into just twenty-four years. With these stages also came spiritual trials. After her second communion at age eleven, Therese experienced the temporary doubt and exile often felt by spiritual aspirants treading the path of complete surrender to God's will. For two years she struggled with her "scruples" and was often withdrawn and sad, being overly self-critical of any earthly frailties. Two events would bring her back to her life of joy, and both related to the love of her family. First, after once again feeling abandoned when her sister Marie left the family home for Carmel, Therese looked to heaven for her solace. She prayed to her little brothers and sisters who had died in infancy and called upon them to console her with their love. "I had not long to wait for the answer: a sweet peace soon inundated my soul and I knew that I was loved, not only on earth but also in Heaven," she wrote in her autobiography. "From that day my devotion towards those blessed ones increased; I loved to talk to them, to tell them of all the sorrows of this exile, and of my great longing to join them soon in our Eternal Home."

The second event took place at Christmas of 1886, when the thirteen year-old Therese experienced what she called her "conversion." After returning home from midnight Mass and preparing to receive the traditional Christmas gifts, Therese overheard her father wishing that her childish antics would end. "These words cut me to the very heart," she later confided. "But Therese was no longer the same—Jesus had transformed her...Therese had once (and) for all regained the strength of mind which had left her when she was four and a half...On this radiant night began the third period of my life, the most beautiful of all, the most filled with heavenly favors...Love and a spirit of self-forgetfulness took complete possession of my heart, and thenceforward I was perfectly happy." The girl of Lisieux was now ready to complete her transformation into a saint.

Therese's wish to enter Carmel was kept a secret between her and Sister Agnes, but she finally confided her heart's most fervent desire to her father when she was fifteen. Louis and Therese together wept tears of joy for the glory of God and sadness for the loss of the family, but Papa gave his firm approval. The problem lay with the approval of the authorities at Carmel and with the local Bishop, both of whom told Therese that she would have to wait until she was twenty-one. This was too much for the aspiring saint to bear, so she went with her father to plead to the Bishop of Bayeux. Later when the family went to Rome on pilgrimage, she took her question all the way to the Pope. Kneeling before the pontiff she broke the usual customary silence by asking him, "Holy Father, in honor of your jubilee, allow me to enter Carmel at fifteen'…He looked fixedly at me, and said clearly, each syllable strongly emphasized: 'Well, child! Well, you will enter if it be God's Will."

Shortly after returning home, in late December of 1887, Therese received a letter from Mother Mary of Gonzaga saying the Bishop of Bayeux approved her admittance and that she could enter the convent at Carmel in April, during Lent. Therese was grateful for the approval but disappointed by the delay. "But the Lord made me understand how valuable those months were, and I resolved to give myself up more than ever to a serious and mortified life…Far from resembling those heroic souls who from their childhood use fast and scourge and chain to discipline the flesh, I made my mortifications consist simply in checking my self-will, keeping back an impatient answer, rendering a small service in a quiet way, and a hundred other similar things. By means of these trifles I prepared myself to become the spouse of Christ." On April 9, 1888, Therese entered Carmel to join her two sisters and take up her cross to follow Jesus. "My desire was now accomplished and my soul was filled with so deep a peace that it baffles all attempt at description." Her saintly demeanor was noticed by her novice mistress who testified during Therese's beatification, "From her entrance, she surprised the community by her bearing, which was marked by a certain dignity that one would not expect in a child of fifteen."

Therese spent the remaining eight and a half years of her life within the walls of Carmel leading an exemplary life, but also one of severe tests and trials—physical, psychological and spiritual. For instance, her relationship with her Superior was difficult, as Mother Mary of Gonzaga was constantly berating the young novice while offering little positive spiritual advice. Even so, Therese took the abuse willingly and grew from the tests. Most importantly, she continued to make great strides in her inner life, learning from all her interactions with the members of her small community and through her service. The twenty or so nuns of Carmel provided an ideal situation for Therese to perfect herself and her "little way."

As Therese approached her nineteenth birthday, an epidemic of influenza struck the community, fatally infecting several of the Sisters. Therese was one of three Sisters able to serve those in need, and performed weeks of endless assistance to those afflicted. In her service, she also received the grace of Christ's presence. "After the influenza epidemic, He came to me daily for several months, a privilege not shared by the Community. I had not sought his favor, but it brought me untold happiness to be united day after day to Him whom my soul loved."

Transept of the Basilica of St. Therese

Many saints speak of infused knowledge, but it is seldom that we receive any insight into the process. Through the writing of Therese, we get a glimpse of this process and an understanding of how we can be open to the same divine inspiration. "The Holy Scriptures and the Imitation (of Christ) are of the greatest assistance; I find in them a hidden manna, pure and genuine. It is from the Gospels, however, that I derive most help in the time of prayer; I find in their pages all that my poor soul needs, and I am always discovering there new lights and hidden mysterious meanings. I know and I have experienced that 'The Kingdom of God is within us,' that Our Master has no need of book or teacher to instruct a soul...I know He is within me, always guiding and inspiring me; and just when I need them, lights, hitherto unseen, break in upon me. As a rule, it is not during prayer that this happens but in the midst of my daily duties."

In 1893, when Therese was twenty, she was appointed assistant novice mistress and worked diligently serving the novices, who were often years older than herself. She shared with them her deep love for God, but also her keen insight into the search for perfection, and at times, she read their innermost thoughts: "I never reprimand you without first invoking Our Blessed Lady, asking her to inspire me with whatever will be for your greatest good. Often I am myself astonished at what I say, but as I say it I feel I make no mistake, and that it is Jesus who speaks by my lips." Through the years, the basis of all her actions gained a single focus: love. "I realized that love includes every vocation, that love is all things, that love is eternal, reaching down through the ages and stretching to the uttermost limits of earth... Beside myself with joy, I cried out: 'O Jesus, my Love, my vocation is found at last—my vocation is love'...I will be love...Thus I shall be all things and my dream will be fulfilled."

Therese's short life was rapidly drawing to its conclusion and her trials seemed never ending. In 1894, Louis Martin died, following three years of institutional confinement after suffering several strokes. But with his passing, the last Martin sister entered Carmel to join the other three, bringing the entire family into the religious life. Of the five sisters, four were at Carmel and the fifth was cloistered in Caen. Therese knew of her coming fate, and in 1895, confided in one of the elder nuns, that she would soon die. "I do not say that it will be in a few months, but in two or three years at most; I know by what is taking place in my soul." Just prior to Easter in 1895, Therese suffered an attack of tuberculosis, coughing up blood, signaling an advanced condition of the disease. Over the next two years, her condition slowly worsened and she physically suffered much, but she remained ever cheerful and full of joy. It is during this time, on orders of her Superior, that she began writing her autobiography, *The Story of a Soul*.

During this time, Therese candidly told her Sisters of her eventual return to earth in order to save souls. One day when a Sister was speaking of the happiness of heaven, Therese interrupted, saying, "It is not that which attracts me... It is Love. To love, to be loved and to return to earth to win love for our Love." "You will look down on us from Heaven?"

she was asked. "No!" came the forceful reply, "I will come down." At another time she told her sister, Mother Agnes, "One hope alone makes my heart beat fast—the love I shall receive and the love I shall be able to give! I feel that my mission is soon to begin—to make others love God as I love Him…to teach souls my little way…I will spend my Heaven in doing good on Earth…there cannot be any rest for me till the end of the world—till the angel shall have said, 'time is no more.' Then I shall take my rest." "And what is the little way that you would teach?" asked Mother Agnes. "It is the way of spiritual childhood, the way of absolute trust and absolute self-surrender," replied Therese. "There is only one thing to do here below—to offer Our Lord the flowers of little sacrifices and win Him by our caresses."

In June of 1897, Therese was moved to the convent infirmary, where she remained for her final months. The pain of her illness was extreme, but to her it was all by God's grace. "When I suffer much," she would say, "when painful and disagreeable things come my way, instead of looking sad, I greet them with a smile. At first I did not

always succeed, but now it has become a habit which I am truly grateful to have acquired…. At each moment He sends me what I am able to bear—nothing more— and if He increases the pain my strength is also increased." After a final three months of agony, Therese was ready to leave her body. On September 30th, with her community and sisters around her, she uttered her last words while looking at her crucifix, "Oh…I love Him!….My God, I…love…Thee!" After leaving her body, a

Reliquary of St. Therese of Lisieux at the Carmel

beatific smile illuminated her face and miracles graced the convent. One Sister, upon kissing the feet of the departed saint was instantly cured of cerebral anemia. Another felt a kiss upon her face from an unseen source while others saw visible signs of blessings. Truly, her promise to return was being immediately realized: "After my death I will let fall a shower of roses."

This little saint was all but unknown outside the walls of Carmel, but the fame of Therese of the Child Jesus and the Holy Face grew rapidly following the publication of her autobiography a year after her death. Printing after printing was ordered and her little way quickly spread throughout the world. Miracles were reported from all corners of the globe and countless souls found comfort in her message and presence. She was beatified in 1923 and canonized two years later. In 1994 her parents were declared Venerable and, in 1997, St. Therese was proclaimed Doctor of the Church. St. Therese continues to touch hearts everywhere through her shower of roses.

THE BASILICA OF ST. THERESE
Basilique du St. Thérèse

Basilique du St. Thérèse

The monumental Basilica of St. Therese was built between 1929 and 1937 and is one of the largest churches built in the twentieth century, seating two thousand people. A highlight of the main sanctuary is the eighteen minor altars, located around the Basilica, that are dedicated by different nations of the world.

As you enter the Basilica, turn to the right, where there are brochures in English.

Continuing along the right side of the Basilica, you will come to the shrine dedicated to St. Therese that contains two bones of her right arm.

Downstairs is the Crypt that consists of a large chapel, decorated in mosaics and marble, and a small quiet Chapel of the Adoration on the left. This is a quiet area for contemplation. St. Therese's knee is in the sacristy and is sometimes brought out for veneration during special celebrations.

Outside the Basilica, there are several things to see. Different exhibitions are shown to the left as you face the Basilica, and down some steps. The film "La vie de sainte Therese" is shown (in different languages) in the cinema to the right of the entrance of the Basilica from May to October. From April to September it is shown in the welcome center (Centre d'Accueil de la Basilique) in front of the Basilica.

The tombs of St. Theresa's parents are behind the Basilica, along with the Stations of the Cross. Initially buried in the Lisieux cemetery, their bodies were transferred to this location in 1958 when the cause for their beatification was introduced. The Lisieux Cemetery can also be visited by continuing up Avenue Jean XXIII. This is where St Theresa was buried until 1923.

Where is the Basilica?
Où est la basilique?

Where is the Carmel?
Où est le Carmel?

Where is Les Buissonnets?
Où sont les Buissonnets?

SHRINE INFORMATION

Shrine: Sanctuary of Lisieux (Sanctuarie de Lisieux)

Address: 31 rue du Carmel/BP 62095/14102 Lisieux cedex/France

Phone: 33 (0)2 31 48 55 08 **Fax:** 33 (0)2 31 48 55 26

E-mail: info@therese-de-lisieux.com

Website: www.therese-de-lisieux.com — Official website for the Sanctuary.

Quiet areas for meditation: The Carmel with the relics of St. Therese is very devotional. The Basilica has a side chapel to the right with the relic of St. Therese's arm, and the Crypt in the Basilica has the Adoration chapel to the left that is very quiet.

English spoken: Rarely. The tourist offices are your best bet.

Hours: Daily July & Aug 9AM–8PM; March, April, Oct 9AM–6PM; May, June, Sept 9AM–7PM; Nov, Dec, Jan, Feb 9:30AM–5:30PM.

Mass at the Carmel: 8AM, 9, 11 (Mass for the Pilgrims),11:30.

Mass at the Basilica: Sunday/Hol: 10:30AM, 5pm in the Crypt; Saturday 5PM July, Aug, Sept; During the week 11AM May-Sept.

Feasts and festivities: October 1 — Feast Day; Sept 25–Oct 10 — St. Therese Festival.

Accessibility: The Carmel has a ramp to the left of the entrance. The Basilica has a ramp to the left of the entrance and an elevator for the underground information office in front of the Basilica. The Buissonnets does not have accessibility.

Information office: The International Pastoral Welcome Center (Centre d'Accueil Pastoral International) is in front of the Basilica in the underground facility, telephone 33 (0)2 31 48 21 06. The Tourist Offices in town are also very informative about everything a pilgrim needs to know in Lisieux (see info below).

Tours: Tours in English can be arranged ahead of time through the local tourist offices. See info below.

Bookstore: There is a bookstore to the left of the Carmel, and in front of the Basilica, in the underground Welcome Center.

Recommended books: *The Story of a Soul* by St. Therese of Lisieux from TAN Books and Publishers.

Lodging: There are two religious houses for lodging, with detailed descriptions on the sanctuary website: www.therese-de-lisieux.com.

Maison d'Accueil des Pèlerins/Ermitage Saint Thérèse/23 rue du Carmel/14100 Lisieux/France Phone: 33 (0)2 31 48 55 10 Fax: 33 (0)2 31 48 55 27 Email: ermitage-ste-therese@therese-de-lisieux.com.

Foyer Louis et Zélie Martin/15 avenue Sainte-Thérèse/14100 Lisieux/France Phone: 33 (0)2 31 62 09 33 Fax: 33 (0)2 31 62 88 65 Email: foyer-martin@therese-de-lisieux.com.

Directions: The Basilica is just south of the center of the city, a ten to fifteen minute walk. At Place Jean-Paul II, at the south side of town, take Avenue Sainte-Therese, and follow the signs to "Basilique Sainte-Therese." There is a large parking lot and information center that is open during the tourist season.

OTHER PLACES OF INTEREST IN LISIEUX

ST. PETER'S CATHEDRAL
Cathédrale St. Pierre

Therese visited St. Peter's Cathedral frequently and this is where she attended Mass daily with her family. She made her first communion and confession here. In the southern ambulatory there is a modern statue that marks the place where St. Therese used to sit when attending High Mass each Sunday. Located in the center of town, this Gothic Norman style church was built in the twelfth and thirteenth centuries. The Cathedral is off rue Henri Cheron and blvd. Jeanne d'Arc behind Square Arnould. There is a large pleasant garden behind the cathedral (Jardin l'Évêché Cour Matignon).

CARMEL CHAPEL
Le Carmel

All that remains of the Carmel Chapel where St. Therese lived is the sanctuary and the choir. The original nave was rebuilt around 1920. The relics of St. Therese were brought here in 1923 from the town cemetery and reside behind an iron grate in a chapel on the right. The wax figure contains some bones of the saint and the rest are housed in a silver casket beneath the reliquary. At the saint's exhumation in 1923 all that remained were her bones, as she had predicted. Once a

Le Carmel

year, on the last Sunday in September, her casket is taken to the Basilica for veneration. Above the reliquary is the statue of the Virgin Mary, Virgin of the Smile, which is the original statue that was in Theresa's room in Les Buissonnets when she was miraculously cured on May 13, 1883. As you enter the chapel, on the right is a brochure and map in English.

On the left side of the entry courtyard is the Relic room (Salle des Reliques) that has personal items of the saint, and an audio guide in English (press #2).

Hours: Easter to Oct 31st 7AM-7PM; Nov 1st to Easter 7AM-6:30PM. Free guided tours in French meet every day in July, August and September (except August 15th and the last Sunday of September) in the courtyard of the Carmel. If arranged ahead of time, there might be a possibility for a tour in English for groups.

LES BUISSONNETS 1877-1888

This is the family home where St. Therese's family moved in 1877, after her mother's death. Therese spent eleven years here until she entered the Carmelite Convent. This charming house allows you to imagine the early life of St. Therese. There is an audiocassette in English that guides you through each room. Les Buissonnets is off Duchesne Fournet Blvd. on Chemin des Buissonnets. The sign "Maison de Ste. Thérèse" leads you to parking. It is about a fifteen-minute walk from the center of town. They do not speak English.

Les Buissonnets

COMING AND GOING

LISIEUX

Car: Lisieux is about one hundred miles northwest of Paris. On A13 from Paris, exit at Pont L'Evêque, drive south for 11 miles (17 km). Lisieux is on N13, the Paris-Caen road, 25 miles (41 km) east of Caen

Train: The Lisieux SNCF station is on the south side of the city and main connections are to Paris, Caen and Rouen.

Plane: There are three small airports in the area. Deauville St. Gatien - 16 miles (25 km) away 33 (0)2 31 65 65 65 . Le Havre Airport, 31 miles (50 km). Caen Carpiquet, 25 miles (40 km), 33 (0)2 31 71 20 10.

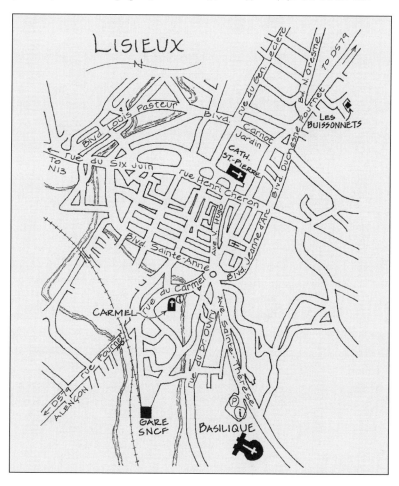

TOURIST INFORMATION

❋ Comité Départemental du tourisme du Calvados/8 rue Renoir/14054 Caen/cedex 4/France Phone: 33 (0)2 31 27 90 30 Fax: 33 (0)2 31 27 90 35 Email: info@cdt-eure.fr www.calvados-tourisme.com French.

❋ Office de Tourisme /11, rue d'Alençon/BP 17197/14107 Lisieux cedex/France Phone: 33 (0)2 31 48 18 10 Fax: 33 (0)2 31 48 18 11 Email: tourisme@ville-lisieux.fr www.ville-lisieux.fr French. Ask for maps and guides in English.

WEBSITES

La Maison du Pèlerin www.lourdes-fr.com — Information about the major shrines in France and Europe including Lisieux.

Sanctuarie de Lisieux http://therese-de-lisieux.cef.fr — Official website for the Sanctuary with comprehensive information on all aspects of your pilgrimage to Lisieux. Email: office-central@therese-de-lisieux.com.

Villes Sanctuaries en France www.villes-sanctuaires.com — The Association of Shrine Towns in France with a suggested tour and contact information.

OTHER PLACES OF INTEREST IN FRANCE

ALENÇON

St. Therese of Lisieux was born in Alençon in 1873 and lived at No. 50 rue Saint-Blaise until 1877, the year of her mother's death. To the left of the house is a chapel built in 1925, the year of St. Therese's canonization. Both are open to the public. The church of Notre-Dame is where St. Therese was baptized on January 4, 1873 and where her parents were married in 1858. There are more places in town related to the saint's family. Contact the tourist information for more information: Phone: 33 (0)2 33 80 66 33 Email: internet@ville-alencon.fr www.ville-alencon.fr. Alençon is 55 miles (88 km) south from Lisieux.

Rouen

Population 400,000

Described by Victor Hugo as the city of a hundred spires, Rouen since World War II has fewer spires to arouse the poets, but just enough to attract the tourists. The Seine River divides Rouen into a Left and Right Bank, with the old city on the Right. There is a youthful buzz with universities and art schools, and a busy port bringing much business to the city. The city is known as home to the famous novelist Gustave Flaubert, who wrote Madame Bovary in 1857, and, of course, St. Joan of Arc, who was burned at the stake here in 1431. A visit to the tourist office on Place de la Cathédrale, directly across from the Notre-Dame Cathedral that Monet painted in different variations, will provide you with two good brochures (*Into the Heart of Rouen's History* and *In the Footsteps of Joan of Arc*) to get you where you want to go in this walkable city. If you don't want to walk, there are frequent 45-minute tours in a small motorized train. *In the Footsteps of Joan of Arc* leads you to areas of town that record her time in Rouen. If you are short on time, be sure to visit the Church of St. Joan of Arc on the square where she died. Then, if you have time, choose from any of the sites listed in your brochures, making sure to include time for the Joan of Arc Chapel in the beautiful Gothic Rouen Cathedral.

Rue du Gros-Horloge, Rouen

ST. JOAN OF ARC
Sainte Jeanne d'Arc 1412–1431

"I must do this thing, because my Lord will have it so."

No saint had a more public or overtly political mission than St. Joan of Arc. Though her life spanned a mere nineteen years, her purpose was very specific, and the impact of her courage and faith influenced the history of the Western world.

Faith is the key to understanding the life of Joan of Arc—for it is her faith in God, faith in His guidance, and faith in her ultimate redemption that drove Joan to accomplish all that she did. With faith to support her, she was able to confront kings, lead thousands of men into battle, and conquer the greatest armies of her day. With faith, she was also able to die a martyr's death with firm knowledge of her own salvation.

Joan's mark on Western history came at a time when the country we now call France was a large territory divided among many kingdoms and controlled by an assortment of kings, earls, dukes, and one dauphin. In 1415, three years after Joan's birth, the English invaded northern France and began a series of wars to reclaim the French throne. The battle for France and the French crown would dictate the life of Joan, and give her a central role in Medieval Western history.

The little village of Domrémy, in current day Lorraine, was home to Jehanne d'Arc. Born to Jacques and Isabelle on January 6, 1412, the young girl grew up with her three brothers and one sister. She learned the typical skills of her era and position—sewing, spinning and caring for the family's livestock. Instruction in reading and writing were not readily available to a peasant girl, but she did get religious instruction—making yearly confession and taking the Sacrament at Easter.

At age thirteen, she had the first experience of hearing voices. "I had a voice from God to help me govern myself. The first time, I was terrified…I heard the voice on my right hand, towards the church. There was a great light all about." She was told to attend church, behave rightly and be a good child. Over the next several years, the voices continued to come to Joan and began telling her of her mission in France.

The voices she heard were those of St. Michael the Archangel and Saints Catherine and Margaret—martyrs of the early church. "He (St. Michael) told me that St. Catherine and St. Margaret would come to me, and that I must follow their counsel... They told me that my King would be restored to his Kingdom, despite his enemies. They promised to lead me to Paradise, for that was what I asked of them...They spoke well and fairly, and their voices are beautiful—sweet and soft." They called her Jehanne the Maid, child of God. After years of Joan's indecision, the voices became more adamant in their instructions, and she finally took action in May of 1428.

St. Joan of Arc - Reims Cathedral

Convincing the men of France that a girl of sixteen was sent from God to lead them to victory over the English would not be a simple task. Twice over the coming months Joan ventured to the nearby garrison at Vaucouleurs to speak with the captain in charge, and each time he refused her request for an escort to see Charles, the Dauphin. Finally, in February of 1429, following the English siege of Orleans and her accurate prediction of a French defeat at Rouvray, the captain submitted to her demand. "The voice said that I would raise the siege before Orleans. And it told me go to Vaucouleurs, to Robert de Baudricourt, captain of the town, who would give me men to go with me."

Joan the Maid, now dressed in men's clothing to protect her identity, traveled with her escort through enemy territory for eleven days and finally arrived at Chinon, the latest home of the Royal Court. After waiting two more days, she was allowed to meet the Dauphin. The twenty-six year old monarch was interested in seeing the visionary peasant girl, for he was curious about her stated mission from God and anxious to reclaim the throne. When she approached Charles, she kneeled before him and said, "I bring you news from God, that our Lord will give you back your kingdom, bringing you to be crowned at Reims, and driving out your enemies." This was good news to his ears, but how was he to believe the young girl before him? Privately, she told him of a very personal prayer he had made to God the year before—a prayer known to no one but himself. With this knowledge, he accepted her as God's messenger. Her full acceptance by the entire court came only after she submitted to three weeks of questioning from a group of theologians at Poitiers. They found her worthy of the Dauphin's trust and agreed that she had indeed received counsel from God.

Now empowered by her king, Joan's first task was to write a letter to the English commanders at Orleans to demand their retreat to England, or else be driven out of France. When they refused her ultimatum, she made ready for battle. She required only three things—a suit of armor, a banner proclaiming her righteous cause, and an army. Her armor was tailor-made to fit her peasant girl body. Her banner was white with a background of gold fleurs-de-lis, embossed with an image of Jesus holding the world in his hand and accompanied by two angels. Finally, Joan's army was waiting for her at Blois, 35 miles south of the besieged city of Orleans.

St. Joan of Arc - Rouen Cathedral

The revived French army arrived at Orleans over a five-day period, and was in full force by the morning of May 4th. Inexplicably, the English did not attack Joan's soldiers as they reinforced the town. Joan arrived on April 29th and was greeted with great excitement and expectation by the citizens. "Hope in God," she told them. "If you have good hope and faith in Him, you shall be delivered from your enemies."

The afternoon of May 4th saw a major contingency of French troops leave the garrison and attack the English a mile west of the city. Joan had no knowledge of the attack, so it caught her by surprise. Upon hearing of the battle, she hurriedly called for her armor and horse, and made her way through the western gate of the city to the field of battle, where the French were beginning to fall back. As the Maid approached on her white steed, with her banner before her, she rallied the men to storm the fortress. The troops responded to her battle cry and quickly turned the battle into a rout of the English. This was the first defeat of the English at Orleans and gave great hope to the town and the militia.

The next day was the Feast of the Ascension, and Joan called for no fighting. She attended Mass and confession, readying herself for the battles to come. The following day, the French again ventured outside the walls and attacked another English fortress, sending the defenders scurrying for refuge. That evening, the War Council made plans for the next day's battle and everyone prepared for the fight. This was to be a decisive day, a day to test the mettle of all involved. Joan told her chaplain, "Keep close to me all day, for tomorrow I shall have much to do and greater things than I have had to do yet. And tomorrow blood will flow from my body, above my breast."

In the dawning light of May 7th, the French attacked the important fortress of Les Tourelles, the primary English stronghold. Joan was one of the first ones to the walls, and as she was moving a scaling ladder into position, an arrow struck her deeply in the right chest. She was taken from the field of battle, where she removed the arrow herself and prayed for strength and healing. As the day wore on, the skirmish was not going well for the French forces. The fortress before them proved impenetrable, and they began losing hope. Joan told them to rest momentarily but be ready to take the offensive. She rode into a nearby vineyard, prayed for ten minutes, and then quickly rushed to the walls. "Watch!" she yelled to her troops. "When you see the wind blow my banner against the bulwark, you shall take it." As her banner struck the wall, the French rose as one, and with a great cry, stormed the towers and scaled the walls. The English were defeated and demoralized. This was the beginning of the end for the English, as they would never again control as much French territory.

Joan's next goal as outlined by her holy voices, was to see Charles crowned King of France at the cathedral in Reims. This was not an easy task, as Reims was well within English controlled territory and many major obstacles remained along the way. But the King's Royal Army began the conquest, taking one city at a time—by force, siege or negotiated peace. The English were becoming demoralized and retreated before the army led by the Maid. Once in Reims, the Dauphin was crowned King Charles VI. Thousands were in attendance, including Joan, who carried her banner and stood near to Charles.

This was the highlight of Joan's life, for it was the culmination of all her dreams and heart-felt desires. From here, it would be much tougher for the Maid. The newly crowned King tried to solicit support from every direction and toured the French countryside, seeking pledges of loyalty. All the while, Joan and the Duke of Alencon, commander of the Royal Army, were trying to engage the English and drive them from the country. Paris was a primary target, and the army reached the walls of the city by the end of August. A siege was begun in early September, but Joan was hit in the leg by a crossbow dart and had to leave the battle. The Duke of Alencon pressed on the siege and wanted to storm the city, but he was undermined by the King, and forced to retreat.

From this point on, the Royal Court no longer supported the French army, leaving Joan and her captains to beg towns for supplies and to recruit their own men. The winter months saw little activity and Joan traveled to many cities with the court, trying to gain support for future battles with the English. By spring, she and a small band of two hundred soldiers marched to join in the battle.

The miracles that occurred around Joan were usually related to her military exploits and premonitions. But one day in April, while marching through the village of Lagny, she was summoned by some young women. "I was told that the girls of the town were gathered before the statue of Our Lady, and wanted me to come and pray to God and Our Lady to bring the baby to life. And I went and prayed with the others. And finally life appeared in him and he yawned three times. Then he was baptized, and soon after, he died and was buried in consecrated ground. For three days, so they said, he had shown no sign of life, and he was as black as my jacket." This is just further evidence that God and the angels walked with Joan.

Joan still heard her voices, often several times a day, but their communications were not always of great outward significance. But in May, they gave her ill tidings. "My voices told me that I would be taken prisoner before St. John's day, and that it must be so, and that I must not be frightened and accept it willingly, and God would help me." Joan continued on with the fight and marched with her army to Compiegne, which had just been besieged by the Duke of Burgundy, an ally of the English. In the morning hours of May 23rd, Joan and her small army quietly slipped past the blockade into the town, and prepared to fight off the Burgundians.

Joan knew what was to come, and during her morning prayers at the church, told some children, "pray for me, for I have been betrayed." Later that day, Joan was fighting outside the walls of the city, and then retreated back towards the gates of the fortress. The gates were prematurely closed before her small contingency made it through, and she was quickly surrounded by enemy troops. She refused to give up, but was pulled off her horse and forced to surrender. It is not certain who betrayed Joan, but most likely it was a group within the Royal Court who wanted her out of the way. Regardless, Joan the Maid was now under the control of her long-time rival, the Duke of Burgundy.

Le Bucher and Pilori - the Site of St. Joan's death

It was customary in medieval times to free captured soldiers upon payment of a ransom. Joan was certainly a prize worthy of ransom, but the Duke had other things in mind. Many attempts were made to rescue Joan, including three military forays by her closest allies and friends, and offers of ransom from King Charles VI but the Duke was set on turning Joan over to the English. The English, too, would pay a ransom, but they would also find ways of eliminating this inspiring leader of the French forces.

Joan remained imprisoned in Burgundy for four months before she was turned over to the English. Her ultimate destination was a prison in Rouen, the center of the English government in occupied France. Unlike other women prisoners who were held in church prisons and guarded by nuns, Joan was held in an English prison and guarded by male soldiers. After more months of imprisonment, she was put on trial before an Inquisitional court and accused of heresy. Her trial was also a sham, as she was intensely questioned for months and never allowed to present any witnesses in her own defense.

To read the records of Joan's trial is to be impressed by this nineteen-year-old woman standing up to the theologians and inquisitors with great conviction and clear thinking. In the end, they were not able to trick her into making heretical statements, but they would still find a way to carry out their evil intentions. After months of questioning, Joan was told she would be released to a church prison if she signed a declaration stating that she would never again carry arms, wear men's clothing, cut her hair short, and several other minor things. Joan could not read, but the bailiff read the statement to her. With much reluctance and foreboding, Joan signed the paper with her customary 'X.' She was immediately returned to her cell in the English prison and given no relief from her plight.

Joan was given a dress to wear in place of her men's clothes, and was soon accosted by her guards and an English Lord. She fought off her assailants, but they eventually took her dress and gave her men's clothing to wear. She argued vehemently with them for hours, but they would not return her dress and her only recourse was to don the men's clothing. Now the trap was sprung—she was immediately accused of being a "relapsed heretic" and sentenced to burn for her crime. A crime with no appeal rights.

The scene of Joan's execution was heart wrenching for all those in attendance. Joan was given a sermon, and then she made her own statement. She forgave her accusers of all their atrocities and for their conviction of her. She also asked for everyone to pray for her soul. She began weeping during her address and many of her accusers and English soldiers were also brought to tears. Then, tied to a post high above a pile of kindling wood, she faced her sentence. She asked for a crucifix and an English soldier produced a makeshift one from the kindling, then a priest gathered one from the nearby church. "Hold it up level with my eyes until I am dead," she cried. "I would have the cross on which God hung be ever before my eyes while life lasts in me." As the flames grew higher and hotter, Joan cried out for Jesus and her saints, and then gave up the spirit.

In 1449, eighteen years after her death, and after the English were driven from Rouen, a new inquisition was called to review the trial. Joan was exonerated from any wrongdoing and the clerics and Englishmen who orchestrated her execution were exposed as the evil men they were. Joan was soon declared a martyr and hero for all of France. In 1909 she was beatified, and she was canonized in 1920. She is now one of the patron saints of France and an inspiration to people throughout the world.

St. Joan of Arc in Rouen Cathedral

THE CHURCH OF ST. JOAN OF ARC
Eglise Saint Jeanne d'Arc

The Church of St. Joan of Arc, built in 1979, stands on place du Vieux Marché, also called the Old Market Square, where Joan was martyred on May 30, 1431. Joan was all but forgotten in the town of Rouen, until her beatification process began in 1891, resulting in her canonization in 1920. Renewed interest in the square brought about plans for a church and memorials. By the nineteen seventies, agreement was made to build a church and a small covered market adjoining it, with a cross erected where Joan had died.

The Church exterior, with its trapezoidal slate covered roof, takes on different shapes when viewed from various angles. When looking at the stained glass windows, the roof takes the shape of a flame. The covered market area represents waves and the fountain looks like a dragon's mouth. With a covered walkway looking like a long tail, it is a strikingly unusual church from the outside. But once inside, the atypical architecture assumes more pleasant lines. The beamed ceiling was inspired by the hull of a ship turned upside-down, creating a nautical ambiance, in combination with the sixteenth century stained glass windows rescued from the church of Saint Vincent before it was destroyed in World War II. The side Chapel of the Saint-Sacrament has old paneling from the ruins of St. Vincent's and is a pleasant place to pray, if it is open. The benches at the back of the church are comfortable for viewing the stained glass windows and meditating on their vivid colors.

Outside the church, facing the entrance, you will see to your right a stainless steel pillar with information in English. Along the storefronts, you will notice the Joan of Arc Museum "Musee Jeanne d'Arc." To your left is the area where Joan met her death with a sign "Le Bucher" and "Pilori." Against the church is a statue of Joan facing the Pilori.

Eglise Saint Jeanne d'Arc

Where is the Church of St. Joan of Arc?
Où est l'église Sainte Jeanne d'Arc?

SHRINE INFORMATION

Shrine: The Church of St. Joan of Arc (Eglise Sainte Jeanne d'Arc)

Address: Place du Vieux Marché/76000 Rouen/France

Phone: 33 (0)2 35 71 85 65 **Fax:** 33 (0)2 35 71 85 66

E-mail: None

Website: None

Quiet areas for meditation: There is a side chapel at the back of the church if it is not roped off. Otherwise, the main church has many tourists coming in and out.

English spoken: Occasionally. It depends if the person on duty at the church entrance speaks English.

Hours: Daily 10AM–12:15PM and 2PM–6PM, except Fri & Sun mornings. Closed Jan 1, May 1, & Nov 11.

Mass: Mon-Fri 6:30PM; Sun 11AM.

Feasts and festivities: May 30 — Feast Day; Second Sunday in May — Civil Ceremony; Sunday closest to May 30 — Fête Jeanne d'Arc.

Accessibility: The church is accessible.

Information office: There is a person on duty at the entrance to the church. If you want more information the tourist office would be best.

Tours: The Rouen Tourist office offers guided tours. Call 33 (0)2 32 08 32 46 Fax 33 (0)2 08 32 49 Email: guidages-tourisme@rouen.fr. Ask for brochures and maps in English, especially *In the footsteps of Joan of Arc*.

Bookstore: Inside the church, to the left as you walk in.

Recommended books: *The Old Market Square and the Martyrdom of Joan of Arc*, by Olivier Chaline, is a booklet sold in the church's bookstore with detailed information about the stained glass windows. *St. Joan of Arc*, by John Beevers, a biography from Tan Books and Publishers, and *In Her Own Words*, a compilation of her quotes from the transcripts of her trial, by Willard Trask from BOOKS & Co. Both these books are not available at the church.

Lodging: None

Directions: The historic area of Rouen is anchored by the Notre-Dame Cathedral (Rouen Cathedral) on the east end and the Market Square, where Joan was burned, on the west end. Rue du Gros Horloge connects the two sites. The tourist office is directly across from the entry to the Cathedral, and rue du Gros Horloge is one block north—turn left. If you follow signs to "Cathedrale Notre Dame" they will get you to the tourist office.

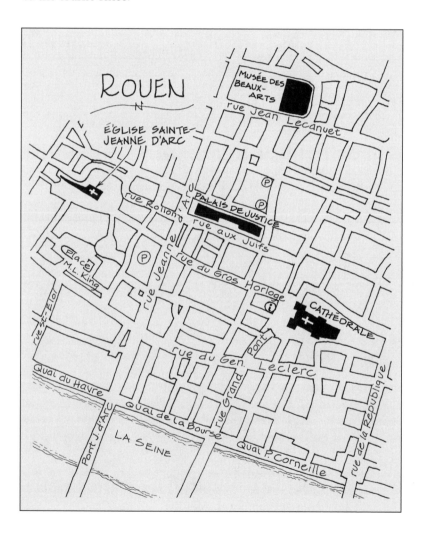

Other places of interest in Rouen

The Notre-Dame Cathedral
La Cathédrale Notre-Dame

The Notre-Dame Cathedral is on place de la Cathédrale across from the tourist office. This is the Cathedral that was made famous by Monet's different versions painted at various times of day. In the middle of this church, to the right, is a chapel dedicated to St. Joan. There is a statue of Joan by the sculptor Saupiqué and modern stained glass windows depicting her life. The church's windows were destroyed in the war, allowing daylight to illuminate this splendid example of Gothic

La Cathédrale Notre-Dame (Rouen Cathedral)

architecture. Open every day, except holidays and during service, from 8AM-6PM, except Monday 2PM-6.

Coming and Going

Rouen

Car: Rouen is 84 miles (135 km) Northwest of Paris on A13. Exit at #22 for Rouen, and follow signs for about 8 miles (12 km) north to Rouen-Centre, which is on the north side (East Bank) of the River Seine. There are three parking garages centrally located, look for "P" signs. Order a map of Rouen from the tourist office ahead of time to locate parking. Parking on the lower quay on the left bank is free and unlimited. You can also park on the street, but it is difficult as this is a busy downtown area.

Train: The main SNCF station is Gare Rive Droite, and is at the north end of rue Jeanne-d' Arc. Take the Metro to the Centre. The station has many daily connections to Paris and all of northern France.

Bus: All local buses, except #2A, from the SNCF station run down rue Jeanne-d' Arc to Centre.

TOURIST INFORMATION

❋ Comité Départemental du tourisme de la Seine Maritime/6 rue Couronné/BP 60/76420 Bihorel/France Phone: 33 (0)2 35 12 10 10 Fax: 33 (0)2 35 59 86 04 Email: seine.maritime.tourisme@wanadoo.fr www.seine-maritime-tourisme.com French.

❋ Rouen Tourisme/25, place de la Cathédrale/BP 666/76008/France Phone: 33 (0)2 32 08 32 40 Fax: 33 (0)2 32 08 32 44 E-mail: tourisme@rouen.fr www.rouentourisme.com Two hour walking tour, or a motorized petit train makes a forty minute loop on a regular basis.

WEBSITES

Joan of Arc Museum www.jeanne-darc.com — The Joan of Arc Wax Museum in Rouen.

International Joan of Arc Society www.smu.edu/ijas — A collection of scholarly documents relating to St. Joan of Arc.

St. Joan of Arc Center www.stjoan-center.com — The purpose of this center is to spread information about, and devotion to, St. Joan of Arc. Email: stjoan@stjoan-center.com.

MORE ST. JOAN OF ARC SHRINES IN FRANCE

ORLEANS
Orléans

Orleans, 74 miles (119 km) southwest of Paris, is the site of Joan of Arc's first victory over the English. This battle was extremely significant in turning the tide of the One Hundred Years war in favor of the French. Each year, from April 29 to May 8, various activities celebrating St. Joan take place in Orleans, as they have almost every year since 1430. The Official website of Orleans offers the dates of the celebrations in English: www.ville-orleans.fr.

The Joan of Arc Center (Centre Jeanne d'Arc) contains many artifacts, manuscripts, and films related to Joan and is open Monday-Thursday 9AM-12PM and 2PM-6: Friday 9AM-12:15PM and 2PM-4:45; Closed Sat/Sun. Address: 24/rue Jeanne d'Arc/45000 Orléans/France. Phone: 33 (0)2 38 79 24 92 Fax: 33 (0)2 38 79 20 82.

The house of Joan of Arc contains reproductions of manuscripts associated with the saint's life and trials. Maison de Jeanne d'Arc/3, place de Gaulle/45000 Orléans/France Phone: 33 (0)2 38 52 99 89 www.jeannedarc.com.fr French.

The Orleans tourist office: Office de Tourisme/6, rue Albert 1er/45000 Orléans/France Phone: 33 (0)2 38 24 05 05 Fax: 33 (0)2 38 54 49 84.

The City of Orleans: Ville d'Orléans/Place de l'Etape/45000/Orléans/France Phone: 33 (0)2 38 79 22 22 Email: infocom@ville-orleans.fr www.ville-orleans.fr.

DOMREMY
Domrémy-la-Pucelle

This village of 180 people is the ancestral home of St. Joan, and contains her birth-home and a basilica dedicated to the saint. The village has changed little over the past centuries and is mostly dedicated to preserving Joan's memory. The house where Joan was born has been maintained as it was and the Joan Centre is under construction near the house. You can also visit the Basilica of Bois Chenu, or the Basilica of St. Joan of Arc, built on the spot where she first heard voices. Her baptismal chapel is also within the village. For information on the internet, Email: Tourisme en Lorraine: crt@cr-lorraine.fr for info about Domremy. The website www.exagonline.com/grand/plus/eng/domrey.htm shows pictures of the sites related to St. Joan in Domremy.

Provence-Alps-Cote d'Azur
Provence-Alpes-Côte d'Azur

Combining the azure waters of the Mediterranean coast, the lavender fields of Provence and the snow-capped mountains of the southern Alps, this beautiful region has it all. It is no wonder Van Gogh and Cézanne ventured here to paint the vibrant landscapes. Throughout the region, ancient Roman ruins are available for exploration and fascination, with the Pont du Gard near Avignon and the Arena at Arles being exquisite examples of Roman-Gallic structures. The Mediterranean laps onto the shore at Cannes and St. Tropez, and also embraces the small town of Saintes-Maries-de-la-Mer, where legend tells of the shipwrecked landing of Mary Magdalene. Her legend also spreads to the cliffs of the Baume Mastiff, where she spent years in seclusion before dying at St. Maxim. The remote village of Cotignac boasts two apparitions of the Holy Family—both the Virgin Mary and St. Joseph appeared here in the sixteenth century. Provence-Alps-Cote d'Azur offers the pilgrim many delights, both spiritual and scenic.

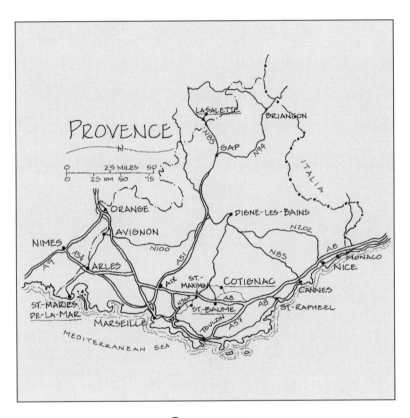

COTIGNAC
St. Joseph of Cotignac
Our Lady of Graces

LA SAINTE-BAUME
St. Mary Magdalene

Cotignac
Population 2,040

Cotignac is located in the hilly center of Provence, about fifty miles from the costal towns of Marseille and Toulon. The town rests at the base of a cliff, dramatically nestling between the steep rock wall and the Cassolle River. A cliff-side waterfall is the backdrop for the village, and fountains are a main ingredient in the cozy atmosphere. Visitors to the old quarter, set next to the cliff, can see houses of the sixteenth and seventeenth centuries, while the rest of the village is mostly from the eighteenth and nineteenth centuries. The town's main "Cours" or courtyard is centered around an ever-flowing fountain and is sheltered under a canopy of trees, providing a place of cool respite if you are here during the summer heat. Restaurants and cafes provide the other needed necessities. For those more adventuresome, visit the ramparts atop the cliffs, or the old quarter with the troglodyte dwellings. But the truly inspirational aspects of Cotignac are found in the apparitions of the Virgin Mary in 1519 and that of St. Joseph in 1660.

ST. JOSEPH
Saint Joseph - June 7, 1660

"I am Joseph."

The summer of 1660 was hot and dry in the hill region of Provence and June 7th promised to be one of the hottest. Herding his sheep onto the sunny east side of Mont Bessillon, twenty-two year old Gaspard Ricard quickly drank his flask of water and was soon in need of more, as was his flock. He was getting increasingly parched as the day wore on, and by one o'clock in the afternoon, the hot sun was high overhead and there was no relief in sight. As Gaspard rested on the rocky slope, an elderly gentleman suddenly appeared before him and said, "I am Joseph." The figure pointed at a large rock, and continued, "Lift it, and you will drink." The startled shepherd looked at the immense rock, then at the man, and knew he could not even budge the weighty boulder. "Lift it, and you will drink," repeated the gentleman. This time Gaspard obeyed the command and found that the rock was surprisingly easy to move. As he pushed the boulder aside, water immediately began to flow from the ground and run down the hillside.

With great delight, the thirsty shepherd drank some of the cool and refreshing elixir, then turned to thank his benefactor. Looking about, he saw no one. The mysterious visitor had disappeared as quickly as he had arrived.

The strange incident unsettled the young shepherd and he hurriedly returned to the village to tell his story. Gaspard was known as a mature and honest man, so the villagers were open to hearing his tale. After he related the events of the afternoon, many returned

Miraculous spring at Monastere Saint Joseph

with Gaspard to the side of Mont Bessillon to see if his story "held water." Indeed, as they approached the previously parched hillside, they witnessed a new spring flowing in an area that was known to be devoid of water. He showed the people the rock he moved, but it took eight men to move it again.

News of the miraculous spring spread swiftly and many pilgrims found their way to the remote site. Reports of miracles were heard throughout the region and people began arriving from distant provinces. That same year, a small chapel was built over the site, but it quickly proved to be too small to accommodate the number of people coming to partake of the miraculous water. In 1661, a larger church was begun and in 1663, St. Joseph's Sanctuary was consecrated. The sanctuary, chapel and spring are preserved for us today, and the water still flows in its own miraculous way.

THE MONASTERY OF ST. JOSEPH OF BESSILLON
Monastere la Font Saint Joseph du Bessillon

Monastere la Font Saint Joseph du Bessillon

The small Monastery of St. Joseph is nestled in the wooded hillside of Mount Bessillon, about two miles northwest of Cotignac. A small community of Benedictine nuns who came here about thirty years ago occupies the remote facility. In 1977, fourteen nuns were looking for a new residence after leaving Algiers and their monastery of St. Benoît of Médéa. Following a long search for a new home, they found the abandoned monastery of St. Joseph in Bessillon and made arrangements to become the new caretakers. They restored the chapel and old buildings that had been in disrepair since the French Revolution, and a new convent was constructed.

The small chapel is open for visitors to share in daily Mass and the Liturgy of the Hours, sung in Latin and Gregorian chant. The spring is still active. Though it sits under the chapel, you can view it through a grilled opening on the outside, lower left of the church. The healing water is available from a tap located next to the sidewalk, near the spring. There is a gift shop with religious articles made by the nuns. You can ring the bell at the door near the spring and a nun will come and show you to the gift shop.

The community of nuns at St. Joseph's is meditative in nature, and you can feel their spiritual depth when praying in the chapel. There is a definite stillness and deep joy that permeates this site and it is worth finding your way here if you are in Provence. The Sister we met here was in her eighties, but her eyes were ageless and full of loving light— a testament to her faith and contemplative lifestyle.

Where is the Monastery of St. Joseph?
Où est le monastère Saint Joseph?

SHRINE INFORMATION

Shrine: St. Joseph Monastery of Bessillon (Monastère Saint Joseph du Bessillon)

Address: 83570 Cotignac/France

Phone: 33 (0)4 94 04 63 44 **Fax:** 33 (0)4 94 04 79 78

E-mail: None

Website: None

Quiet areas for meditation: The church and surrounding woods are very quiet.

English spoken: Occasionally

Hours: Morning and afternoon.

Mass: Daily 11AM

Feasts and festivities: March 19 — Feast of St. Joseph of Cotignac (Fête de Saint Joseph à Cotignac).

Accessibility: The path is accessible except it is gravel and at an incline.

Information office: None

Tours: None

Bookstore: A small room with items for sale is inside the monastery. You will have to ring the bell at the door near the spring and wait patiently.

Lodging: Women and girls on religious retreat only are welcome to stay in the guesthouse and share in the silence and prayer of the sisters.

Directions: From Cotignac, drive northwest 2 miles (3.5 km) on D13 in direction of Barjols. Turn left at the sign to "Monastere de St. Joseph" or "Ch. de Saint Joseph". Follow the signs for 1.5 miles (2 km) to the Monastery. (Don't follow sign to "le Hameau de St. Joseph").

OUR LADY OF GRACES
Notre Dame de Grâce 1519

"Receive the gifts I wish to bestow."

The early years of the sixteenth century in Europe were rife with change and this held true in Provence as well. The region had recently become part of the developing French Kingdom and the Reformation was just beginning. Provence was still devoutly Catholic and Jean de la Baume, a woodcutter from Cotignac, was one of the faithful. In August of 1519, both John and Cotignac would be thrust into history.

On August 10th, John went up to the top of Verdaille hill to chop wood and take it back to sell in the village. As usual, he began his day in prayer, kneeling on the ground. After completing his supplications, he rose to begin work when he saw an image of the Virgin Mary appear from a cloud. Standing atop a crescent moon, she held in her arms the Christ Child, and was accompanied by St. Michael the Archangel, St. Bernard, and St. Catherine the martyr. While the woodsman gazed in awe, the Blessed One said, "I am the Virgin Mary. Go and tell the clergy and the Consuls of Cotignac to build me a church on this place in the name of Our Lady of Graces, and that they should come in procession to receive the gifts which I wish to bestow." The vision immediately disappeared and John was left to wonder if he really understood what he had just witnessed. He decided to keep the vision to himself.

The next morning, John returned to the hill to complete his work. Again, after finishing his prayers, he beheld the same vision and heard the same message. This time he had no doubt, and immediately ran to the village to relay the message to all who would listen. John was known as a serious man, not given to mischief, so the clergy and townspeople believed in the truth of his vision. A chapel was soon built on the site of the apparitions, but within five years, it was deemed too small to accommodate the growing numbers of pilgrims coming to seek intercession of the Blessed Mary. A new and larger church was needed.

By 1537, a new sanctuary was completed, similar in size and location to the present day church. The shrine was alive with many pilgrims, but the clergy of the small parish in Cotignac had difficulty serving the great number of people, so in 1586, a small community of priests came to staff the shrine. The priests organized themselves around the Oratory, a new rule developed by Philip Neri in Rome, and became the first such organization in France. But that is just the beginning of the story. Our Lady of Graces had yet to bestow her most famous gift of grace.

A century later, Louis XIII was king of France and had yet to father an heir. For twenty-two years, the King and his wife, Anne of Austria, had attempted to have children, but found no success. The Queen prayed constantly, but it seemed as if a special grace would be required for the couple to bear any offspring. The grace began to manifest on October 27, 1637, when Brother Fiacre was praying at Our Lady of Victories, in Paris. While deep in prayer, the Brother experienced a revelation that told him that the Queen would receive the grace of bearing a son if the people said three novenas for her.

The vision of Our Lady and the Christ Child

The novenas were to be prayed at Our Lady of Graces in Provence, Notre Dame de Paris, and at Our Lady of Victories. Brother Fiacre had received this same inspiration two years before, but did not have the conviction to tell his superiors. This time, after courageously telling them of his revelation, he was told to keep his dreams to himself. What proof had he of the validity of his revelation? They would get their answer in six days.

In the early morning hours of November 3rd, Brother Fiacre was

Notre Dame de Grâce

again praying in the monastery when he was drawn to the sound of a crying child. Opening his eyes to investigate the source of the cries, the brother was astonished to find himself before the Blessed Virgin, who held a crying infant in her arms. "Don't be afraid," she said, "I am the Mother of God, and the baby that you see is the Prince which God wants to give to France." The vision disappeared, and then reappeared for another moment. Brother Fiacre remained in prayer through the night trying to understand the apparition. Two hours later, Mary appeared once again, this time alone, and said, "Dispel any doubts, my child, in what you have told your confessor. To show you that I want the Queen to make three novenas to me, here is the same picture which is at Our Lady of Graces in Provence, and the appearance of the church." Before the Brother appeared the likeness of the painting of Our Lady displayed in Provence, along with a detailed vision of the church.

Neither Brother Fiacre nor his superiors had ever been to Provence. When he told them of his latest vision, other Brothers who had been to Our Lady of Graces corroborated the exact details of the painting and church, and Brother Fiacre's vision was accepted as indeed coming from the Blessed Mother. The Cardinal was informed of the apparition, and after a time, the King and Queen heard of the prophetic occurrence. Meanwhile, Brother Fiacre took it upon himself to begin the novenas, and discreetly began them on November 8th, completing them on December 5th. Nine months later, on September 5, 1638, the Queen bore her first son, and named him Louis Dieudonne—Godgiven.

The Queen was forever grateful to Brother Fiacre, and when she met him for the first time, she bowed at his feet. After King Louis XIII died in 1644, Brother Fiacre remained in distant service to the young Louis XIV, and went to Our Lady of Graces on two occasions to deliver items to the church. King Louis XIV himself visited Our Lady of Graces, accompanied by his mother, when he was twenty-one. A plaque, given by Louis XIV commemorating the memory and faith of his mother, is in the church. Brother Fiacre is also present, for he wished that his heart be sent to Our Lady of Graces after his passing, and it rested here until the Revolution. Now, only the lead casket that held his heart remains in the church. Also present is the very painting that appeared before Brother Fiacre and initiated the miraculous conception of the future king.

The church was badly damaged during the French Revolution and many stones were removed to construct new buildings. But Our Lady of Graces has since been restored to its pre-Revolution state and Our Lady is once again receiving pilgrims and granting their supplications.

SHRINE INFORMATION

Shrine: Sanctuary of Our Lady of Graces (Sanctuaire Notre-Dame de Grâces)

Address: 83570 Cotignac/France

Phone: 33 (0)4 94 69 64 90 **Fax:** 33 (0)4 94 69 64 91

E-mail: nd-de-graces@wanadoo.fr

Website: www.nd-de-graces.com — Official website

Quiet areas for meditation: The church and surrounding grounds are quiet.

English spoken: Occasionally

Hours: 7AM-7PM

Mass: Weekly 11:30AM; Sun 11AM.

Feasts and festivities: March 19 — Feast of St. Joseph of Cotignac; August 9 — Anniversary of the Apparitions; December 27 & 28 — Feast of St. John.

Accessibility: Contact the Sanctuary for information.

Bookstore: At the front of the complex of buildings to the right.

Lodging: Foyer de Sainte Famille J.M.J. Quartier Notre Dame/83570 Cotignac/France Phone 33 (0)4 94 04 65 28 Fax: 33 (0)4 94 04 71 68 Lodging for family retreats.

Directions: Driving south out of Cotignac on D13, turn right immediately after crossing the river at small sign "Ch. de Notre Dame." If approaching Cotignac from the south, make a sharp U-turn just before crossing the river. Sign is small and difficult to see.

COMING AND GOING

COTIGNAC

Car: Cotignac is 13 miles (20 km) north of Brignoles. Exit A8-E80 to Brignoles, take D554 north in direction of Barjols. After 2.5 miles (4 km), at le Val, take D562 east for 7 miles (12 km) to Carces, then D13 north for 4 miles (7 km) to Cotignac.

Train: The nearest train stations are in Toulon and Marseille, (approx. 50 miles away).

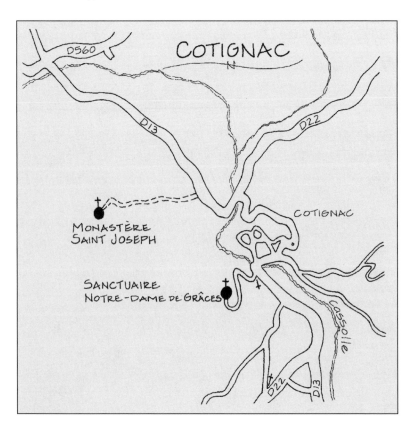

Bus: Cotignac is available by bus from Toulon and Marseille. Take a taxi to the shrines.

TOURIST INFORMATION

✤ Provence Web www.provenceweb.com/f/var/cotignac/cotignac.htm Click on English version on bottom of page.

✤ Conseil Général des Bouches-du-Rhône région Provence Alpes Cote Azur /13 hôtel du département/52 av Saint Just/13004Marseille/ France Phone: 33 (0)4 91 21 13 13 Email: cdt13@visitprovence.com www.visitprovence.com.

WEBSITES

Sanctuaire Notre-Dame de Grâce www.nd-de-graces.com — Official website with history of Cotignac in English.

La Sainte-Baume
Population 1000

The Sainte-Baume massif is an eight-mile long rocky outcropping that rises above the hills of south-central Provence. The most notable feature of the north-facing cliffs is the legendary cave of St. Mary Magdalene. It is said to have been her secluded home for the last thirty-three years of her life and has been a celebrated pilgrimage destination since the fifth century. Kings, saints and pilgrims of all nations have climbed the rocky paths to this famous cave and have made it a place of sacred devotion.

ST. MARY MAGDALENE
Sainte Marie Madeleine 1st Century

Mary Magdalene is known as the "Apostle to the Apostles," for it was she who first witnessed the risen Christ and was instructed to tell the Apostles of his resurrection. The Gospels tell many stories of this important figure in Christian history and Christ himself said of her, "I tell you the truth, wherever this gospel is preached throughout the world, what she has done will also be told, in memory of her." (Matt. 26:13 NIV) It was Mary Magdalene who anointed Jesus' feet with oil, sat at his feet to receive his teachings, and was one of the few disciples

St. Mary Magdalene raised up by the angels

to follow him to Calvary. After the crucifixion, the disciples of Christ began to spread the "Good News" around the world and the evangelistic journey of Mary Magdalene became a story of legend. Most probably, she traveled with St. John to Ephesus, in Asia Minor, where she preached until her death, but the tradition of Provence places another ending on this story.

Following the Pentecost, the disciples began preaching throughout Palestine and the East, but they were not always well received. The legend relates that Mary Magdalene, her sister Martha, brother Lazarus, Maximin, and several others, were placed aboard a ship without mast or oars, and put out to sea to die. The ship sailed by the will of God to the southern shores of what is now France, and shipwrecked at the mouth of the Rhone. From here, the shipmates began to evangelize Provence, with Martha settling in Tarascon, Maximin in Aix-en-Provence, and Mary Magdalene and Lazarus spreading the gospel in Marseille. Soon, Mary would move to the remote region where Maximin was bishop and seclude herself in a cave on the cliffs of the Baume massif.

A mythology developed around the life of Mary Magdalene, and though it lacks authority, it is inspirational at its heart. Mary would spend her days in prayer and contemplation, living in the cave with the barest of necessities. It is said that the angels would come down from heaven seven times a day and raise her up to the heights of the mountains so she could hear the angel choirs of heaven. Maximin remained in close contact with Mary, and when she knew she was near death, Mary traveled down the mountainside one last time to take Holy Communion from her saintly friend. After receiving the blessed host, she died peacefully in his arms.

The legend continues that Mary Magdalene was buried in a crypt in Villa Latta, which is now St. Maximin, and that, in 710 A.D., the Christian people were afraid about invading Saracens and chose to hide her remains. In the next century, a monk of Vezelay went and took some of the few remains that were not hidden. In 1279, a sarcophagus was discovered in St. Maximin and inside was found a skeleton with a manuscript (dated 710 A.D.) claiming that these were the remains of Mary Magdalene. To solve the mystery, a jawbone given to the Pope more than five hundred years before was retrieved and found to fit perfectly into the jaw of the skeleton in St. Maximin. The bones were declared the true relics of Mary Magdalene. In 1295, a great basilica was built in St. Maximin, with pilgrimage housing constructed, and the flood of pilgrims began. Mary Magdalene's relics were kept in the fourth century crypt in St. Maximin, with her femur bone and a few hairs placed in a reliquary in her secluded cave in La Baume in the nineteenth century.

The high altar inside the Cave of St. Baume

Cliff-side Sanctuary of St. Baume

Over the centuries, the Basilica of St. Maximin and the cave of La Baume have been visited by a who's who of famous personages. The site was especially popular among the line of French King Louises! First King Louis the IX visited in 1254, then King Louis XI, XIII and XIV all paid homage to St. Mary Magdalene, as did Charles IX, Henry III and Francois I. Many saints took the long hike up the path to St. Mary Magdalene's cave, including St. Catherine of Sienna, St. Jeannne de Chantal, St. Jean-Baptiste de la Salle, and many others. Today, the site has been restored after being plundered during the French Revolution, and the inspirational story of Mary Magdalene lives on.

THE CAVE OF ST. BAUME
Grotte la Sainte-Baume

The Cave is on the north-facing cliffs of the La Baume Massif and a 45-minute walk from the parking area. The walk is mostly in an old, shaded forest with the latter half of the walk being uphill. Hiking boots are recommended but not necessary for the 90-minutes of hiking. It's a pleasant walk, with the reward of a great view, refreshingly cool cave and the sacred grotto. If you go to the Chapel St. Pilon at the top of the cliffs, you will need at least an additional hour.

As you reach the final ascent towards the Cave, the Stations of the Cross are built into the stairway, and they culminate with carved statuary of the crucifixion. The Cave is at the top of the stairs and is fronted by a flat courtyard that overlooks the valley below. A bronze

Pieta and spectacular view are the highlight of the courtyard. Facing the cave, there is a pilgrim's store on the left and the Dominican Convent (Couvent Sainte Marie Madeleine) on the right.

Grotte la Sainte-Baume

The Cave is rather large, and contains several altars, statues and a reliquary. The central High Altar is carved in stone and is in front of the Rock of Penitence. On the right side is the reliquary of St. Mary Magdalene that contains her femur bone and a few hairs. Several sculptures are located throughout the grotto with small areas for prayer in front of them. To the right of the High Altar is the statue of St. Mary Magdalene being raised up by angels, and on the lower right level is the statue of "The Meditation of St. Mary Magdalene." There are many opportunities to sit quietly and contemplate the sacred life of this legendary saint.

Where is the cave of St. Mary Magdalene?
Où est la grotte de Sainte Marie-Madeleine?

SHRINE INFORMATION

Shrine: Dominican Fathers of Sainte Baume (Dominicains de la Sainte Baume)

Address: Maison Sainte-Marie-Madeleine/83640 Le Plan d'Aups - Sainte Baume/France

Phone: 33 (0)4 42 04 53 19 **Fax:** 33 (0)4 42 04 53 40

E-mail: sainte-baume@dominicains.com

Website: http://saintebaume.dominicains.com French

Quiet areas for meditation: The cave and surrounding forest are very peaceful.

English spoken: Occasionally

Hours: Summer and Winter 7:30AM–6:30PM

274 THE PILGRIM'S FRANCE

Mass: Daily 10:30AM

Feasts and festivities: Whitmonday — Pilgrimage from all over Provence (High Mass 10:30AM); July 22 — Feast of St. Mary Magdalene (High Mass 10:30AM); December 24 — Midnight Mass (procession starting at 10:30PM)

Accessibility: None

Information office: There is an information office (Accueil de l'Association des Amis des Dominicains) across from the Hostelry.

Tours: At the Grotto the Dominican Fathers are available to lead tours.

Bookstore: Hôtellerie gift shop and the "Boutique de la Grotte" with a few books in English.

Recommended books: *The Sainte Baume: A Mountain Steeped in Geological and Religious History* by Father Philippe Decouvoux Dubuysson available at the Hôtellerie gift shop.

Lodging: Hôtellerie de la Ste. Baume/La Sainte-Baume/83640 Le Plan d'Aups-Saint Baume/France Phone: 33 (0)4 42 04 54 84 Fax: 33 (0)4 42 62 55 56.

Directions: The Hostelry and beginning of the walking path is about 2 miles (3 km) east of the small town of Plan d'Aups-St.-Baume. From the Hostelry and the parking area, there is a path to the east of the Hostelry that leads toward the cliffs. Once reaching the forest and the main trail, there are signs for two paths. "Chemin du Canapé" is to the right and the shorter of the two paths, about forty minutes to the Cave. The other, "Chemin des Roys," goes left and is much longer.

COMING AND GOING

LA SAINTE-BAUME

Car: The Hostelry at the foot of la St. Baume is 13 miles (21 km) south of St. Maximin and 2 miles (3 km) east of Plan d'Aups-St.-Baume. Exit A8 at St. Maximin, take D560 south for 6 miles (10 km), then continue south on D80 for 2 miles (3 km) to Nans-les-Pins. Continue on D80 for 5 miles (8 km), turn right at the "T" intersection, and go .6 miles (1 km) to the Hostelry at the foot of the cliffs. From the west, take A50 from Marseille, exit on A520 toward St. Zacharie and St. Maximin. Follow D560 for 4 miles (6 km) east to St. Zacharie, then turn south on D480 for 7 miles (11 km) to D80.Turn left at the "T" intersection and go 2 miles (3 km) to the Hostelry. For the more adventuresome, exit A50 for Gemenos, and follow the curvy D2 up the side of the Massif. It takes an additional hour, but offers many great vistas. Whichever way you go, get a very detailed Michelin map, for exact directions are difficult to describe.

Train: Since the site is remote, reaching it by public transportation is a lengthy process. The nearest train station or airport is in Marseille. There is bus service to Nans-les-Pins, and taxi service is available for the seven miles (11 km) to la Sainte-Baume.

Plane: Marseille Provence airport, 53 miles (85 km) Phone: 33 (0)4 42 78 21 00.

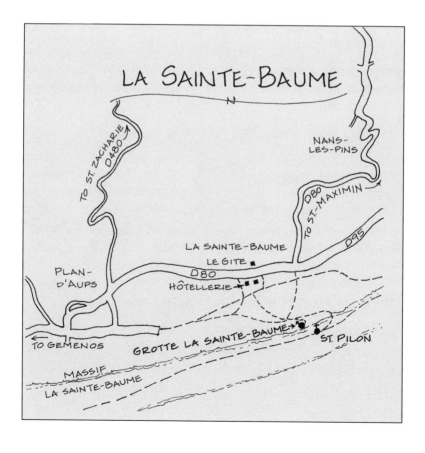

TOURIST INFORMATION

❋ Comité Régional de Tourisme Provence-Alpes-Côte d'Azur/Les Docks, 10 place de la Joliette/Atrium 10.5/BP 46214/13567 Marseille/France Phone: 33 (0)4 91 56 47 00 Fax: 33 (0)4 91 56 47 01 Email: information@crt-paca.fr www.crt-paca.fr.

❋ Conseil Général des Bouches-du-Rhône région Provence Alpes Cote Azur /13 hôtel du département/52 av Saint Just/13004 Marseille/France Phone: 33 (0)4 91 21 13 13 Email: cdt13@visit-provence.com www.visitprovence.com.

❋ Hôtel de Ville/83470 Saint-Maximin-la Sainte-Baume/France Phone: 33 (0)4 94 59 84 59 Fax: 33 (0)4 94 59 82 92 Email: office.tourisme.stmaximin@wanadoo.fr www.hotelfp-saintmaximin.com This hotel was once the convent adjoining the Basilica of Saint Maximin and is a good place to stay when visiting the caves in La Sainte-Baume thirteen miles away.

❋ Office of Tourism/Couvent Royal/Place Jean Salcisse/83470 Saint Maximin/France Phone: 33 (0)4 94 59 84 59 Fax: 33 (0)4 94 59 82 92.

❋ Office de Tourisme/Place de la Mairie/83640 Plan d'Aups Ste Baume/France Phone/Fax: 33 (0)4 42 62 57 57.

WEBSITES

Dominicains de la Sainte Baume http://saintebaume.dominicains.com French — Dominican Fathers of Sainte Baume.

Sainte Baume: Grotte de Sainte Marie Madeleine http://saintebaume.dominicains.com French — Official Site of the Cave of St. Mary Magdalene.

OTHER PLACES OF INTEREST IN PROVENCE

ST. MAXIMIN OF ST. BAUME
Saint Maximin la Sainte Baume

The Basilica of St. Maximin was built in the fourteenth century and legend says the remains of St. Mary Magdalene are in its fourth century crypt. Mary Magdalene is purported to have descended from her cave in the St. Baume cliffs and to have died here in the arms of St. Maximin during the first century. In 710, Cassian monks removed her relics for safe keeping during the Saracen invasion. They hid most of the relics, but some were sent to Rome and others to Vézelay. In 1279, Prince Charles de Salernes, the nephew of King Louis IX, discovered a sarcophagus that contained written proof that the skeleton inside was Mary Magdalene's. The Pope declared the relics authentic when the bone from Rome fit perfectly in the jaw of the skeleton. The Basilica was built to house these relics and to welcome the flood of pilgrims to the area. See tourist information above.

SAINTS MARYS OF THE SEA
Saintes-Maries-de-la-Mer

Saintes-Maries-de-la-Mer on the central Mediterranean coast of France is located in the heart of the Camargue—marshland abundant with wildlife and white horses that roam freely in the national park. The town was named in the nineteenth century for the three Marys— Mary Jacob, Mary Salome and Mary Magdalene—who, according to legend, landed here after being set adrift from Palestine (see story about St. Mary Magdalene above). The seaside town is famous for the annual pilgrimage of gypsies (Pèlerinage des Gitans) on May 24 & 25, when gypsies from all over Europe come and pay homage to Sara, their patron saint. There are several legends about the dark-skinned Sara's origin. One is that she was an Ethiopian servant to the three Marys, while another says that she was a local queen who

Fortress Church of Saintes-Maries-de-la-Mer

welcomed and housed the three Marys when they were shipwrecked in Provence. The relics of these women reside in the town's church.

The Romanesque Fortress Church dates from the twelfth century, with an upper chapel added in the fourteenth and fifteenth centuries. In 1448, King René discovered relics under the crypt floor, believed to be those of St. Mary Jacob, Mary Salome and Sara. The present day reliquaries are in the upper chapel and contain what remains of these relics, after they were burned during the Revolution. Three times a year the reliquaries are lowered on ropes from their upstairs location and a procession including a model of the saints' boat is carried to the sea. Guardians on horseback lead the crowd of revelers.

The church is entered on the left side, and the interior is very dark. On the left is the model ship used in the processions, while the crypt is below the main altar. The crypt includes a statue of Sara, and she is always adorned in festive attire. Near the ceiling of the church, above the crypt, is the opening where the reliquaries are lowered for feast days.

The town was built near the mouth of the Petit Rhône River, and the church acted as a fortress to protect the people during the Saracen raids. The roof served as a watchtower, and can be visited for a view of the area (enter on the outside of the church). This is a very lively town, and unfortunately, you must be wary of aggressive panhandlers around the church. Visit the Tourist Office for a brochure in English on the Fortress Church of Saintes–Maries de la Mer and a map of the city and area.

Office du Tourisme/5 Avenue Van Gogh/BP 16/13460 Les Saintes Maries de la Mer/France Phone: 33 (0)4 90 97 82 55 Fax: 33 (0)4 90 97 71 15 Email: info@saintesmaries.com www.saintesmaries.com Directions: 22 miles (36 km) southwest of Arles on D570.

A chapel inside the fortress church of Saintes-Maries-de-la-Mer

Rhone Alps

Rhône Alpes

The region of the Rhone Alps is situated in southeastern France, embraced on its eastern border by Switzerland and Italy. This border displays the majestic peak of Mont Blanc, the highest in Europe. To the west lie two serene alpine lakes, Lac d'Annecy and Lac du Bourget, which attract Europeans and foreign tourists in all seasons. Lyon is the major city in the region and is known as the capital of French gastronomy, boasting famous chefs and three hundred and sixty-five local wines. The beauty of the national parks, famous vineyards, gorges along the river Ardèche and the snowy summits of the Alps all contribute to the diverse terrain and grandeur of this region. To arrive at the pilgrimage towns of Annecy, La Salette and La Louvesc, you will experience stunning drives through the mountains and countless expansive vistas. The small country village of Ars-sur-Formans provides an excellent location for quiet retreat even though it is located near Lyon, the second largest city in France. With these four shrines to explore, you can easily combine inspiring pilgrimage and breathtaking sightseeing on a visit to the Rhone Alps.

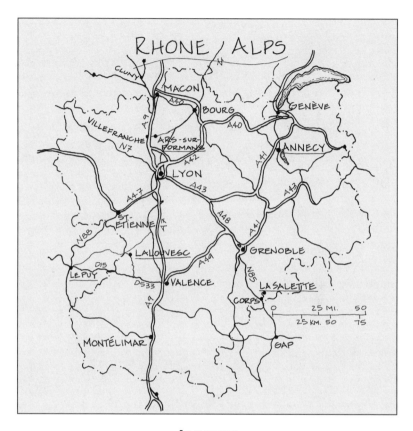

ANNECY
St. Francis de Sales
St. Jane de Chantal

ARS-SUR-FORMANS
St. John Vianney

LA LOUVESC
St. John Francis Regis
St. Therese Couderc

LA SALETTE
Our Lady of La Salette

Annecy

Population 125,000

Lake Annecy (Lac d'Annecy) is one of the most beautiful areas in which to enjoy the French Alps. Though a popular and busy vacation spot for Europeans, the tourist/pilgrim can still find quiet accommodations around the lake. Château de Menthon, on the eastern side of the lake, is the birthplace of St. Bernard, patron saint of mountaineers, and is open for tours. Ancient chateaux are seen along the shoreline while hang gliders float on mountain drafts, creating a picturesque juxtaposition of the old and new. The charming town of Annecy, at the lake's northern end, has a quaint medieval quarter with markets and Venice-like canals, offering a unique opportunity for relaxed strolling. Excellent views over the town and lake can be seen from the Château d'Annecy and walking or biking the lakefront is peaceful and pleasant. Many boats leave Annecy for various destinations around this pristine lake. A boat tour presents the best views of the scenery in the shortest amount of time, but buses also make the loop. The Basilica of the Visitation can be visited on foot from the town center of Annecy, but may also be reached by bus or by car. After visiting this Basilica and the relics of St. Francis de Sales and St. Jane de Chantal, explore the town of Annecy for other points of interest for the pilgrim following in the footsteps of these two saints. The French Alps will beckon you to stay longer, so be sure to make time to do so. For hikers, a beautiful two-hour hike actually starts at the Basilica of the Visitation and rises into the peaks above the town and lake.

ST. FRANCIS DE SALES
Saint François de Sales 1567–1622

"By turning your eyes on God in meditation,
your whole soul will be filled with God."

St. Francis de Sales saw every soul as a special being, capable of achieving spiritual union with God. While many preachers and philosophers of his day professed that man is inherently evil—fallen from the grace of God, Francis believed that man is innately good—made in the image of God. To this end he focused his preaching and copious writings on showing people how to live in the material world while also living a life of devotion and love for God. He understood that it is possible to live a life of sanctity in any worldly position or profession.

Born to a noble family in the Château de Sales in Savoy, nestled in the foothills of the Alps of eastern France, Francis lived a life surrounded by material comforts, worldly pleasures and people of high education and social stature. The eldest son of the family, he was expected to become a nobleman of great power and prestige, carrying on the family name and tradition. To prepare young Francis for his rise to power, he was sent at age eight to study at the College of Chapuisien in Annecy, and at age fourteen to Paris, to attend the College of Clermont. As a member of the upper class, he took the appropriate lessons in riding, fencing and dancing, and worked hard to please his father. But deep inside, Francis felt he had another destiny. His love for God filled his heart, but he kept this secret from his father—who was determined that his boy would make his mark in the secular world.

The College of Clermont was a Jesuit school chosen specifically by Francis so he could attend classes on theology as well as the required classes on law, language and the arts. He excelled in rhetoric and philosophy, and by age eighteen, he often debated his fellow classmates on the hottest topics of the day. As a result of one of these exchanges on the concept of predestination, Francis fell into a deep depression. He had previously felt a sweet love for God and a reciprocal loving presence, but now that feeling had vanished. Was he predestined for eternal damnation? Since he did not constantly

Visitation Monastery, Moncalieri, Italy

St. Francis de Sales

feel the living presence of God in his heart, was he destined to live for eternity in the fires of hell?

Francis fought with these doubts and feelings for many weeks, becoming weak and despondent. "Lord," he prayed, "If I may not love Thee in the other world—for in Hell, none praise Thee—let me at least in every instant of my brief existence here love Thee as much as I can." Shortly after crying this heartfelt prayer, Francis went to pray before his favorite statue of Our Lady at St. Étienne des Grés. While in prayer, he felt the overwhelming unconditional love of God and the complete acceptance of his soul. His despair was instantly relieved, replaced by great joy and gratitude, feelings he would harbor for the remainder of his life. This was a pivotal lesson for the young Francis, for in the future he would always treat his fellow seekers with tenderness and understanding whenever they were undergoing spiritual difficulties or trials of doubt.

Francis continued with his studies and graduated, at age twenty-four, with a doctorate in law from the University of Padua and returned home to the family chateau on Lake Annecy. For the next eighteen months he contemplated his future, while his father worked on his own vision for Francis—arranging for his marriage and a seat in the senate of Savoy. Francis refused both of these arrangements, much to the dismay of his father, whom Francis still had not informed of his desire to devote his life to God. At this time, the provost of the Geneva diocese passed away and the Bishop of Geneva, without the family's knowledge, petitioned the Pope in Rome to appoint Francis to the vacant post. When the appointment was approved, Francis's father was extremely upset and refused to hear of it, but eventually relented. Francis took the post and was ordained a priest in December 1583.

The mission of Francis could have been a simple one—preaching in the large churches of the cities and taking care of ecclesiastical business. But instead, he was chosen by his bishop to convert the people of the nearby mountainous region of Chablais—a region steeped in Calvinism since the Reformation, and a place of danger for a man of his position. Francis's father begged him not to take on this dangerous mission, but Francis would not change his mind. For three years, Francis and his collaborators tried to reach the people of the remote region with little success. His difficulties were exacerbated by two assassination attempts, as well as the bitter cold and austere conditions. The tide turned when he began writing pamphlets and literally put them under the doors of the houses for people to read. In his writings, he did not try to convert them or say they were wrong, he simply wrote of the love of God and how to experience that love. People responded to his message of love and began coming to his services to hear his inspirational sermons. Over time, he opened many doors and brought scores of souls back to the Catholic Church.

In 1602, at age thirty-five, Francis was appointed Bishop of Geneva, and began reorganizing the diocese and bringing the teachings directly to the people. He developed a "Bishop's Catechism" for instructing lay people and began writing books about living a spiritual life. Francis believed that all people are able to live a life for God, regardless of their position in the world. One does not need to be a cloistered monk or nun to live a devout life—one simply has to live for God.

A major part of Francis's mission was writing and answering letters from his faithful congregants, and this correspondence became the basis for his books. *Introduction to the Devout Life*, published in 1609, was based on letters he wrote to Marie de Charmoisy, wife of a courtier in the court of Henri de Genevois-Nemours, who sought advice on living for God while maintaining her rank in the world. Francis taught her how to live in high society while preserving a sacred inner life. He wrote, "As the mother pearls live in the sea without taking one drop of salt water…and as huge flies fly in the flames without burning their wings, so a vigorous and constant soul can live in the world without receiving any worldly taint … and can fly among the flames of earthly desires without burning the wings of the holy aspirations for the devout life." Francis stressed prayer and meditation, and keeping God's presence alive in our hearts while we undertake all the ordinary activities of the day. "At the conclusion of your prayer," he wrote, "walk about a little and gather a little nosegay of devotion from the considerations that you have made, in order to inhale its perfume throughout the day." Francis's book was immediately popular with the masses and was soon translated into many languages, making Francis and his teachings universally known.

Another important chapter in Francis's life began in 1604, when he met Jane de Chantal, a young widow in search of spiritual direction. In her, Francis found a kindred soul searching for ultimate fulfillment in the bosom of God's love. Francis became Jane's director and

286 THE PILGRIM'S FRANCE

confidant, and they exchanged many letters of encouragement and spiritual direction. The development of their inner lives was the basis of their relationship, but together they created a work greater than either one of them.

In 1610, Jane and two of her daughters moved to Annecy where Francis and Jane instituted a new order of nuns. The order was called the Visitation of Holy Mary, and was open to all women—regardless of their status, age or health. Their path to God was one of a deep interior life in ordinary surroundings. The Order was originally organized to allow the women to live and serve in the community, but soon became a cloistered order to better support their contemplative lifestyle. Under Jane's care and the direction of Francis, the Order quickly grew in reputation as a deeply rich spiritual environment, and many sister communities were founded in later years.

As director of the Visitation nuns, Francis had many opportunities to teach his form of devout living in sermons, conferences and correspondence. The thoughts he expressed during this time evolved into his most ambitious book, the *Treatise on the Love of God*. Here he expounded on the soul's inevitable progress towards God, the perfection of God's love and the soul's union with God. He emphasized that all souls are created to realize their oneness with the Divine, and that God is ever pursuing us to that end. "See the divine love at the entrance," Francis wrote. "He does not simply knock once. He continues to knock. He calls the soul: come, arise my beloved, make haste! And he puts his hand on the lock to see whether he can open it."

The heart was the key to the spiritual life for Francis, for the heart is where we experience the love of God and the source of all intuition. When describing preparation for prayer and meditation, Francis wrote, "When therefore you come to prayer, you must say with all your heart, and to your heart: O my heart, my heart, God is truly here....think that not only is God in the place where you are, but that he is in a very special manner in your heart and in the depth of your spirit, which he quickens and animates with his divine presence, since he is there as the heart of your heart, and the spirit of your spirit." Francis summed up his teachings by writing at the head of every letter, "Live Jesus," to say that in every moment we should live in the divine presence that resides within our hearts, and act from that center.

In November of 1622, Francis left Annecy after intuitively putting all his affairs in order. He was ordered by the duke of Savoy to accompany his court to Avignon to meet with Louis XIII, king of France. On the return journey he stopped in Lyon where he inhabited the gardener's cottage at the convent of the Visitation. Weak and exhausted from the decades of service, Francis still continued to give himself to all who asked for his help. After a month, he suffered a stroke and was partially paralyzed. In hopes of healing the dying saint, the doctors subjected Francis to the latest treatments—bloodletting and cauterization by a hot iron—both to no avail. On December 28th, Francis passed away with the word "Jesus" on his lips.

The process of canonization was started immediately for the saintly bishop, and his beatification was the first one celebrated in the newly completed St. Peter's Basilica in Rome in 1662. Three years later, he was canonized, and in 1877 declared doctor of the Church. His feast day is January 24th, the day his body was returned to Annecy, where it is venerated along with that of his companion in God, Jane de Chantal.

ST. JANE FRANCES DE CHANTAL
Sainte Jeanne Françoise de Chantal 1572–1641

"Once divine love takes possession of your heart,
oh! how easy all the rest will be!"

All of us desire a caring, attentive mother, and even more, the nurturing of our divine Mother. Jane de Chantal fulfilled that role for many souls—for her own children as well as those of her spiritual family. A strong soul who humbly placed the spiritual needs of others before her own, she gave great solace and advice to all the Sisters under her wing and left a spiritual legacy of universal love.

Jane's own mother died when she was eighteen months old, leaving her to be raised by her loving father and aunt. Her aristocratic father was the president of the Burgundian parliament and the family home was an environment rich in education and spirituality. As Jane grew up with her brother and sisters, they were given the opportunity to openly discuss many lively topics, developing in Jane the ability to stand up for herself and her beliefs.

When she reached her twentieth year, Jane's father arranged her marriage to the Baron de Chantal, Christopher de Rabutin, an officer in the French army and seven years her senior. The young couple moved to his family home in Bourbilly, where she found the estate and its finances in need of much repair. Jane was asked by her husband to right the family ship, meanwhile giving birth to six children, four of whom survived their infancy. After eight years of marriage, the two were still deeply in love and enjoying their family life together when Christopher was killed in a hunting accident. This sent Jane into an extended period of grieving, but also brought to the forefront her inner longing for God.

St. Jane de Chantal

A major hurdle for Jane was to forgive her husband's accidental killer. Christopher had forgiven his friend before he passed, but it took Jane several years to open up her heart enough to forgive the man who took her beloved. She finally came to terms with her own grief and the man's sincere sorrow, and forgave him completely, to the point of becoming the godmother of one of his children. Jane realized for herself that we must forgive others their mistakes, as we ask God repeatedly to forgive our own. Her compassion and love for others would be the hallmark of her future mission.

With her dearest human love departed, Jane began to focus on the real love of her life, God. Her desire to live devoutly was difficult to realize, as she found herself living with her children in the home of her overbearing father-in-law and his cantankerous housekeeper. Her family responsibilities required her to stay in this living situation for several years, but she never complained and worked to keep harmony in the household.

Jane's longing for God led her to experience several visions. One was of a mysterious man whom she saw while riding horseback around her lands. Her soul was filled with peace and she understood that this was the spiritual guide she longed for. She had another vision when she was near a church in a deep wood. It was made clear to her that "Like the son of God, Jesus, who was obedient, she was destined to be obedient." The first vision foretold of the meeting with her mentor, Francis de Sales, while the second led her to understand that she would have many trials throughout her life, and that an all-consuming divine love was to be her lot.

Three years after the loss of her husband, Jane went to Dijon to visit her father and hear the Lenten sermons of a well-known bishop. Attending the service, Jane immediately recognized Francis de Sales as the man of her vision—the realized answer to her prayers for a true mentor. She and Francis were immediately attracted to each other as they saw in each other the goodness of man, and the deep desire to serve God alone. Their friendship in God matured over the years and blossomed into a beautiful flower of divine love that inspired many of their peers and fellow seekers.

In the next few years, Jane's longing for a monastic life grew ever more intense. She was in constant communication with Francis and he understood her dilemma. She had four small children to attend to, and, she was a woman approaching forty years of age—hardly a candidate for the typical convent. Francis empathized with Jane's strong desire for the devout life, and suggested to her that they begin their own religious order, one that would accept women of Jane's position, and promote a life of piety and service.

With this new concept, the two founded the Order of the Visitation of Holy Mary, in Annecy in 1610. They began the community with Jane and two other women. Within several months, the community grew to ten members and, in a few years, many sister communities began forming all over France.

The essence of the community life was contemplation and assistance to the poor, especially ill women. Jane's role as Mother Superior was perfect for her temperament, as she was able to transform her motherly instincts and love into divine friendship and direct the spiritual progress of the members of her community. As the Order expanded over the years, Jane worked tirelessly to communicate with the Sisters, frequently writing letters of encouragement and advice on spiritual matters, and other down-to-earth concerns. "Should you fall fifty times a day," she wrote to one Sister, "never, on any account, should that surprise or worry you. Instead, ever so gently, set your heart back in the right direction and practice the opposite virtue, my darling Péronne, all the time speaking words of love and trust to our Lord after you have committed a thousand faults, as much as if you had just committed one... No matter what happens, be gentle and patient with yourself."

The new Visitation Order was well received by many people as it filled a great need for a simple interior life. But there was still controversy surrounding the moderately cloistered way of life. After the community in Annecy was well established, Francis accepted the invitation of the Archbishop of Lyons to found a new community in his diocese. Following a number of exchanges between Francis and the Archbishop, the Order of the Visitation took on the rule of St. Augustine and became an entirely cloistered order.

The virtues of the Visitation Order may be best understood through the words of Jane, as written to a novice mistress: "It seems to me, my dear Sister, that you should try to make your own spirituality, and that of your novices, generous, noble, straightforward and sincere. Try to foster that spirit...founded on that deep humility which results in sincere obedience, sweet charity which supports and excuses all, and an innocent guileless simplicity which makes us even-tempered and friendly towards everyone...This way is very narrow, my dear Sister, but it is solid, short, simple and sure, and soon leads the soul to its goal: total union with God...I beg Him in His goodness to guide you to perfection in His most pure love. My soul cherishes yours more than I can say; be absolutely assured of this, and pray for her who is yours unreservedly."

The relationship of Jane de Chantal and Francis de Sales was always one of divine love, and they maintained a respectful distance. They mutually cherished each other, but understood that their individual search for God was their only vocation. In 1616, Jane arranged to take a retreat for spiritual recharging and private contemplation. At this time, Francis was ill, and Jane found her mind turning always to her unwell mentor instead of focusing on her inward goals. They both understood that her thoughts should be centered on God, and that their relationship was hindering her spiritual evolution. They mutually agreed to "let each other go" and base their relationship solely on the business of the Order.

Within nine years of its inception, the Visitation Order had communities at Annecy, Lyon, Moulins, Grenoble and Bourges. In 1619, Francis asked Jane to move to Paris to found a community in the French capital. There was great opposition and hostility towards the Order because of its popularity, so it required all of her skills of humility, patience and perseverance, but she finally succeeded in winning over all her antagonists. Francis also asked Vincent de Paul to be director of the new community. He joyfully accepted, and thus became Jane's confessor and confidant. She spent three years in Paris before returning to Annecy.

In her later years, Jane spent her time nurturing the Sisters of the Order, but she also had to deal with great personal sadness. In 1622, Francis de Sales passed away in Lyon while Jane was traveling to various convents of the Order. This event, along with the death of her son a few years later, was difficult for Jane, but she placed it all in God's hands saying, "Destroy, cut, burn, whatever opposes Thy holy will." A year after her son's death, a severe plague ravaged France and made its way to Annecy. Much of the town evacuated. But Jane offered great comfort and compassion to the sick and dying who remained.

Souls sincerely treading the path to God often find times of spiritual dryness, when they do not feel their connection with Him. Jane de Chantal experienced many years of this feeling of abandonment, but steadfastly kept her consciousness elevated and continually strove to help others. St. Vincent de Paul said of her, "While apparently enjoying that peace and easiness of mind of souls who have reached a high state of virtue, she suffered such interior trials that she often told me her mind was so filled with all sorts of temptations and abominations that she had to strive not to look within herself, for she could not bear it … But for all that suffering her face never lost its serenity, nor did she once relax in the fidelity God asked of her. And so I regard her as one of the holiest souls I have ever met on this earth."

By 1635, the Visitandines had founded seventy-one communities, and Jane continued to travel for the affairs of the Order that could not be regulated by correspondence. She wrote many letters of encouragement and sometimes of admonition. She directed many souls—religious and lay people alike—on the straight and narrow path that she and Francis de Sales had outlined so many years before. On December 13, 1641, while returning from a trip to Paris, Jane fell deathly ill in

Moulins. St. Vincent de Paul, upon hearing of her illness, prayed for the dying saint and beheld a vision. He saw a fireball of light ascend into the heavens to join another fireball, and together, they ascended and merged into one great light. Intuitively he knew these were the souls of Jane de Chantal and Francis de Sales finally uniting with the great light of God.

Jane died in Moulins at the age of sixty-nine. Her body was taken to Annecy, where she was buried beside Francis de Sales. During the French Revolution, their bodies were secretly removed from their crypts to protect them from possible desecration, but they were ultimately returned, and now they rest together in the Basilica of the Visitation. Jane de Chantal was canonized in 1767.

THE BASILICA OF THE VISITATION
La Basilique de la Visitation

The Basilica of the Visitation contains the relics of St. Francis de Sales and St. Jane de Chantal in bronze reliquaries on either side of the main altar. Built between 1922-1930, on a hill overlooking the city of Annecy, the Basilica is illuminated at night, creating a beacon of light for all to see. The stained glass windows illustrate the life of

St. Francis de Sales on one side of the Basilica and that of St. Jane de Chantal on the other. There is an information office (Accueil) on the left as you enter the Basilica, that is staffed by volunteers who speak only French. Two brochures in English are available to the right as you enter the Basilica. One describes the Basilica and the other is titled *In the Footsteps of Francis de Sales in Annecy,* which

La Basilique de la Visitation

includes a map of relevant places to visit in the town. Refer to "Other places of interest in Annecy" below.

A museum outside the Basilica, to the right of the bookstore, contains reliquaries with wax figures of the two saints. Photographs and many objects once owned by the saints are also displayed there, with descriptions in English. The museum is open from 9AM-12PM and 2PM-5.

The Visitation nuns have lived in the adjacent monastery since 1911, after living in various locations in Annecy throughout the centuries. All of the 151 Visitation monasteries in existence today originated from this cloister in Annecy. The community of nuns live within the cloister, practice silence while they work, and pray the Divine Office for four hours every day. The nuns share liturgical prayer with visitors each day, either in their chapel located to the right of the sanctuary, or via loudspeakers, positioned in the Basilica.

The relics of both saints were initially kept in the Church of the Visitation in Annecy, now called the Church of St. Francis, until the Revolution in 1793, when they were secreted across Lake Annecy to Château de Duingt for safe-keeping. The following year they were installed in St. Peter's Cathedral, until several good citizens, fearing desecration, hid them between the floors of one of their houses until 1806. To cover up, they replaced the missing relics with skeletons taken from the Poor Clare cemetery.

After the terrors of the Revolution died down, St. Francis's relics were placed in St. Peter's Cathedral and St. Jane's in the Church of St. Maurice in 1806. The Visitation community returned to Annecy in 1822 and, when the Church of the Visitation was completed in 1826, the relics were placed there on rue Royale (this church was later demolished). In 1911, they were translated to the new monastery of the Visitation until the Basilica was complete in the 1930s.

St. Francis' body remained incorrupt for ten years after his death, though not in subsequent investigations. St. Jane's tomb was opened in 1716 and 1724 as part of the process of beatification and canonization, revealing no signs of incorruptibility in her body. The bronze sculptures of the saints covering their reliquaries were fashioned after paintings, as were the wax figures in the museum. Now resting peacefully after experiencing many translations over the years, both saints' bones lie inside their bronze reliquaries.

Where is the Basilica of the Visitation?
Où est la Basilique de la Visitation?

SHRINE INFORMATION

Shrine: The Basilica of the Visitation (Basilique de la Visitation)

Address: 20, avenue de la Visitation/74000 Annecy/France

Phone: 33 (0)4 50 45 22 76 **Fax:** 33 (0)4 50 45 68 94

E-mail: visitation.annecy@wanadoo.fr

Website: None

Quiet areas for meditation: Pilgrim tour buses come and go, but otherwise the Basilica is quiet.

English spoken: Rarely

Hours: Summer 8AM–12PM, 2PM–6.

Mass: Weekdays 7:25AM; Sun/Hol 9:30AM. Weekdays: Visitors can join the sisters in their chapel for Mass and for Laudes afterwards; Also Vespers, except on Sunday.

Feasts and festivities: January 24 — Feast of St. Francis de Sales; December 12 — Feast of St. Jane de Chantal.

Accessibility: There is a ramp to the right side of the Basilica.

Information office: As you walk into the Basilica, to the left you will see "Accueil." It is staffed by volunteers who do not usually speak English.

Museum: Open 9AM-12PM; 2PM-5, no charge. Wax figures of the saints in reliquaries, personal items and photographs with English descriptions fill this small museum.

Tours: If you call ahead to make arrangements, there is a possibility that someone can take you on a tour in English. There are brochures in English on the right side of the Basilica as you enter, and on the left side of the altar near the crypt of St. Francis de Sales.

Bookstore: Souvenirs de Pélerinage is located to the right of the Basilica as you face it. No books in English.

Recommended books: *Introduction to the Devout Life* by St. Francis de Sales, Vintage Books, 2002; *Treatise on the Love of God*, Tan Books, 1988; *Francis de Sales, Jane de Chantal: Letters of Spiritual Direction*

edited by Classics of Spirituality. None of these books are available at the shrine in Annecy. At the tourist office in town the brochure, *Town Walks*, contains a chapter on "The Churches" that includes the sites that relate to the Visitation Order.

Lodging: None

Directions: The Basilica is on the Avenue de la Visitation, and is located south of the Centre Ville Mairie. It is less than a one-mile walk mostly uphill, from the center of town. From Pont Perrière, walk south on Faubourg Perrière, then Ch. de la Tour la Reine, which leads to the Avenue de la Visitation. Follow the road up the hill, and watch for the pathway shortcut that leads more directly to the Basilica. By car, from the turnabout at the Hospital, head uphill on Avenue de Tresum, then left on Avenue de la Corniche, and finally, the next left on Avenue de la Visitation. Coming from the other direction on Avenue du Rhone and Avenue du Cret du Maure, turn right on the Avenue de la Visitation.

OTHER PLACES OF INTEREST IN ANNECY

THE CHURCH OF SAINT MAURICE
Eglise Saint Maurice

The church of Saint Maurice, patron saint of Annecy, is where St. Francis made his First Communion and Confirmation, where he preached, and where the remains of St. Jane de Chantal were venerated from 1806-1826. The church is located across from the Town Hall (Hôtel de Ville) and the park on the lake (Les Jardins de l'Europe) on Place St. Maurice in the Old Town area of Annecy.

ST. PETER'S CATHEDRAL
Cathédral Saint Pierre

St. Peter's Cathedral, built in 1535, is where Francis de Sales was ordained, served as Bishop from 1602 until his death in 1622, and where his remains were venerated from 1806-1826. The pulpit illustrates St. Francis de Sales preaching to the Senate of Savoy, while the stained glass windows in the apse relate his life story. The Cathedral is located on rue J.J. Rousseau in the Old Town area of Annecy.

CHURCH OF ST. JOSEPH AND THE GALLERY HOUSE
Eglise St. Joseph e la Maison de la Galerie

Statue of St. Francis de Sales at Eglise St. Joseph

The Church of St. Joseph (Eglise St. Joseph) is now the Convent and Chapel of the Sisters of St. Joseph. This is where the second monastery of the Visitation was founded in 1634. Next door is the Gallery House (Maison de la Galerie) where the Visitation Order was founded by Francis de Sales and Jane de Chantal on June 6, 1610. The Gallery House is now managed by the Sisters of St. Joseph. If you call ahead, you may be able to arrange a visit to see the Chapel and the bedroom of St. Jane de Chantal. After making arrangements, go to the Church of St. Joseph (Eglise St. Joseph) and the Sisters will escort you to the Maison next door. Located on rue de la Providence next to the Church of St. Joseph; Phone: 33 (0)4 50 45 03 30.

THE CHURCH OF ST. FRANCIS DE SALES
Eglise Saint François de Sales

Built for Jane de Chantal in 1612 and consecrated by Francis de Sales in 1617, this was the site of the first Visitation Order Monastery and the burial place for both saints until the revolution in 1793. Used as a textile factory in the nineteenth century, it is now the Italian Church of Annecy. The saints' previous burial places are marked and there is a gilded wooden statue of St. Jane de Chantal. A Black Madonna in the church is similar to the one which was revered by St. Francis de Sales. Located on place Saint-Maurice, in the Old Town area of Annecy. Phone: 33 (0)4 50 45 06 92.

MORE SHRINES IN EUROPE

TREVISO, ITALY

CHURCH OF THE VISITATION
Monasterio de la Visitazione

The heart of St. Francis de Sales was given to the community of the Visitation in Lyon, where the saint died in 1622. The community emigrated to Italy during the French Revolution. The incorrupt heart, along with other relics of the saint, now rest in the Monastery of the Visitation in Treviso, Italy, north of Venice. The monastery does not provide lodging, but there are hotels in the area. Address: Madre Superiora, Monastero de la Visitazione, via Mandruzzato, 22, 31100 Treviso, Italy. Phone: 39 (0)4 22 30 22 23 Fax: 39 (0)4 22 30 09 12.

COMING AND GOING

ANNECY

Car: Located on A41, 63 miles (101 km) northeast of Lyon and 32 miles (51 km) south of Geneva (Switzerland). Traffic in Annecy can be heavy. Exit off A41 on Sortie 16, Annecy Sud. Follow signs to Annecy Centre, taking a left at the turnabout below the hospital to reach the centre ville. Do not follow signs to Annecy-le-Vieux, for this is another town. Note that you will pass the Avenue de la Visitation on your right as you get near the hospital.

Train: TGV from Paris via Lyon to Annecy takes 3.5 hours. www.tgv.com SNCF; Phone: 33 (0)8 36 35 35 35 www.sncf.fr Taxis are available at the railway station. Call 33 (0)4 50 45 05 67.

Bus: SIBRA Phone: 33 (0)4 50 10 04 04 for local buses.

Plane: Geneva-Cointrin International in Geneva Switzerland www.gva.ch 33; Lyon-Saint Exupéry International www.lyon.aeroport.fr; Annecy-Meythet in Metz-Tessy with regular flights between Annecy and Paris and other towns in France. www.annecy.aeroport.fr.

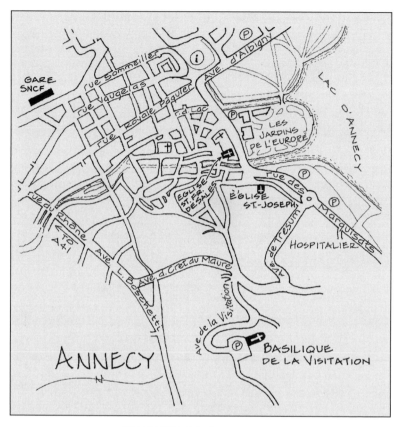

TOURIST INFORMATION

✱ Agence Touristique departmentale de Haute-Savoie/56, rue Sommeiller/BP 348/74012 Annecy Cedex/France Phone: 33 (0)4 50 51 32 31 Fax: 33 (0)4 50 45 81 99 E-Mail: tourisme@cdt-haute-savoie.fr www.hautesavoie-tourisme.com Informative website for the area. Go to "Cultural sites; monuments" for more churches to visit in the department of Haute-Savoie.

✱ Office de tourisme/1, rue Jean Jaurès/Bonlieu/74000 Annecy/France Phone: 33 (0)4 50 45 00 33 Fax: 33 (0)4 50 51 87 20 E-mail: ancytour@noos.fr www.lac-annecy.com. Located at pl. de la Libération in the Bonlieu shopping mall. Detailed maps and a *Town Walks* brochure. English tours by appointment.

Ars~Sur~Formans
Population 1100

The small town of Ars-sur-Formans lies nineteen miles north of Lyon. The surrounding area offers nature reserves, "Saracen chimneys" perched on the roofs of ancient Bresse farms, and the restored medieval city of Pérouges. The town of Ars literally was put on the map after the humble St. John Vianney moved there in 1818 and became the cherished parish priest for more than forty years. During his lifetime, the existing church was restored and enlarged, and he founded an orphanage, served the poor, and attracted thousands of pilgrims day and night to his confessional. Today, the shrine of the Curé d'Ars attracts 400,000 pilgrims each year, including 10,000 priests and seminarians who visit the Foyer Sacerdotal John Paul II for rest and retreat. All points of interest for the pilgrim, including the saint's house and garden, are conveniently centered around the Basilica, with pleasant religious lodging at "La Providence" across the street. The special grace of St. John Vianney can be felt even today in this village; his tireless work for the salvation of souls is still ongoing.

ST. JOHN VIANNEY - CURATE OF ARS
Saint Jean Vianney - Curé d'Ars 1786–1859

"It is in solitude that God speaks to us."

The life of John Vianney reads more like a historical novel than that of a saint, for his life's path was a winding road to sanctity. John's sojourn and his personal search for God were interwoven with the French Revolution, the Days of Terror, and Napoleon Bonaparte, creating a colorful tapestry of nineteenth century religious life. In the end, John became a beacon of light for the French people, living a life of purity and service, and showing thousands of souls the way home to God.

Trouble was brewing throughout France in the late eighteenth century as the people overthrew the ruling class of the French aristocracy. They stormed the Bastille, removed the heads of state from their posts and banished the practice of organized religion. At first, rural areas were not much affected by these events in Paris, but this soon changed, as the priests of the local parishes were not allowed to perform worship services and rituals unless they swore an oath of loyalty to the Revolutionary government. Churches were closed or destroyed, and the priests were exiled or executed, so the remaining faithful had to go underground to practice their beliefs. This was the atmosphere that young John found swirling around him in his youth.

Born into a prosperous farming family three years before the beginning of the Revolution, John was the fourth of six children born to Matthieu and Marie Vianney in the small village of Dardilly, near Lyon. His early years were spent in the family home, hearing stories of saints from the Bible, while learning to perform family chores on the farm. At age four, his mother gave him a statue of the Virgin Mary, which instantly became his prize possession. He would carry it with him always, and was often found kneeling before his statue in prayer. "Oh, how I loved that statue," he related nearly seventy years later; "neither by day nor by night would I be parted from it. I should not have slept had I not had it beside me in my little bed...the Blessed Virgin was the object of my earliest affections; I loved her before I knew her."

In the years immediately following the Revolution, those devout people wishing to practice their faith had to do so in secrecy, risking punishment and exile. The Vianney family was one of many who waited anxiously each week to hear word of a secret location where they could go to celebrate Mass with a renegade priest and their fellow Catholics. John was seven when he was quietly ushered through dark back streets and into clandestine services held in dimly lit barns, houses and other discrete meeting places. Here devout people quietly received the blessings and support of their faith, while longing for their churches to reopen.

John's days were spent in the fields tending to the family flocks and enjoying the natural beauty that characterized his native lands. He always found time to create a little altar for his favorite statue and pray before his beloved Mary. Each day was dedicated to living for God and performing all duties as a way of inward service. Even at this young age, John felt a deep calling and connection with God. He wrote in his catechism, "Oh what a beautiful thing it is to do all things in union with the good God! Courage my soul, if you work with God; you shall indeed do the work, but He will bless it; you shall walk, and He shall bless your steps."

What was not present in his life was a means of receiving a formal education. The Revolution made a point of promoting free compulsory education, but it had closed all the schools, requiring teachers to take a loyalty oath before they could teach in the classrooms. In the rural areas such as Dardilly, two years passed before teachers and schools found a way to open their doors and educate the children, and John was nine before he resumed his limited education. He continued to receive instruction until his thirteenth year, when he had to return to the fields full-time to support the family. Religion was still practiced only behind closed doors, so John took his first communion in secret when he was thirteen. He later wrote of the

St. John Vianney - Curé d'Ars

blessing, "When we receive Holy Communion, we experience something extraordinary—a joy—fragrance—a well being that thrills the whole body and causes it to exalt."

In 1799 Napoleon Bonaparte gained control of the government and instituted his own version of the revolution. One positive result was the liberation of the churches and the right to practice religion in public. This increased John's religious fervor and he longed to enter the priesthood. His mother enthusiastically supported him in this vocation, but his father was completely opposed. John was needed to work the family farm, and there were no funds to educate the teenager. He continued to toil in the fields until he was nineteen, when a presbytery school was opened in nearby Ecully, and his father finally relented, allowing John to pursue his dream of serving God through the priesthood.

John had much difficulty in advancing in his studies after so many years of educational neglect. Latin was especially challenging, and he struggled greatly to master the ancient language. His teacher, M. Balley, worked closely with his favorite student, but was unable to help him. Feeling frustrated and fearing that he would not be accepted into the priesthood, John embarked on a pilgrimage to the shrine of St. John Regis in La Louvesc, to pray for guidance and help. He made his way on foot to the mountainous shrine and met there with an encouraging Jesuit priest. Upon returning to Ecully, he still found his Latin studies difficult, but he approached everything with a new joy and acceptance. This joy was his hallmark, for all the teachers and examiners were impressed by the young man, and felt that his pious nature would serve him well in the priesthood. In 1807, at age twenty-one, he was confirmed and took the name John Marie Baptiste.

Things were looking up for the young seminary student but fate would soon change his course. In 1809, Napoleon was fiercely fighting Spain and Austria, and required more troops for his campaigns. All eligible men were called up in the draft and ordered to report to duty. John was safely enrolled in the seminary, but his teacher had forgotten to submit his name on the list of students, so he was mistakenly included in the draft. No argument would dissuade the officials, so John had to report to duty in October 1809. Within two days, he became very ill and was assigned to a hospital to recover. In November, he was ordered to leave with his regiment, but after several days of marching, he became ill again, and was placed in a hospital run by the Sisters of Augustine. In January, he was once more given marching orders. As he prepared to leave, he first went to a nearby church to pray and offer himself to God. "There," he wrote later, "all my sorrows melted away like snow under the sun."

Returning to his post, he found that the troops had already departed. The following morning he set off to catch his unit, but was unable to make up the lost time through the rugged mountains. Tired of the chase, John stopped for a rest along the mountain road. When a young man approached and picked up John's knapsack, and headed up into the hills. John followed, soon finding himself in the company of deserters who were hiding in the remote countryside. The thought of being labeled a deserter worried the young man, and he soon turned himself in to the local mayor. The mayor was a kindly man who took no joy in seeing young men head off to war, so he took John under his wing and sheltered him for the next fourteen months. The first months were spent hiding in barns and haylofts. Eventually, John found refuge in the home of the mayor's cousin, where he continued to study his Latin, and earned his keep by teaching the young children. John's fugitive life was punctuated by frequent visits by the gendarmes who were constantly searching the area for deserters. On one occasion, he was surprised by a sudden arrival of soldiers but quickly made his way into a secure hiding place under some hay. The diligent troops searched the barn and began poking the stack of hay with their swords. John suddenly felt a thrusting saber between his ribs but was able to maintain his silence and avoid detection. The gendarmes soon left to have drinks with the friendly mayor!

In 1810, Napoleon's foray into Austria proved successful, and by way of celebrating his marriage to Archduchess Marie Louise, he granted amnesty to all deserters. John was now free to return home, even though he still had to meet his military obligation. To his good fortune, his younger brother agreed to join the army in his place, so John was free to continue his studies for the priesthood.

The next years were spent in Verrières and Lyons, studying philosophy and theology in preparation for ordination. John continued to struggle with his studies, but impressed everyone with his devout character. He finally returned to the school of M. Balley in Ecully to take his final courses before his examination. The Latin exam proved too difficult for John so he failed to receive approval, and was told to try another diocese. Convinced of his student's sanctity, M. Balley privately appealed to the Archbishop of Lyon. Known for his leniency, he asked some simple questions about the candidate: "Is the Abbé Vianney pious? Has he devotion for Our Lady? Does he know how to say his rosary?" "He is a model of piety," came the reply. "Very well" declared the pundit. "I summon him to come up for ordination. The grace of God will do the rest." By August 1815, John Mary Baptist Vianney was fully ordained into the priesthood at age twenty-nine, and returned to Ecully to serve as vicar under M. Balley. Within two years, John's beloved teacher M. Balley died, and John was soon assigned to be parish priest in the tiny village known as Ars-en-Dombes.

In February of 1818, John left Ecully on foot with two companions to travel the nineteen miles to Ars. The day was cold and misty, and the small band soon lost their way. Happening upon three children playing in a field, John asked directions to his new parish. Upon receiving direction on the right path, the new Curé of Ars replied, "My young friend. You have shown me the way to Ars. I will show you the way to heaven."

Monument of the Encounter

The Curé of Ars had his work cut out for him, as the people of the village were more apt to go to a dance at a local tavern than attend Mass on Sunday. The people of the area were not necessarily bad; they had simply lapsed in the practices of their faith, and chose to live more worldly lives. The first years of the Curé's mission were mostly spent in bringing the faithful back to the church and preaching of the pitfalls of worldly entertainments. The Curé of Ars openly spoke against blasphemy, working on Sunday, and the evils of drinking and dancing, and worked hard to change the habits of his parishioners. He expected people to live a life with God as the center, and he used his own life as a living example. His life was a life of constant work, service, mortification and prayer. Within a few years, the townspeople were responding to the love and direction of their Curé, and a noticeable change slowly took place. Taverns closed, many people became openly pious, and Sunday again became a sacred day of religious celebration. Of course, the Curé of Ars had his detractors, as he was preaching against all the "pleasures" of life, but his message opened the hearts of many souls.

Within six years of his arrival at Ars, the Curé began to attract attention as a devout healer, intuitive confessor and miracle worker. An increasing number of pilgrims began arriving at the tiny village to experience the holiness of this man of God, and to seek his guidance. The Curé of Ars put all his energy into serving his expanding flock at the cost of his own solitude. He had always wanted to lead a more solitary life of prayer, but his mission was now one of outward service. To this end, he put service to God first in his life and neglected his own body. He ate very little, often fasting for days on end, and slept only three hours a night, spending most of his time tending to the people's needs. On a typical day, he would rise at midnight and hear confessions till dawn, when he would perform the rites of the day. He would continue to preach, teach, and hear confessions through the afternoon, then eat a small meal at evening, and finally read the lives of the saints before heading to bed at nine. Such is the life of a saint!

Thousands of pilgrims made their way to Ars every year, and the reputation of the Curé of Ars spread throughout Europe. The saving of many souls also attracted the attention of another powerful force, namely, Satan. For over thirty years, beginning in 1824, demonic visitations were common for the Curé, as he would have almost nightly encounters with the devil. These occurrences consisted mostly of loud noises and voices, but on occasion they manifested as physical attacks. In one instance, when he was not present, his bed inexplicably burst into flames. "At the beginning I felt afraid," he confessed to a fellow priest: "I did not then know what it was, but now I am quite happy. It is a good sign: there is always a good haul of fish the next day." At another time he was heard to say, "The devil gave me a good shaking last night. We shall have a great number of people tomorrow." For the Curé, it was all in a day's work.

In 1824 the Curé founded a home for orphans and wayward girls, called La Providence. With the assistance of two young women of the community, the home soon served sixty children, subsisting entirely on charitable contributions. It was a difficult undertaking for all involved, but the grace of God was ever present. In two different instances, food miraculously appeared at the orphanage. On one occasion, the empty grain loft was suddenly filled with supplies. Another time the bakers were able to make ten 20-pound loaves of bread from a few pounds of flour that was blessed by the Curé of Ars. The miracles of the Curé became legend throughout France, and the number of pilgrims coming to Ars increased every year, keeping him in constant demand.

The Curé of Ars was not happy to receive the attention drawn to him by miracles and cures. He soon began to preach of the holiness and powers of St. Philomena, and asked the people to pray to her for intercession. Creating an altar to the ancient martyred saint within the parish church at Ars, he invoked her presence whenever anything was requested of him. He was becoming so popular that it would often take him twenty minutes to cross the plaza between the presbytery and the church, past hundreds of souls seeking guidance or healing who seized his hands and ripped at his cassock. "What misguided devotion," he exclaimed at the sight. "I do not work miracles. I am a poor ignorant man who once upon a time tended sheep. Address yourselves to St. Philomena—I have never asked anything through her without being answered."

The confessional was the primary place of service for the Curé of Ars, as he often spent over twelve hours a day hearing confessions. His attraction to the confessional was the opportunity to work directly with individual souls, while the parishioner's attraction was the Curé's uncanny ability to intuitively read their souls and give them guidance. On many occasions he knew of a person's plight before talking with them. He once confided to a peer that his intuitive insights seemed like an awakening of memory. "I once said to a certain woman," he related, " 'So it is you who have left your husband in hospital and who refuse to join him.' 'How do you know that?' she replied, 'I have not mentioned it to a soul.' I was more surprised than she was; I imagined that she had already told me the whole story."

As the years passed, the extraordinarily busy life of the Curé changed little, and he still longed for a life of solitude. On three different occasions he attempted to leave Ars to pursue a more inward life, but always returned to his post. "Since the age of eleven I have asked God to let me live in solitude," he confided to the Mayor of Ars. "But my prayers have never been answered." The last attempt occurred in 1853, when at age sixty-seven, he secretly accepted an offer from the Bishop to retire, and made plans to leave the village under the cover of night. As he was endeavoring to make his way out of town, his assistant vicars and nuns, who insisted that he stay, thwarted his efforts. The church bell was rung in warning and the townspeople arose to see the cause of the disturbance. Upon hearing of the Curé's plans, they surrounded the elder saint and fell to their knees, barring his departure. Many tears were shed before he relented and agreed to stay on as their shepherd.

The Curé of Ars was now feeble and feeling his age, but continued with his mission. In 1859, the last year of his life, over one hundred thousand pilgrims journeyed to Ars to behold the saintly priest before he passed away. By the end of July, he knew his time was approaching and called his fellow priests and vicars to pray with him. After receiving

The reliquary of St. John Vianney

the sacraments he murmured, "It is sad to receive Holy Communion for the last time." In the early morning hours of August 4th, with the sound of thunder echoing in the skies, the Curé of Ars peacefully left his body.

The process of canonization was swiftly undertaken for the saintly Curé, as miraculous healings followed his death and thousands of pilgrims continued to make their way to Ars. In 1925, Pius IX canonized John Vianney. Four years later, in 1929, he was named the patron saint of parish priests throughout the world.

THE BASILICA OF ARS
La basilique d'Ars

If approaching the village of Ars from the west, you will see the Basilica with its octagonal dome and two circular chapels with green roofs. As you enter the town, you will see the old church with its simple brick façade facing the street, and behind it, the red brick bell tower. This original church, consisting of just the nave, was in need of repair when John Vianney first arrived in 1818. He quickly made plans to restore the church, starting with the addition of the bell tower and side chapels. By the end of his life, he had approved plans to build a bigger church, dedicated to St. Philomena, in order to accommodate the growing number of pilgrims, but he did not live to see it constructed. In 1862, four years after his death, the new church was begun. It was completed in 1878, after the original plans were altered in order to connect the new church with the old, as demanded by the parishioners.

La basilique d'Ars

As you enter the old church from the front, you will see on the left the pulpit from which the saint preached, and on the right, the pulpit where he taught catechism. St. Vianney built the side chapels on either side of this nave. The saint was interred in the center of the floor until 1904.

The men's confessional is on the right hand side in the former sacristy and the women's is on the left, in the Chapel of St. John the Baptist. These confessionals are where the Curé spent most of his time, sometimes as much as 17 hours a day. Preaching from the pulpit one day, the priest said, referring to the St. John the Baptist chapel, "If you knew all that happened in this chapel, you would not dare step in. I do not add another word; had God wanted it, he would have let you know."

There are a few steps up into the Basilica from the old church. As you enter the Basilica, you will see immediately to your right the beautiful gilt bronze and glass reliquary containing the incorrupt body of St. John Vianney. This reliquary was donated by the priests of France on his canonization in 1925. His body was examined in 1904, forty-five years after his death, and found to be darkened and dry but completely intact. His face, which was still recognizable but showing signs of deterioration, was covered with a wax mask and his body clothed in religious vestments. His incorrupt heart was removed in the year of his beatification and installed in the Shrine of the Curé's Heart just outside the Basilica.

To the left in the Basilica is the Chapel of the Glorification, with a statue of the saint. Over the main altar is the richly decorated octagonal dome with three radiating chapels. The Basilica has been under repair inside and out since 1999, having suffered from pollution and previous alterations. The result is the creation of an uplifting, bright interior, and lovely, decorative exterior. As you exit on the left side of the Basilica, you will find the saint's charming house (Maison du Curé d'Ars), which has been maintained as it was on the day that he died. The first floor contains the bedroom where he died and, as you exit, you will see the kitchen where Catherine Lassagne, his confidante and helper, made his meals after she moved to Ars in 1848. The Maison du Curé d'Ars is open from 6:30AM–7PM.

As you exit the house, you will be on a side street that contains a souvenir/bookshop (Magasin du Pèlerinage) that sells the small guide in English, *Ars: Pilgrim's Guide*. It would be wise to purchase this guide when you arrive in Ars, before visiting the sites. At the end of this street is the Chapel of the Heart (la Chapelle du Coeur) erected in 1930 for St. Vianney's canonization and to house his incorrupt heart that rests in a reliquary. To the right of the Chapel is the audio-visual room (Audio-vidéo).

As you exit this small street, turn left towards the back of the Basilica, noticing the renovated exterior, and continue until you reach a small plaza. Down some stairs and across the street, you will come upon the Chapel of the Providence (Chapelle de la Providence) inaugurated in 1848 as part of the pilgrim's lodging of La Providence. The Curé intended this chapel to be a retreat for himself upon his retirement, which never occurred. The pilgrim can now enjoy his good intentions in this quiet chapel, which is suitable for prayer and contemplation. The hours vary, so you need to check if it is open or ask in La Providence up the street. La Providence was founded by the Curé as an orphanage for girls and was operated by Catherine Lassagne from 1824-1848. It was transferred to the Sisters of St. Joseph of Bourg until 1975, when the girls were relocated to the Institutes of Specialized Education. La Providence then became a welcoming center for pilgrims. The Musée de Cires is up rue Jean Marie Vianney, and contains a wax museum (diorama) of the Curé's life.

The underground church that houses 2500 pilgrims is called the Crypt and was built in 1959 to celebrate the hundred-year anniversary of the Curé's passing. It is open on weekends for Sunday Mass and feast days. The entrance is across the street from the Chapel of the Providence or on your way out of town toward the Monument of the Encounter (le Monument de la Rencontre), on the right. The Crypt opens onto a meadow that contains the Way of the Cross. To reach the Monument of the Encounter continue out of town over the river, and turn right at the fork. At the tennis courts, keep to the left. The Monument is just up the road on the right. This is where John Vianney asked the way to Ars of a young shepherd and said, "My friend, you have shown me the way to Ars, I will show you the way to Heaven."

Where is the Basilica of Ars?
Où est la basilique d'Ars?

Where is the Chapel of the Providence?
Où est la Chapelle de la Providence?

Where is the Monument of the Encounter?
Où est le Monument de la Rencontre?

SHRINE INFORMATION

Shrine: Secretary of Pilgrimages

Address: Rue Jean-Marie Vianney/01480 Ars-sur-Formans/France

Phone: 33 (0)4 74 08 17 17 **Fax:** 33 (0)4 74 00 75 50

E-mail: info@arsnet.org

Website: www.arsnet.org — Official website: parts of website in English.

Quiet areas for meditation: The Basilica with the reliquary of St. John Vianney, and in the same building, the side chapels of the old church. Chapel of the Providence (Chapelle de la Providence) connected to "La Providence," the pilgrim lodging behind the Basilica, but the hours are not regular. The monument of the Encounter (Monument de la Rencontre) is a walk (or drive) out of town, less than a mile to a statue of the Curé asking a shepherd boy for directions. There are a couple of benches under shaded trees for an outside meditation. Ars is a quiet town; you will find someplace that is peaceful.

English spoken: Occasionally

Hours: Daily 6:30AM–9PM, Easter to All Saints Day; 8AM–7PM, Nov. 1 to Easter.

Mass: Weekdays 8:45AM, 11, 6PM; Sun/Hol 8AM, 10, 11, 6PM.

Feasts and festivities: August 4 — Feast Day St. John Vianney; Second Sunday in February — Anniversary of the saint's arrival in Ars.

Accessibility: The old church is accessible, but not the new church.

Pilgrimage office: Accueil du Pèlerinage on rue Jean-Marie Vianney across from the old church side of the Basilica. They have information, a good map and a video in English.

Tours: Inquire at the Accueil du Pèlerinage on rue Jean-Marie Vianney across from the old church. Phone: 33 (0)4 74 08 17 17 Fax: 33 (0)4 74 00 75 50

Bookstore: There is a Pilgrimage Bookshop (Magasin du Pèlerinage) next to the information office (Accueil du Pèlerinage) on rue Jean-Marie Vianney, and also one near the Chapel of the Curé's Heart.

Recommended books: In the bookstores (Magasin du Pèlerinage) is the *Ars Pilgrim's Guide* that has pictures and short descriptions of everything to visit. They also have other books, a video in English and the most respected book on the life of St. John Vianney, *The Curé d'Ars* by Abbé Francis Trochu, from Tan Books with 586 pages.

Lodging: Maison La Providence/rue des Ecoles/01480 Ars-sur-Formans/France. Phone: 33 (0)4 74 00 71 65 Fax: 33 (0)4 74 08 10 79 Email: accueil@ars-providence.com www.ars-providence.com. Once you drive past the Basilica, follow the arrows to La Providence. At rue des Écoles turn left even though it says one-way. The one-way street does not begin until after the entrance to La Providence. Turn right through the iron gate. Other religious housing: Maison Saint Jean/01480 Ars-sur-Formas/France.

Directions: As you enter town from the west, the tourist office will be on your left and a big parking lot on the right. Stop and get a map. It is a very small town with good signs, so you won't get lost. You can park across from the tourist office and walk into the center of town, which is not far. You may want to drive through town to get your bearings and then find parking. Ars-sur-Formans is 19 miles (30 kms) north of Lyon and 4.5 miles (7 kms) from Villefranche-sur-Saône.

COMING AND GOING

ARS-SUR-FORMANS

Car: Take A6 to the Villefranche-sur-Saône exit (no. 31) then follow signs to Bourg, then Ars.

Train: The train station is located 4.5 miles (7 km) from Ars at Villefranche-sur-Saône. From Paris, transfer at Mâcon-Loché to the TGV shuttle to Villefranche. From Lyon go to Villefranche-sur-Saône. Then take a taxi or a bus to Ars.

Bus: From Monday through Saturday from Villefranche take the Villefranche-Ars-A.R. Régie de l'Ain to Ars. Call 33 (0)4 74 60 76 11 for times.

Air: Lyon-Saint Exupéry International Airport. Phone: 33 (0)4 72 22 72 21 www.lyon.aeroport.fr. Then a taxi or train is 37 miles (60 km) to Villefranche and a taxi 5 miles (8 km) to Ars.

TOURIST INFORMATION

✻Ars Office de Tourisme/rue Jean-Marie Vianney/01480 Ars-sur-Formans/France Phone: 33 (0)4 74 08 10 76 Fax: 33 (0)4 74 08 15 42 Email: ot.ars.pod@wanadoo.fr www.cc-porteouestdeladombes.com French. Open from April 1st to October 31st.

✻ Comité departmental de l'Ain/ 34 Rue Général Delestraint/BP 78 - 01002 Bourg en Bresse Cedex/France Phone: 33 (0)4 74 32 31 30 Fax: 33 (0)4 74 21 45 69 E-mail: tourisme@cdt-ain.fr www.ain-tourisme.com.

WEBSITES

Ars Tour www.webspan.net/~ronnieb/Arshome.html — Personal website by Ronnie B. with many good pictures of the Ars shrine.

Department of Ain www.ain-tourisme.com — Tourist information for the department of Ain.

Sanctuaire d'Ars www.arsnet.org — Official website for the Sanctuary of Ars; parts of website in English.

MORE ST. JOHN VIANNEY SHRINES IN FRANCE

DARDILLY

Dardilly, in the northwest suburbs of Lyon, is where St. John Vianney spent the first twenty years of his life. The house where he grew up is now a museum and open limited hours: Wed–Sat 10AM–11:30; Tues–Sun 2PM–5. Address: 2 Curé d'Ars Street, Dardilly. For group tours call in advance: Phone: 33 (0)4 78 66 19 09.

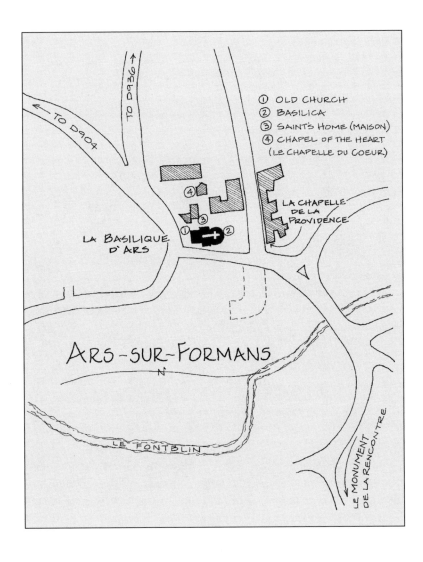

La Louvesc

Population 495

At an altitude of 3,543 feet, the small town of La Louvesc is situated in the mountains of the Ardèche, offering a lovely vista that extends between the Alps and the Cévennes. Surrounded by forests featuring abundant bilberry bushes and mushrooms, the area attracts hikers and cross-country skiers to over one hundred miles of trails. What has attracted pilgrims here since the seventeenth century are two saints: John Francis Regis and Therese Couderc. St. Regis Basilica, which houses the saint's relics, is in the center of town, facing a panoramic view of the valley. There is also a number of other sites adjacent to the Basilica that relate to St. Regis. Therese Couderc is interred in the Chapel at the Sisters of the Cenacle Convent, several blocks from the Basilica. Though out-of-the-way, this small village rewards the pilgrim with peaceful surroundings and the inspiration of two God-filled souls.

ST. JOHN FRANCIS REGIS

Saint Jean François Régis 1597–1640

St. Regis was always focused on the salvation and comfort of others, especially the poor and disenfranchised. He saw it as his duty to serve all in need while doing so only with the greatest humility. It was said that he vilified himself to great extremes while he treated everyone he encountered as a saint.

Born in the small village of Fontcourverte near Narbonne, Regis was raised in a family of landed gentry and well educated at local Jesuit schools. Even at a young age he was not interested in typical entertainment and games, but chose to spend his time reading spiritual materials and in devotions at home and in church. Though he imposed a very austere life upon himself, he related to his classmates and acquaintances with humor, good will and humility, and was well liked by his peers.

At the age of nineteen, Regis became a novice in the Jesuit order and began his ecclesiastical education in Toulouse. After his first year, he went to Cahors and then Tournon to continue his studies. He split his time between studies and devotion, but preferred to spend much of his time in prayer. A roommate told his superior that Regis spent all his nights praying in the chapel and was told, "Take care not to disturb his devotions, nor hinder his communion with God. He is a saint—and if I am not greatly mistaken, the Society will some day celebrate a feast in his honor." During the weekends, he would accompany a priest to the neighboring villages, where he would teach the catechism to the local children and preach to the adults. Everyone was greatly impressed by the pious young man of twenty-two, and many hearts were opened by his clear love of God and his honest expression of divine joy. "The interior fire of his breast appeared in his looks. He was often seen at the foot of the altar without motion as in a kind of rapture; and he spoke of God with such a feeling unction, that he inspired all that heard him with his holy love, and excited the most tepid to fervor."

Over the next years, Regis taught at several colleges and continued his own education. In 1628, at age 31, he began his theological studies to prepare for the priesthood. He was ordained in 1631. At his first celebration of Mass, Father Regis' deep devotion brought on a torrent of tears, which persisted throughout the Mass, and deeply touched his fellow priests. His first years of service were spent at the Jesuit college of Montpellier and in the surrounding communities.

Eglise de Fontcouverte

St. John Francis Regis

Father Regis now began to see his personal mission as one of service to the poor, and of converting lapsed Catholics, and Calvinists. He spent his mornings in the church hearing confession, praying and performing Mass. In the afternoons, he frequented the prisons and hospitals, giving care and comfort to the needy. He also organized the women of the community to assist in caring for these destitute citizens. As a tireless worker for God, he slept little, ate little, and always found time to inspire souls through his outward activities and his saintly demeanor. Through the years he made countless friends, but he also made enemies, as he worked to help prostitutes turn their lives around. He would offer them new jobs and new living situations, and this did not make their previous "employers" very happy. There were several instances where he was threatened with violence, but treated his assailants with such tenderness that they were unable to carry out their threats, and often converted to his cause.

Reliquary of St. John Francis Regis

The one desire that persisted for Father Regis was to travel to the New World and convert the Native American Indians. He saw the life of the missionary and potential martyr as the ultimate offering in service to God. As it turned out, his destiny was to become a missionary, but much closer to home. Like the New World, there were "wild" areas of France where no priests had penetrated for decades, and where religious and civil strife had decimated the morality of the villages. The mountainous regions of southeast France, known as the Vivarais and the Velay, became the focus of Father Regis' missionary work.

Beginning in 1633, Father Regis put all his energy into serving the people of this region. His summers were spent in Le Puy, where he continued his work with hospitals, prisons and prostitutes, as well as with his traditional congregation. His saintly countenance attracted great attention and there were often more than four thousand parishioners at his services. He was always wanted in the confessional, and devoted countless hours to counseling his flock. He also saw to the physical needs of his people, as he helped create a soup kitchen during the plague of 1438, and also established a granary for the poor. The granary was the site of one of the many miracles associated with him, as there were three instances where the stores of grain were nearly depleted, but through his intercession the vats were miraculously filled with fresh supplies.

His winter months were spent on "missions" to the remote villages of the area, where he would teach, preach and hear confessions from all in need. Nothing could stop the energetic priest as he made his way from village to village regardless of rain, snow or bandits. On one occasion, he was trapped in a snow bank for three weeks before he could make his way out to safety. When people heard that "the saint" was in the vicinity, they would seek him out, and great hordes of people would hike through the rough mountains in search of salvation. His missions became legend in the region, and even his fellow priests noticed the power of his presence. "After the mission I did not recognize my own parishioners, so completely had he reformed them," stated the Curé of Marlhes. "I have seen him stop in the middle of a forest to satisfy a crowd who wished to hear him. I have seen him stand all day on a heap of snow at the top of a mountain, instructing and preaching, and then spend the whole night hearing confessions."

Miracles seemed to surround the young priest—sometimes blessing others, sometimes, himself. While visiting a family at their home in his parish, he was introduced to a young boy who had been blind for six months. Father Regis gathered the family in prayer to ask for a healing, and before he completed his devotions, the child regained his sight. On another occasion, he healed an older gentleman who was also blind. The physical aspects of his mountain missions were at times daunting to Father Regis, but he always made his appointments. Even when he fell and broke his leg, he made his way to the congregation waiting for his appearance. He immediately went to the confessional and administered to his people. When he left the confessional many hours later, his leg was completely healed.

In early winter of 1640, Father Regis was making ready to leave Le Puy for a mission in La Louvesc, and spent three days in retreat at the college of Le Puy before starting for the mountain village. As he was leaving Le Puy, he was asked if he would stay longer and renew his vows with his brothers. "The Master does not wish it," he replied. "He wishes me to leave tomorrow. I shall not be back for the renewal of vows – my companion will." So he and his constant companion, Brother Bideau, set off in severe weather to complete his mission. They soon became lost in the inclement weather, and spent the night in an open barn, subject to whipping winds and icy rain. Father Regis was already weak from the years of torturous work and was hit hard by the intense conditions. He arose the next morning with an intense case of pleurisy, but managed to drag himself to La Louvesc to begin his mission.

He preached three times on Christmas, three times on St. Stephens's Day, and spent the remainder of the time hearing confessions. After preaching to his congregation, as he was returning to the confessional, he fainted two times before he was taken from the church, and carried to the house of the Curé by Brother Bideau. All day December 31st, 1640, Father Regis gazed at the crucifix and communed with the Divine. In the evening hours he exclaimed, "Brother! I see our Lord and His Mother opening Heaven for me! .... Into Thy hands I commend my spirit." With these words, he left his body at the age of forty-three.

Father Regis' body remained in La Louvesc and has since been entombed in the Basilica built specifically for his veneration. The process for canonization began immediately after his death, and he was canonized in 1737. Over the years, millions of pilgrims have paid tribute to this saint, with perhaps the most famous being St. Jean Vianney, the Curé d'Ars. Following his pilgrimage to La Louvesc and the shrine of St. Regis, St. Vianney realized his vocation as a priest and gave much credit to this saint of the mountains. On his deathbed, St. Vianney said of St. Regis, "Everything good that I have done, I owe to him."

THE BASILICA OF ST. REGIS
Basilique St. Régis

Immediately after his death, John Francis Regis was venerated as a saint by the many pilgrims who crossed the mountains to visit his tomb. The church was declared a Basilica in 1888 and is operated by the Jesuit Fathers. The stained-glass windows illustrate the saint's life and the paintings in the choir depict famous men and women who came as pilgrims to this shrine.

The original crypt is entered from the outside on the left side of the Basilica. The body of St. Regis was placed here in 1641. The crypt can be cold and dark, but there is a light switch on the wall to the right of the altar. In 1716, his relics were taken for safekeeping to Grangeneuve, a few miles from La Louvesc, and hidden deep in the floor of a church. The Saint's remains were brought back to La Louvesc and installed in the Basilica in 1873. They now rest in a reliquary (châsse) to the right of the main altar.

Basilique St. Régis

The Chapel where he died, Chapel of St. Regis, is in another building to the right of the Basilica. The side street turns to the right with the tourist office on the left. Next to it is the Museum/Diorama, then the Chapel of St. Regis. The Miraculous Fountain (Fontaine miraculeuse) is in between the Basilica and the Chapel. When St. Regis arrived in La Louvesc on December 24, 1640, it is said that he drank from the fountain and since then miraculous cures have been attributed to the water. There is a Pilgrim's Park (Parc des Pèlerins) within walking distance from the Basilica. As you face the Basilica, to the left is the street "Chemin de Croix." Walk a couple of blocks to a large staircase that leads to the park and way of the cross. The house of St. Regis (Maison St. Regis) behind the Basilica is the residence for the Jesuit Fathers.

CHAPEL OF ST. REGIS

The Chapel of St. Regis is where the saint died. It is located off the small pedestrian street to the right of the Basilica. It was previously the presbytery of the church. There are a few chairs and a replica of his deathbed. This is a sweet place to sit and meditate. You can buy votive candles next door at the Museum.

Where is the crypt of St. John Francis Regis?
Où est la crypte de Saint Régis?

Where is the Chapel of St. Regis?
Où est la chapelle de Saint Régis?

Do you have information in English?
Avez-vous des informations en anglais?

MUSEUM DIORAMA
Diorama

On the small street to the right of the Basilica, between the tourist office and the Chapel of St. Regis, this small museum operated by the church contains a diorama on the life of St Regis. They have postcards and information in English if you ask for it. You can buy votive candles here to light in the Chapel of St. Regis next door. Phone: 33 (0)4 75 67 82 00 Fax: 33 (0)4 75 67 81 23 E-mail: Sjlalouvesc@post.club-internet.fr

SHRINE INFORMATION

Shrine: The Basilica of St. Francis Regis (Basilique St. Régis)

Address: House of Fathers Jesuits (Maison St. Régis)/rue St. Jean Françoise Régis/07520 La Louvesc/France

Phone: 33 (0)4 75 67 82 00 **Fax:** 33 (0)4 75 67 81 23

E-mail: sjlalouvesc@post.club-internet.fr

Website: None

Quiet areas for meditation: The Basilica of St. Regis and the Chapel of St. Regis.

English spoken: Occasionally

Hours: Daily 8AM–7PM.

Mass: Weekdays 9AM July 1–August 24; Daily 11AM, Mon-Fri 6PM.

Feasts and festivities: June 16 — Feast of St. Regis; July 31 — St. Ignatius of Loyola; August 15 — Feast of the Assumption; Last Sunday of August — Solemnity of St. Therese Couderc.

Accessibility: Ramp on left side of Basilica.

Information office: Tourist office to the right of the Basilica, then down the first small pedestrian street. To the right of the tourist office is the museum of St. Regis. Expect to speak French in both locations.

Tours: Available in French with advance reservations.

Bookstore: Next to the Chapel of St. Regis. They have a map of La Louvesc.

Recommended books: No books available in English.

Lodging: Abri du Pèlerin Phone: 33 (0)4 75 67 82 63 Run by the Jesuit fathers of the House of St. Regis.

Directions: La Louvesc is a small town with the Basilica standing in its center.

ST. THERESE COUDERC
Sainte Thérèse Couderc 1805–1885

"There is sweetness and peace when one gives himself totally to God, and by doing this, the soul finds Heaven on earth."

Therese Couderc moved to La Louvesc in 1826 to join the little community of Teaching Sisters, known as the "Religious of St. Regis," founded by Fr. Stephen Terme. The community served the needs of women coming to the shrine of St. Francis Regis, taught school and received religious training from the Jesuit fathers. Father Terme, who brought her to La Louvesc, said Therese had "good sense and sound judgment." She was appointed Mother Superior when she was only twenty-three years old.

Within a few years, Therese saw the mission of the community shifting towards serving as a center for religious retreat for the lay population—a new concept in nineteenth century France. The community divided into two branches, with Therese becoming Superior of the "Religious of the Cenacle," the branch serving the retreatants. The community grew but also struggled with internal differences. After a failed attempt to enlarge the facilities of the community, Mother Therese resigned her position as Superior, but continued to work in the background. She spent many years in the convent at Fourvière, and later was Superior for a short time at Paris and Tournon. Throughout her life's work, she was a humble servant and worked tirelessly to aid her fellow sisters in attaining "goodness." The primary tenet of her teaching was complete surrender to the will of God.

St. Therese Couderc

A pivotal event in her life occurred one day after Mass, when she had a mystical vision of goodness. "I saw written as in letters of gold this word 'Goodness,' which I repeated for a long while with an indescribable sweetness," she related. "I saw it, I say, written on all creatures, animate and inanimate, rational or not, all bore this name of goodness. I saw it even on the chair I was using as a kneeler. I understood then that all these creatures have a good, and all the services and help that we receive from each of them is a blessing that we owe to the goodness of our God, who has communicated to them something of his infinite goodness, so that we may meet it in every thing and everywhere."

Therese's life was dedicated solely to making Jesus Christ known and loved, and in this dedication she found utter sweetness and joy. Complete surrender brought her the greatest happiness. "Oh! If people could understand beforehand the sweetness and the peace enjoyed by those who hold nothing back from the Good God. How he communicates himself to the soul who sincerely seeks him and who knows how to surrender herself. Let them just experience it, and they will see that therein is found the true happiness which they are vainly seeking elsewhere."

The final surrender of Therese Couderc took place in September 1885, when she gave up her body after many months of suffering. She was beatified in 1951 and canonized in 1970. But a true testimonial to her life is the legacy of her mission. The Sisters of the Cenacle have spread her message of universal goodness and divine surrender throughout the world. Their mission is one of awakening and deepening faith through retreat work, spiritual direction, and religious education.

Where is the house of St. Therese Couderc?

Où est la maison de Sainte Thérèse Couderc

CHAPEL OF ST. THERESE COUDERC

Maison Thérèse Couderc

Fr. Stephen Terme founded the Convent of the Cenacle in 1826 as the Institute of the Sisters of St. Regis. Today the convent operates as the foundation house for the Nuns of the Cenacle, who have Centers around the world, with the motherhouse in Rome. Pilgrims are welcome during the day to visit, but lodging is only for French-speaking individuals or groups who are on silent directed retreats. The Chapel of St. Therese Couderc contains the incorrupt remains of the saint along with a video in French about her life. There is a souvenir shop with pictures of the saint but no books in English.

SHRINE INFORMATION

Shrine: Maison Thérèse Couderc

Address: 14 rue de la Fontaine/BP 13/07520 La Louvesc/France

Phone: 33 (0)4 75 67 83 01 **Fax:** 33 (0)4 75 67 8635

E-mail: cenacle.lalouvesc@wanadoo.fr

Website: http://ndcenacle.free.fr/ — Official website, French. www.cenaclesisters.org — Cenacle Sisters in North America.

Quiet areas for meditation: The chapel and choir adjacent to the chapel.

English spoken: Rarely. Simple English for directions, but otherwise French only.

Hours: 9AM–6:30PM

Mass: Mon–Sat 11:30AM

Feasts and festivities: June 26 — Open to the public; September 26 — Feast Day

Accessibility: Call (in French) and ask for directions. The entrance is through the garden.

Information office: The souvenir shop but little English is spoken.

Tours: None

Bookstore: The souvenir shop has pictures of the saint, prayer cards, and books in French.

Recommended books: *Therese Couderc: Woman and Saint* by Paule de Lassus, ordered through Cenacle, North American Province, 513 West Fullerton Parkway, Chicago, IL. 60614-5999, send a check for $13.85.

Lodging: There are single, double and family rooms (approximately 60 total) but only available only for those making retreats.

Directions: There is a sign in the village that points to the maison Thèrése Couderc at 14 rue de la Fontaine, and a sign on the building "Soeurs de Notre Dame du Cénacle."

Where is the house of St. Therese Couderc?
Où est la maison Thérèse Couderc?

COMING AND GOING

LA LOUVESC

Car: There is no easy way to reach La Louvesc. The mountainous roads lead to beautiful vistas, but traveling is slow, so take your time and enjoy the scenery. The town is 45 miles (72 km) east of Le Puy and 60 miles (97 km) southwest of Lyon on D532. This narrow winding road runs west from Tournon, near the #13 exit of A7-E15. We highly recommend that you purchase a detailed map before driving in these mountains, and give yourself plenty of time to traverse the area.

TOURIST INFORMATION

✤ Comité departmental de l'Ardèche/4 Cours du Palais/BP 221/07002 Privas/France Phone: 33 (0)4 75 64 04 66 Fax: 33 (0)4 75 64 23 93 E-mail: cdt07@ardeche-guide.com www.ardeche-guide.com A booklet in French titled *Pèleriner en Ardèche* is available for pilgrim hikes in the Ardèche.

❀ Office de Tourisme/rue St. Régis/07520 La Louvesc/France Phone: 33 (0)4 75 67 84 20 Fax: 33 (0)4 75 67 80 09 E-mail: ot.lalouvesc@wandadoo.fr / lalouvesc@fnotsi.net www.ardeche-verte.com.

WEBSITES

Catholic Encyclopedia www.newadvent.org — Biography of St. John Francis Regis and Religious of the Cenacle.

Catholic Online www.catholic.org/saints — Biography of St. John Francis Regis.

Cenacle Sisters of North America www.cenaclesisters.org — Biography of St. Therese Couderc and lists of the Cenacle Sisters organizations around the world.

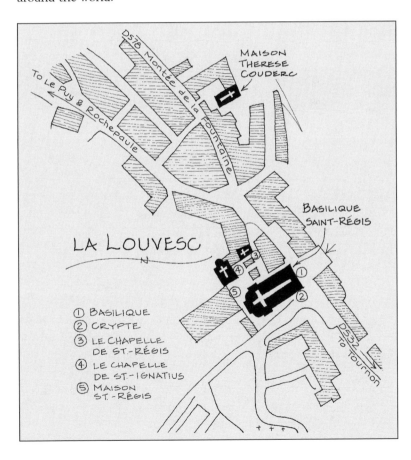

Society of Saint Pius X Canada www.sspx.ca — Biography of St. Therese Couderc, click on saints.

Soeurs de Notre Dame du Cénacle http://ndcenacle.free.fr/ — Official website of the Sisters of Our Lady of the Cenacle, French.

PLACES OF INTEREST NEAR LA LOUVESC

OUR LADY OF LE PUY
Le Puy-en-Velay

By the fifth century, Le Puy-en-Velay was well known in Europe for its shrine to the Black Virgin. In the tenth century, Le Puy became one of the four starting points for the route to Santiago de Compostela, the shrine of St. James in Spain, after Bishop Gothescalk became known as one of the first pilgrims to walk there in 951. After miraculous healings on Fever Rock (Pierre des Fièvres), an ancient Druid ceremonial stone, and a number of apparitions of the Virgin Mary, the cathedral of Notre-Dame was built in the twelfth century to receive the increasing numbers of pilgrims. Refer to the chapter on Auvergne for more information.

OUR LADY OF AY
Notre Dame d'Ay

The Sanctuary of Our Lady of Ay is 10 miles (16 km) northeast of La Louvesc, overlooking the Ay valley. The eleventh century chapel contains a late sixteenth century statue of the Black Madonna to the left of the choir. This statue has been visited by Saints John Francis Regis and Therese Couderc among others. Annual pilgrimages occur on August 15 and September 8 with Marian processions on the evenings of August 14 and September 14. Address: Our Lady of Ay (Sanctuaire Notre-Dame d'Ay)/ 07290 Saint-Romain d'Ay (Ardèche)/France Phone/Fax: 33 (0)4 75 34 58 04 Lodging: Small groups, only 15-20 people. Contact the Sanctuary: Chaplain of Our Lady of Ay/Presbytery/07290 Satillieu/France Phone/Fax: 33 (0)4 75 34 94 85.

La Salette

Population 200

The Shrine of Our Lady of La Salette rests in the beautiful French Alps in the department of Isere, at an altitude of over 6,000 feet. Just off the historic "Route Napoléan" at Corps and 46 miles south of Grenoble, snow-capped mountains and luscious fields of springtime wildflowers encircle La Salette. The Blessed Virgin Mary appeared here in 1846 to two shepherd children and six years later construction of the shrine was begun. The Valley of the Apparition, where the children saw the vision and heard the message, is just outside the Basilica. The shrine is the only point of interest in this small township, so we recommend staying overnight to have the time to visit the shrine and walk the surrounding hillsides. There are many designated trails that lead to beautiful mountain vistas and views of the shrine, and a hike with a picnic lunch makes for a very memorable experience. 250,000 pilgrims visit La Salette each year and attest to the power of Our Lady, who came to give her message to all those who will hear it, high in the Alps.

OUR LADY OF LA SALETTE

Notre Dame de La Salette - September 19, 1846

"If my Son is not to abandon you,
I am obliged to entreat him without ceasing."

The Blessed Virgin Mary has appeared for centuries to people all over the globe, and has been a herald of a wide variety of messages. Often she talks of love, hope and peace. But sometimes she comes to give dire warning to those who are retreating from their spiritual life. Her appearance in La Salette in the mid-nineteenth century brought such a warning to a world that was becoming increasingly secularized, and turning away from a life centered in Spirit.

The September days of 1846 were warm and pleasant in the alpine foothills surrounding the tiny community of Corps, and the meadows were speckled with herds of grazing cattle. Shepherds wandered the gentle terrain, keeping track of their charges and enjoying the beautiful fall weather. On this particular day, two of these young shepherds, Maximin and Mélanie, were urging their cows up the slopes of Mont sous-les Baisses, leading them to the lush grasses above.

328 THE PILGRIM'S FRANCE

Maximin Giraud, an overly active boy of eleven, played with his dog and goat as he made his way up the slopes. He was looking forward to another day away from his uncaring home and to spending time with his new friend, Mélanie. Since his mother's death when he was an infant, his father Germain had shown little affection toward him or his sister. Work for a wheelwright seemed difficult to acquire, so Germain Giraud spent his time doing odd jobs and supporting the local taverns. Maximin was happy to get away for a few days and work as a shepherd in the mountains above Corps, in the village of Albandins. He had just met Mélanie the previous day, and discovered they were both from Corps. Now he would have a companion for the final days in the mountains.

Melanie Calvat quietly made her way up the path, shooing the cows before her. At fifteen, she was much older than Maximin, but her quiet and timid ways were in stark contrast to those of the feisty boy, and she hoped she would not be pressed into too much conversation. She was the fourth of ten children, and her poor family had to send her away to seek work just so she might feed herself. She was tired of begging on the streets and enjoyed the respite of the shepherdess's life. In the cool crisp air above Corps she could find peace away from the misery and poverty of her home.

The two children followed their eight cows wandering through the grass, and made their way up the hillside. After a short break for a snack, the companions nestled into the grass for a brief nap. Mélanie awoke with a start and excitedly looked about. "Get up!" she cried to Maximin: "Let's go look for our cows. I don't know where they are!" They quickly scrambled up the hillock in search of their charges. They could certainly ill afford to lose something as valuable as a cow! Making their way over the crest, they spied their heifers peacefully feeding below. Relieved, they retreated back toward a small spring down the hillside with two stone benches perched beside it. As they approached, Mélanie looked up and saw a blazing globe of light on one of the benches. Dropping her shepherd's staff she called to Maximin, "Look over there, a light!" The boy ran to her side and together they witnessed the light slowly transform into the image of a beautiful lady sitting on the bench. Within this globe of light, they saw the woman with her head in her hands, her elbows on her knees, and tears streaming down her face.

As the lady rose, she spoke to them in French, "Come near, my children, do not be afraid. I am here to tell you great news." The beautiful lady of light was clothed as a woman of the mountainous region. Her long dress hung to her feet, with an apron wrapped around her waist, and she had a shawl draped across her shoulders, tied in the back. Roses ringed her head like a crown, bordered her shawl and adorned her shoes. A heavy chain was also around her shoulders and a finer chain encircled her neck, from which hung a glowing crucifix, with a hammer on one side and tongs on the other. Certainly the children had never seen a lady such as this before.

The children gazed in amazement as the glowing figure spoke to them. She spoke of her son, and how she was trying to restrain his wrath, because the people were not obeying the holy laws. Working on Sunday and swearing were forbidden, yet these were common practices among the people, and this was making her son unhappy. "If my people do not obey, I shall be compelled to loose the arm of my Son. It is so heavy that I can no longer restrain it…. I have given you six days

Statue of the Apparition at La Salette

to work. The seventh I have reserved for myself, yet no one will give it to me…. The cart drivers cannot swear without bringing in my Son's name. These are the two things which make my son's arm so heavy."

Continuing to address the children, the lady of light spoke of a famine and how the famine would persist as long as the people lived in sin and did not respect her wishes. She spoke to the young ones both in French and in their native dialect, so they could clearly understand her message. "Do you say your prayers well, my children?" she asked in dialect. When their reply was negative, she responded: "Ah, my children, it is very important to do so, at night and in the morning. When you don't have time, at least say an "Our Father" and a "Hail Mary," and when you can, say more."

Maximin Giraud and Melanie Calvat

She went on to talk of the importance of attending Mass and respecting the Sabbath, and then spoke more of famine. Speaking directly to Maximin, she reminded him of an incident in the previous year when he had seen spoiled wheat while traveling with his father. "It is very true, Madame," Maximin replied.

Finally, she addressed them both in French, "Well, children, you will make it known to all my people." Maximin stepped aside to allow her to pass, and she proceeded to cross the brook and climb the hill before her. Without turning to face them, she repeated, "Please, children, be sure to make this known to all my people."

As she walked up the ravine, the lady began to rise in the air, and the children chased after her. At the top of the hill, she rose five feet above the ground and gazed upward towards heaven. Still enveloped in light, the luminescent figure began to melt into that light, starting with her head, and moving down to her feet. Maximin attempted to leap up and touch the roses of her feet as she was dissolving from sight, but gained nothing in his grasp. She was gone.

After the light vanished, Mélanie was first to speak, "It was perhaps a great saint!" Maximin responded, "If only we had known, we would have asked her to bring us with her."

The children did not comprehend their vision, and returned to the village of Les Albandins to tell their story to their neighbors. The next day was Sunday, and the children were taken to the local priest who listened intently to their story, and immediately believed them. He tearfully spoke of the vision in his sermon, and the story of the apparition spread from there like wildfire. Upon hearing of the story, the mayor of Corps went to Les Albandins to interrogate the children, but only Mélanie remained, for Maximin had returned to his home in Corps. The mayor talked with Mélanie all afternoon and attempted to trap her into contradicting herself, but she remained firm and exacting in her retelling of the experience. When the mayor endeavored to bribe her into remaining silent about the event, Mélanie replied, "The Lady told me to say it, and I will say it!" That evening, Mélanie dictated her story to three local men who dutifully wrote down her testimony word for word, then signed the document, swearing to its authenticity.

Five years of investigation passed before the Bishop of Grenoble issued a doctorial pronouncement regarding the apparition. He wrote, "We judge that the apparition of the Blessed Virgin to two shepherds on September 19, 1846 on a mountain of the Alpine chain, situated in the parish of La Salette, of the archpresbytery of Corps, bears all the characteristics of truth, and that the faithful have grounds for believing it to be undeniable and certain." Pilgrims from all over the world began flocking to the remote site and the construction of the shrine was initiated the following year. Through the years, La Salette has remained a constant source of inspiration to countless pilgrims, still attracting many thousands of faithful each year to personally experience the message of the Blessed Virgin.

But what became of Mélanie and Maximin? Unlike St. Bernadette, who also witnessed the living presence of the Virgin Mary, the children of La Salette did not lead particularly saintly lives. Maximin fell under the spell of several unscrupulous people who attempted to use his notoriety for their own financial gain and advancement, but found little success. Unable to commit to a religious life, Maximin wandered the continent, taking on a variety of jobs, and finally returned to Corps in 1875. Following a visit to the site of the new shrine at La Salette, he died at the age of thirty-nine.

Mélanie longed for a devout lifestyle, and made several attempts to live as a reclusive nun in different Carmelite monasteries, but was unable to deal with the attention given her as a result of the apparition. Making her way in the secular world, she began to espouse her own prophecies and mystical dogmas, and unsuccessfully tried to develop a personal following. She, too, returned to visit La Salette in her later years, but soon departed for Bari, Italy, where she died in 1904. Here she was buried under a marble column with a bas-relief of the Blessed Virgin escorting the little shepherdess into heaven.

THE SANCTUARY OF OUR LADY OF LA SALETTE
Sanctuaire de Notre Dame de La Salette

After the apparition of the Virgin Mary was deemed authentic in 1851, the Church announced in 1852 the construction of a shrine on the mountain. The new church was completed in 1865 and consecrated as a Basilica in 1879. The entry to the Basilica is flanked by two tall towers, which rise like the mountains of the region. The interior is modern in feeling for there is limited ornamentation. The central nave is bordered by two rows of Byzantine columns supporting the Roman vaulted ceiling. A mosaic of Christ crowns the apse, at the termination of the nave. The transept exhibits three medallions that represent the stages of the apparition, and the stained glass windows along the side isles tell other stories of Christ and the Virgin Mary. Ten small side chapels were added to the basilica in 1894 and form these side aisles. As you enter the Basilica, there is a door to the right that leads downstairs to a small museum. Here, the history of La Salette is chronicled with pictures and memorabilia. The Missionaries and Sisters of Our Lady of La Salette maintain and operate the Shrine.

Just outside of the Basilica, you will see the Valley of the Apparition and a path that follows in the footsteps of the two shepherd children and the "Beautiful Lady." Start at the Virgin's Fountain where you will find a spring that was present at the time of the apparition. Walk toward the Way of the Cross and the bronze statues, installed in 1864, that represent the apparition's three stages. The first group of statues includes one of Our Lady crying with her head in her hands, grieving for the spiritual famine of her people. In the second group, called the

"Meeting," Our Lady is relaying her message to the children. Then, up the hill, toward the Basilica, the third group is called the "Assumption" and depicts Our Lady's departure, at the location marked by Maximin shortly after the apparition.

Leading from the plaza in front of the Basilica are several hiking paths that wind gently up the sides of the mountains. One path leads to the top of the adjacent promontories, while another leads to the cemetery and oratory chapel. This oratory was first built in 1857 on the spot where the statue of the Virgin of the Assumption now stands, but was moved to its present location in 1864, when the statues were installed. A statue that previously

Sanctuaire de Notre Dame de La Salette

stood on top of the oratory is now inside the structure. Fr. Jean Berthier (1840-1908), founder of the Missionaries of the Holy Family is buried to the left of the chapel. On the right side is the vault of the La Salette missionaries.

The Basilica is attached to a large lodging complex with 250 rooms, cafeterias, bookstore, and meeting rooms. Connected to the lodging on the main floor there is a modern "meeting chapel" built in 1995 for pilgrims to celebrate Mass in their own language. Hundreds of pilgrims come with tour groups, but many come individually and in small groups. We suggest you stay at least one night to have time to visit the site of the apparition and the Basilica, and climb the surrounding hills, perhaps with a picnic lunch. Two nights would be more restful, leaving a full day to enjoy this beautiful shrine in the French Alps.

Where is the site of the apparition?
Où est le lieu de l'apparition?

SHRINE INFORMATION

Shrine: Sanctuary of Our Lady of La Salette (Sanctuaire de Notre Dame de la Salette)

Address: 38970 La Salette/France

Sanctuary: Phone: 33 (0)4 76 30 00 11 Fax: None

Shrine Lodging: Phone: 33 (0)4 76 30 32 90 Fax: 33 (0)4 76 30 03 65

E-mail: infos@nd-la-salette.com or reception@nd-lasalette.com

Website: www.nd-la-salette.com — Official website: Scheduled events under "Pèlerinage." French.

Quiet areas for meditation: The shrine is large with many groups of pilgrims coming and going, but it is generally quiet. The atmosphere in the Valley of the Apparition is typically reverent and peaceful. The modern "Meeting Chapel" connected to the lodging on the first floor is usually a place of activity. In good weather, a hike up the mountain on designated paths leads to the quietest places for meditation.

English spoken: Occasionally

Hours: Basilica daily: 7AM–11PM; Lodging reception desk daily: 8AM–9PM Summer; 8:30AM–7PM Winter. Open all year; weather permitting, except closed October 31 through November 30.

Mass: Summer: Sunday 7AM, 10:15, 11:45, 4PM; Weekly 7AM, 10:15; Winter: Sunday 10:45AM; Weekly 6PM; Eucharistic procession every Sunday outside at 2PM, followed by adoration inside the Basilica; Marian procession every evening at 8:30PM from July to October.

Feasts and festivities: August 15 — Assumption of Our Lady; September 8 — Birthday of Our Lady; September 19 — Feast Day of Our Lady of La Salette; Check out their website www.nd-la-salette.com French, under "Pèlerinage, Actualités and Horaires des messes" for festivities planned for every month and hours of celebrations.

Accessibility: There is a special lift for wheelchairs, and an elevator.

Information office: The reception desk at the hotel also serves as the information desk for the shrine. Money can be exchanged at the hotel. Open 9AM–12, 2PM–5:30. Closed Sunday.

Tours: When you make your reservation, arrange a guided tour in English at that time. A video in English is shown in Salle Notre Dame.

Bookstore: The bookstore is off the main lobby of the Hotel.

Recommended books: *A Short Guide to Notre-Dame de La Salette* by Albert Hari is available at the shrine and describes what to visit. The book *A Grace Called La Salette* by J. Jaouen is available from the Missionaries of La Salette in Hartford, CT on their website, www.lasalette.org.

Lodging: The Sanctuary of Our Lady of la Salette (Sanctuarie de Notre Dame de la Salette) is a 250-room facility that accommodates up to 650 pilgrims. See contact information above.

Directions: From Corps, La Salette is approximately 10 miles (16 km), 25 minutes northeast. Follow signs to "Le Sanctuaire."

COMING AND GOING

LA SALETTE

Car: From Grenoble, take Route N75, then N85 south 46 miles (74 km) to Corps. From Gap, take the same N85 north 33 miles (53 km). From Corps, follow signs to "Le Sanctuaire" (The Sanctuary) on D212C. La Salette (not the same as the hamlet of La Salette-Fallavaux) is approximately 10 miles (16 km), or 25 minutes, from Corps. In winter, the route is kept clear of snow, except in extremely bad weather.

Train: The nearest train stations are in Grenoble 45 miles (72 km) or Gap 33 miles (53 km) www.ter-sncf.com/UK/Default_uk.htm SNCF for train info in English.

Taxis from Grenoble train station: Phone: 33 (0)6 08 42 32 33 for advanced reservations.

Bus: In summer an early morning bus leaves Grenoble for La Salette. Other times of the year, the bus ends in Corps. You must then take a taxi the ten miles to the sanctuary. On the homepage of the shrine website, click on the bus schedule (Horaires de car) from Grenoble and Gap. It is in French, but you can figure it out, or translate it at www.systranbox.com. From Grenoble to Corps, take bus line 4100, then from Corps to Salette VFD 401. To contact coach lines: SCAL 33 (0)4 76 87 90 31 and VFD 33 (0)4 76 47 77 77.

TOURIST INFORMATION

✳ Comité Departemental du Tourisme Isere Phone: 33 (0)4 76 54 34 36 Fax: 33 (0)4 76 51 57 19 Email: informations.cdt@isere-tourisme.com www.isere-tourisme.com.

✳ Grenoble Tourist Information Centre/14, rue de la République/Grenoble/France Phone: 33 (0)4 76 42 41 41 Email: welcome@grenoble-isere.info www.grenoble-isere-tourisme.com.

WEBSITES

Missionaries of La Salette www.lasalette.org — Hartford, CT, USA 1 860 956-8870 Email: asalettecom@aol.com.

New Advent Catholic Encyclopedia www.newadvent.org/cathen/09008b.htm — History of La Salette.

Sanctuary of Our Lady of La Salette www.nd-la-salette.com — Official website of the shrine, French. Check under "Pèlerinage, Actualités and Horaires des messes" for festivities planned for every month and hours of celebrations. Translate using www.systransoft.com.

PLACES OF INTEREST NEAR LA SALETTE

OUR LADY OF LAUS
Notre Dame du Laus

The Blessed Virgin appeared in the Alps centuries before the apparition at La Salette. In 1664 she appeared to the seventeen year-old shepherdess Benoîte Rencurel in a pasture near the village of St. Étienne, and subsequently, at a small chapel in Laus. Benoite was blessed with "an incalculable number" of visions of Mary over the next fifty-four years of her life, and lived as a devout Dominican Tertiary. Many pilgrims came to this remote village during her lifetime, and received blessings and healings. Benoîte Rencurel was proclaimed "Venerable Servant of God" in 1872, and the Basilica was proclaimed a minor

Basilica in 1893. 45,000 pilgrims find their way here each year and experience the deep blessings of this secluded site. There are no "tourist" amenities at Notre Dame du Laus except for pilgrimage housing for 250 and a small bookstore.

Sanctuary Notre Dame du Laus/05130 Saint-Étienne-du-Laus/France Phone: 33 (0)4 92 50 30 73 Fax: 33 (0)4 92 50 90 77 E-mail: sanctuary@notre-dame-du-laus.com. Lodging: accueil@notre-dame-du-laus.com Website: www.notre-dame-du-laus.com — Official website French; www.ewtn.com/library/MARY/LAUS.htm — Description of Shrine in English from Eternal Word Television Network.

Directions: Shrine is 13 miles (20 km) southeast of Gap on Route D942 and is accessible by car or hotel shuttle from the Gap SNCF railway station.

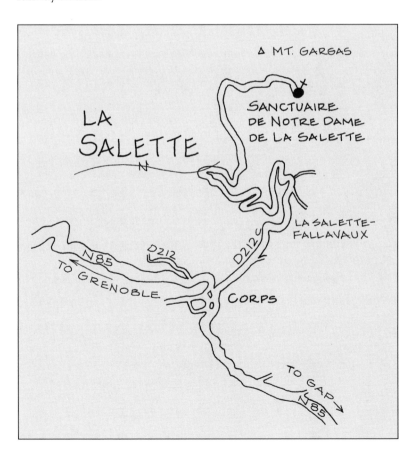

A Guide to Meditating with the Saints

PRACTICE BEFORE YOU GO

Meditation is best practiced in a peaceful environment. A peaceful environment is usually necessary for meditation. Unfortunately, with their many distractions, the shrines are not always the most suitable environments for focusing inwardly. But, with practice, you will learn to shut out most external disturbances. You also do not need to visit saints' shrines to experience their grace. In fact, you should practice before going on pilgrimage by meditating on the saints you will be visiting. Because the large shrines are filled with many pilgrims and tourists, you will sometimes feel like you have connected to a saint better at home than halfway around the world in a noisy environment. Each way of experiencing the saints is valid. Even with a lot of noise, we have often felt the saints' special presence pierce through the commotion and move us to tears by their sweetness.

It is a good idea to start meditating at home for short periods of time (five to ten minutes), and then lengthen the time as your body becomes accustomed to sitting quietly for longer periods (half hour to an hour). As with any new behavior, it is a good idea to form the habit of meditating at the same time of day or night. Good times to meditate are upon awakening, before lunch, after work, or before retiring at night. Make the time convenient for yourself, and when you won't be disturbed.

When you are ready to meditate, find a quiet room, unplug the phone, and use headphones or earplugs if your surroundings are noisy. Dress comfortably or loosen your belt, and use a light blanket for warmth if needed. Sit on a straight-backed chair with your spine upright, and away from the back of the chair. Experiment with using a small pillow under your sit bones, to slightly raise and tilt the pelvis forward. Your feet should be flat on the floor. Put your hands, palms up, resting on the crease between the thighs and the hip. This will help keep your shoulders back and chest open.

If you are accustomed to sitting on a cushion on the floor, or you have special needs, experiment and choose the sitting position that works best for you. On pilgrimage, you will mostly be sitting on hard wooden benches or standing. So, even though you might not think that sitting with your spine straight is comfortable now, you will have less creature comforts at the shrines. That is why sitting for longer and longer periods will train your body to be accustomed to meditation, and after awhile it will not protest so much.

RELAX

When you are comfortable, close your eyes and mentally relax each body part, slowly, one by one. Focus on relaxing your head, neck, face, and jaw and so on, all the way down through your body to your toes. You will be surprised how much tension you hold in the different muscles.

If you find it difficult to relax, do some yogic stretching that involves deep breathing and slow, conscious movements. A simple stretch is bending forward from the waist while standing, until your upper body is hanging loosely with neck and shoulders relaxed. Continue to breathe and relax a bit more with each exhalation, allowing your head and shoulders to sink toward the floor. Then, on a final exhalation, slowly return to standing, bringing your arms up over your head and slightly back with your palms together, bending

St. Remi Basilica side chapel in Reims

the spine just a few inches in the opposite direction of the forward bend. Return to standing with your arms down at your side. Only go as far as is comfortable, never forcing the movement or bouncing.

Another easy technique for relaxation is to take a deep inhalation, hold the breath and tense the entire body. Then release the tension by forcing the breath out on the exhalation. Do this two or three times. When you feel relaxed, return to sitting upright with eyes closed.

In order to meditate, the body must be relaxed, or it will distract you with all its aches and pains. But you don't want to be so relaxed that you fall asleep. That is why it is important that you remain in an upright position with your spine straight, shoulders slightly back and chin parallel to the floor. In the beginning, you might spend more time relaxing than focusing inwardly, but eventually you will be able to develop the habit of relaxation immediately upon sitting.

FOCUS INWARD

Sitting in an upright position, begin to be aware of your breathing by focusing on your breath going in and out of the lungs. Follow the breath from the nostrils into your lungs, and then follow the breath

out again. Instead of just breathing from the top of your chest, your chest and stomach should move in and out together, stretching the diaphragm. If your stomach is not moving in and out, practice breathing into your stomach by gently pushing it out on the inhale. Eventually, your breaths will become longer and deeper, similar to when you are sleeping, which in turn will help you to relax even more. Check in with your body from time to time to see if it is relaxed, with a

St. Joseph's miraculous spring in Cotignac

straight spine. If you continue to be tense, imagine breathing into that area of tension, and letting go of the tension on the exhale. Then return your attention to the breath.

Another simple technique to help you focus is to inhale through the nose to a count that is comfortable for you (6-8 or 8-10), hold the breath for the same count, and then exhale through the nose on the same count. Continue immediately with your next inhalation. You can practice this three or more times.

As you continue to watch the breath, you are learning how to focus. It seems like a very simple exercise and that not much is happening. But as you try to meditate on your breath for any length of time, you will notice how much your mind can wander. This can be frustrating in the beginning because the mind, like a wild horse, does not want to be tamed. But, with patience, and most of all practice, you will begin to notice that you are more peaceful and calm. Each time you catch your mind going hither and yon, gently bring it back to your breathing.

OPEN YOUR HEART

We have all had the feeling of openheartedness when we see a smiling baby, a playful puppy, or a beautiful sunset. This feeling is in us all the time, and we can practice in meditation opening up to our inner sweetness and joy. Because of the hurts and traumas we have experienced in life, our hearts may have protective layers defending us against further pain. Through meditation and feeling the unconditional love of the Divine, the heart will begin to relax more. This might mean that tears of pain could flow, releasing old wounds. This is one of the great benefits of meditation. Our hearts learn to expand instead of contract, and we become more open and loving.

Humans want to be loved more than anything else, and when the heart contains so much pain, it is unable to receive the love we desire. The unconditional love of the Divine heals all wounds. The saints are good examples of how to let go of our attachments to the past and feel the presence of God in the present. Visualize offering your pain to the Divine on the exhalation, and then allow unconditional love to replenish your heart on the inhalation. Continue imagining the Source of all Love filling you completely. Eventually, your tears will turn from those of grief to tears of gratitude. The heart will be touched with so much love your pain will eventually melt into joy.

After you are calm, relaxed and focused, visualize your heart open and loving. Imagine this love expanding out in concentric circles beyond your body to include at first your loved ones, then your community, and eventually the world. Breathe naturally and be receptive to what feelings or intuitions come.

THE SPIRITUAL EYE OR CHRIST CENTER

As you become more focused in meditation, you may see some form of light when your eyes are closed. Within each of us is a spark of the Divine, and inherent in this spark is the ability to feel connected to the Divine light. In order to perceive this light, we need to practice bringing our focus inward toward the spine and upward toward this

inner light. We can do this by focusing on what is called the spiritual eye, third eye, or Christ Center—located at the point between the eyebrows. You see this portrayed in pictures of the saints with their eyes lifted upwards. The Eastern saints are sometimes represented with a ray of light radiating from their spiritual eye. Jesus explained this technique when he said, "If therefore thine eye be single, thy whole body shall be full of light." (Matthew 6:22)

Candles in Les Jacobins, Toulouse

With eyes closed, turn your eyes slightly upward, focused about an arm's length away, but looking through the point between the eyebrows. Do not strain or cross your eyes; your eyes should feel comfortable and relaxed. As your practice deepens, you may feel sensation or a slight tingling at the point between the eyebrows. At some point, you may begin to see light at the spiritual eye, and eventually a five-pointed silver star in a field of blue, surrounded by a golden halo. This representation is apparent to people of all faiths. Some people see this light early on in their meditation practices and others never see it. It is not necessary to see this light to feel a Divine connection, so don't be concerned if you are not able to. It is not an overt sign of the depth of your spirituality. Focus on the spiritual eye as often as you can, especially while practicing all your meditation techniques.

Bring your attention now to the air passing through your nostrils, and focus on it flowing to the point between the eyebrows. It might help to put your finger at the point between the eyebrows at first to help you visualize the air reaching its destination. As you do this, repeat silently two or three words that have spiritual meaning to you. For example, on the inhale mentally repeat "Jesus" and on the out breath "Christ" or "A" – "men" or "I am" – "Spirit." Practice this for several minutes, or as long as you want, always bringing your attention back to the spiritual eye if it wanders.

FEEL THE SAINTS' PRESENCE

By using the above techniques of relaxation, focusing inward and opening, we are now more receptive to the saints' blessings. When you are open and calm it is a good time to pray to the saints, asking to feel their presence. Some qualities you might experience when feeling the saints' presence are joy, sweetness, unconditional love, or peace. These are actually manifestations of God's consciousness within us. Imagine that you are absorbing these qualities into every cell of your body. Open your mind, body and soul, absorbing the gift of grace that you have prayed for. Try not to let your mind wander and miss out on this opportunity. This special grace can disappear in a flash, and you will want to take advantage of each moment, bathing in the rays of the saints' blessings. Then hold on to the experience, carrying it with you as you go about your day. Any time, anywhere, by closing your eyes, and focusing on the spiritual eye, you can recall the particular qualities you have felt.

ADDITIONAL TIPS

In the beginning of practicing meditation, the mind wants to stay active, so it helps to have some additional tools to train the mind to maintain focus.

1. Listening to, or singing, quiet devotional songs helps to open the heart and invoke the presence of the Divine before meditation.

2. Creating an altar with pictures of your favorite saints or holy ones will assist you in focusing. Look into the eyes of the saints, and feel that they are sitting in front of you. Talk out loud or silently to them, recite prayers, mantras, or the rosary when your mind is distracted. If you are unfamiliar with praying, just converse with the saints, speaking to them from your heart: "I want to know you," or "Show me how to love God as you do." Then, close your eyes and bring your attention inward and upward, imagining the picture of one of the saints at the point between your eyebrows, the spiritual eye.

3. Another useful tool is to create a personal relationship with a saint. As you read about the saints' lives in this book, feel as if you know them and are familiar with what kind of people they were. What aspects of their experiences can you personally relate to? You might sense that a particular saint seems like a father, mother, grandmother or grandfather to you. Then, as you meditate on them, you will begin to know their unique vibration. When you visit their shrines, you will find it easier to tune into their vibration because it will already be familiar.

4. It is generally not a good idea to meditate after a meal, when your body is preoccupied with digestion. Better to wait at least a half hour, or up to three hours, depending on how big the meal is. Caffeinated beverages speed up the body and mind, and are not conducive to a calm, meditative, mental state. We once made the mistake of having a strong cappuccino before we visited a shrine. Unfortunately, we were too wound up to focus inwardly and ended up leaving. Depending on how you react to caffeine, you might want to wait a half hour to an hour after consuming the stuff.

5. When visiting the shrines, try to look for quiet places to sit and meditate. In the description of the shrines at the end of each chapter,

we make note of suitable places available for quiet contemplation. If one is not available, you won't regret bringing earplugs to help block out most sound.

For the purposes of experiencing pilgrimage, you will need just the basic meditation techniques described above. More in-depth methods are taught in many excellent books on meditation, some of which are listed in the resources section in the appendix. For further instruction, please refer to them when you are ready to move beyond these simple techniques. Joining a meditation group can be helpful not only because it is easier to learn to meditate with others, but also because a good group leader can guide you through the learning process. Meditation groups can be found through churches, spiritual bookstores and on the Internet.

TYPICAL MEDITATION ROUTINE

1. Find a quiet room where you will not be disturbed.

2. Do several stretches to release tension in your body, or inhale, tense and exhale the tension.

3. Sit on a chair with your spine erect and not touching the back of the chair. Your chin should be parallel to the floor, feet flat on the floor, and hands, palms facing upwards, resting on the crease between your thighs and hip. Begin with a prayer from your own heart.

4. Close your eyes, breathe naturally, and check your body from head to toe for tension. Breathe into any areas of tension, relaxing the tension on the exhalation. Mentally relax by letting go of all worries, thoughts and distractions.

5. Inhale slowly through the nose to a count that is comfortable, hold the breath for the same count, exhale for the same count. Repeat for several rounds.

6. Follow the breath entering the nostrils, traveling into the lungs, and out again. The relaxation steps 1 – 6 should take about three to five minutes. With eyes closed, turn your eyes upward, looking through the point between your eyebrows (spiritual eye). Your focus should be fixed about an arm's length away and relaxed. Gaze at this point throughout your meditation.

7. Follow the air passing through the nose, to the point between the eyebrows, then back out again. Repeat "A – men," or other words that have spiritual meaning to you, on the inhalation and exhalation. Do this technique for half of your remaining meditation time.

8. When you feel calm and peaceful, invoke the presence of the saint by asking: "St. _____, help me to feel your presence and the grace of God that flows through you. Bless me and (others you are praying for), by guiding us on our spiritual path." Or pray in your tradition through the saint you have called upon. After invoking their presence, sit in the silence and absorb the peace and grace they are sharing with you. This should constitute the final half of your meditation time. End with a prayer of gratitude, bringing the peace and inner calmness of meditation into your activities.

Chapel of the Heart in Ars

Tips for Traveling in France

Traveling in France is simple because the language barrier is not as difficult as it was years ago and transportation is very good. Almost everyone speaks a little English, and where they don't, you can use a good phrase book to get by. We recommend Rick Steves' *French Phrase Book & Dictionary* that has phonetic spellings. Pronouncing French can be a challenge, so the burden is on the traveler to listen to some language CDs to become familiar with the language. But, with a small amount of study, anyone can travel around France easily and enjoy this beautiful country and its friendly people.

The French are formal in their greetings and always say either "Bonjour Madame/Monsieur" "Good day Ma'am/Sir." or "Bonsoir Madame/Monsieur" "Good Evening Ma'am/Sir." These phrases will get you far, along with the obligatory "please – s'il vous plaît" and "thank you – merci."

To reiterate what we said in the beginning of this book, this book is not intended to be a complete travel reference with general tourist advice. We suggest you purchase a guidebook that is published yearly; giving all the pertinent and up-to-date information you will need to plan your trip. There are many excellent guidebooks that cater to different budgets and interests, so visit a bookstore with a large travel section and purchase a book that appeals to your brand of travel.

There are some issues to be aware of in France, and one is cigarette smoke. It seems that almost everyone smokes in France, and they are only recently starting non-smoking campaigns. So, until massive changes are made (don't hold your breath), assume that restaurants will be smoky, even with non-smoking sections. If the weather is good, choose outdoor cafes, or buy picnic food to eat elsewhere. Otherwise, there are only minor quirks, like sometimes getting only one bath towel for two people, "runny" omelets, and a fondness for wax museums!

France is divided into regions, departments and then cantons and communes. There are tourist offices (Office de Tourisme) for each region and department. In travel literature, some regions are combined, for example, Upper and Lower Normandy are usually called Normandy. Paris is divided into twenty "arrondissements" or districts, and you will quickly learn to ask for these numbers in locating addresses.

The tips below will help prepare you for some of the differences in France. The French people love to talk and will attempt to include you in their conversation, even with limited English. If you ask if they speak English, their typical reply is "a little," but when they hear your French, they will be conversing in very good English in no time (unless they really don't speak any English).

TRAVEL IN FRANCE

Driving is not difficult if you stay out of the big cities and learn the basic rules of driving in France. It is important to learn what the French traffic signs mean. Most travel guides will provide these or you can do a search on the Internet for "drive France." The toll roads (autoroutes à péage) are expensive but worth it if you are doing a lot of driving. They also have convenient places to eat at the rest stops along the way. Some small cities do not allow parking inside the city except for unloading luggage. In this case, there are usually ample parking lots outside the city. When making your lodging reservations ask about parking and how much it costs.

It is essential to buy a good map of France. If you are traveling by car, you need a detailed map that shows all the small roads and highways. The maps provided by the rental agencies are fine for major roads, but if you want to venture into the countryside to find some of the small shrines described in this book, you will need a more detailed map. We like Michelin motoring or road atlases that are spiral bound, because they are easy to use in the car. Even though the *France Michelin Atlas* is huge, it is invaluable if you are doing a lot of driving. The foldout maps are good too, but we found that they became torn, and are difficult to fold up in the car, though they are adequate for short driving trips.

Locals having fun in the Jardins de l'Europe in Annecy

When looking for a city in the index of a map be aware that sometimes a city's common name is a shortened version, for example, "Ars." In your map index, there are many cities with the name Ars, like Ars-sur-Formans. That is why we use the long version of city names for easy reference. Look for a map store in your yellow pages, major bookstores, or do a search for maps on the Internet. Here are a few sites: www.maps.com / www.viamichelin.com / www.randmcnally.com.

Trains are a good way to travel in France, except when you want to visit small towns that are not on the train routes. Research your transportation options for out-of-the-way towns on your itinerary. The French National Railway is SNFC and they also operate the TGV trains, which are the high-speed trains (185mph/300km). If you are traveling by train, make sure the map you get shows train routes.

In Paris, the RER train serves the outlying suburbs and regions of Paris and has fewer stops than the Metro, which is the most efficient way to get around within Paris itself. We highly recommend getting a Metro map. BE FOREWARNED! Paris is notorious for pickpockets and you are tempting fate if you don't keep your valuables safe in a money belt or security wallet that can be worn under your clothes. This means that women do not use purses and men do not put wallets in pockets. It might not feel stylish, but you can relax and enjoy the sites knowing your money and passport are safe.

Local buses usually originate at a town's train station. Some bus lines are included in your rail pass because they are run by SNCF. Inquire at the local tourist information office for bus schedules.

Getting around the cities of France is a bit of a challenge. In France, street names often change every block, so finding a specific address can take research. Maps are essential but do not always show all the street name changes. You can save time wandering around looking for a shrine by getting a town or city map before you arrive in the city. We have included many maps in this book, but a greater level of detail will be necessary. Contact the local tourist offices of the cities you will be visiting, and request a city map at least three months before you leave. Or, upon your arrival, go directly to the local tourist office and get a local map. Then you will have a map of France, the city, and the map in this book for locating the shrine.

When traveling, always give yourself enough time to get lost. Even with a map, you will find one-way streets going in the wrong direction, or there will be signs showing the way to a shrine that suddenly leaves you guessing at the next crossroads. Take a deep breath and relax— you're on pilgrimage! If you learn any French before you go, learn to ask directions and be able to understand the reply. You can always ask, "Où est la Sanctuaire…(insert the saint or shrine's name)?"

LANGUAGE

English is spoken quite often in the big cities, but in the smaller towns it will be less likely. The French people are very helpful, but it is worth the effort to try to speak their language.

Always be prepared with an English/French phrasebook. We provide some French phrases in the book, but you will need an English/French phrase book to learn how to pronounce the words. Even better, it is a good idea to listen to language CD's before you leave to accustom your ear to the French language.

LODGING

Staying in monasteries and convents is a wonderful way to make a trip to France affordable. You must understand though, these are not hotels, and they do not have the amenities of a hotel. The rooms are plain and simple, and there is no room service. However, we have found them to be clean, safe, and affordable. You can share a bathroom down the hall or sometimes they have private bathrooms for an additional cost. The Sisters or Brothers are very sweet and add to the quiet ambiance of the lodging. Some monasteries/convents are just for people on spiritual retreat and we mention this when applicable. Most monasteries have a curfew, so ask about this when you check in. If you are not back in time, you will be locked out for the night! Curfews are usually late enough to accommodate most pilgrims' lifestyles. See Resources in the Appendix for books and websites on lodging in monasteries and convents in France.

We found Laundromats easy to find in most cities in France. Ask where you staying: "Où est laverie?"

Church Etiquette

When Mass is being conducted, please be respectful. Do not walk around looking at the artwork, talking loudly or taking pictures. The churches are usually owned by the government in France and administered by a Catholic Order. So, many churches feel more like museums, but they continue to be a house of God for the local people and all due respect is appreciated. Talking should be kept to a minimum, and whispering is preferred. When you light a votive candle, it is expected that you make a monetary offering. Also, please turn off your cell phone before entering a church.

Hours of Operation

Some churches are closed for lunch from 12PM-2. Check the hours in this book before heading out. Know what holidays occur during your visit; as listed below. Many businesses are closed on Monday or close early. If your itinerary is tight, you will need to check before you go, or at least upon arrival in town, so you won't be disappointed. The month of August is vacation for most French people, and many places are closed or have limited hours.

National Holidays

The national holidays in France are: January 1, New Year's Day; Easter Monday; April 30, Great Prayer Day; May 8, VE Day; July 14, Bastille Day; August 15, Feast of the Assumption; November 1, All Saints' Day; November 11, Armistice Day; December 25, Christmas Day. Dates are listed day first, then month and year, as in 15/08/04 for August 15, 2004.

CHURCH CELEBRATIONS

All Cathedrals with the name "Notre Dame" celebrate the Feast Days honoring the Blessed Virgin Mary: March 25, Feast of the Annunciation; July 1, Feast of the Visitation; August 15, Feast of the Assumption; September 8, The Nativity of the Blessed Virgin Mary.

TELEPHONES/FAXES/EMAILS

The country code of France is 33. The first zero of a phone number is used when calling within the country, but is omitted when calling from outside France. In this book we listed phone numbers with parentheses around the zero to remind you to omit it if you are calling from outside France. For example: 33 (0)4 63 45 54 23. For calls within France, use your own phone card or buy a phone card (télécarte or carte téléphonique) at local newsstands (tabacs), train stations, or post offices.

Almost all the shrines have an email address, but there are a few that don't. When there is not an email, you can fax. Whether calling, emailing or faxing ask if they speak English (parlez vous Englais?). If they don't, you will have to communicate in French. Travel guides often list the questions you need to make reservations in French, either over the phone or in writing. You will quickly learn the French words for making reservations and get to practice speaking French. If they don't understand you, just say, "Merci, Au revoir—Thank you, good bye."

Internet cafes are in almost every town, but they are called "cyber cafes." Ask: "Is there a cyber cafe near here? (Y a-t-il un cyber café près d'ici?) Cyber is pronounced "see-behr." Some travel guides, like Lets Go, list Internet cafes. Be aware that the Internet cafes are very smoky, although we found one in Toulouse that was smoke-free. Also consider that sending emails back home will take longer because the keyboards in Europe are different.

MONEY

When the Euro was first issued the exchange rate was close to the U.S. dollar, so it was pretty easy to understand the cost of things. But now, the Euro is worth about 20% more than the dollar. For current exchange rates and a currency converter for the Euro, check out the website www.xe.com. The French use a comma as a decimal point (2,50 = 2.50) and ones, fours and sevens are written differently.

We found out the hard way about sending items purchased in

France back to the United States. If it is over $200, you will be charged by customs. We were charged $75, so what we thought was a deal was not. If you plan to ship items home, check with customs regulations before you leave. US Customs: www.customs.gov/travel/travel.htm.

TOURIST INFORMATION

Tourist information offices in France are most often called "Office de Tourisme," but they can also be named "Bureau de Tourisme," "Syndicat d'Initiative," or "Information Touristique." The Official Government Tourist Offices for France are called "Maison de la France" www.franceguide.com. You can contact an office in your area below:

New York City, USA
Phone: 1 410 286 8310 Fax: 1 212 838 78 55
Email: info.us@francequide.com

Miami, USA
Phone: 1 305 373 81 77 Fax : 1 305 373 58 28
E-mail : info.miami@franceguide.com

Los Angeles, USA
Phone: 1 310 271 66 65 Fax : 1 310 276 28 35
E-mail : info.losangeles@franceguide.com

Chicago, USA
Phone: 1 312 751 78 00 Fax : 1 312 337 63 39
E-mail : info.chicago@franceguide.com

London, UK
Phone: 090 68 244 123 Fax : 020 74 936 594
E-mail : info.uk@franceguide.com

Montreal, Canada
Phone: 514 876 9881 Fax : 514 845 48 68
E-mail : canada@franceguide.com

VEGETARIANS

If you travel without doing any research, you might think it is hard being vegetarian in France. But, when you use the books and websites we list in the Resource section, you can locate vegetarian restaurants in most major cities.

We include this topic because we are vegetarians. We see that more people are interested in learning how to eat well in general, but when traveling it can be more of a challenge. Fortunately, the French always have good salads (salade), bread (baguette) and cheese (fromage). There are also ethnic foods in the larger cities, like Chinese and Indian, that serve many vegetarian entrees. The typical French menu does not usually have meatless dishes, so we always read a menu before we sit down at a restaurant. We let them know we are vegetarians, "Je suis végétarien (male) végétarienne (female)", and always ask if each thing we are ordering has no meat, "No viande?" Vegans and people who are allergic to wheat or dairy will have to do their research on what is edible in the different regions of France. Refer to our Resources in the Appendix for Vegetarian Travel. There are websites that list vegetarian and vegetarian friendly restaurants in France.

If you don't drink caffeinated beverages, bring your own tea bags and ask for hot water; herbal teas are not usually available. If you want to eat protein at breakfast, it will be difficult to find in France. Breakfast typically consists of a croissant and coffee or black tea. So, if you need protein, bring your own or purchase food the day before. We bring our own protein powder and mix it with water or juice so we don't run out of energy in the morning. All French cities have bakeries, "Boulangerie," and there are many small produce markets, "Alimentation." Typically, you don't touch or pick out the produce yourself. You wait in line and tell them each item you want, unless it is a supermarket. Omelets are served at lunch and dinner, but not in the morning. Be prepared to understand the foods and customs of France, and you will have much more fun! Check out our resource section on Vegetarian Travel, especially the book *Vegetarian France: Over 150 Places to Eat and Sleep* by Alex Bourke.

TRAVELERS WITH DISABILITIES

Increasing numbers of people with disabilities are traveling and there are increasing numbers of resources available for them. For example, a well-researched guide called *Access in Paris* is available at no charge (they request a donation) from Access Projects, 39 Bradley Gardens, London W13 8HE, United Kingdom. This guide is for anyone with mobility issues visiting Paris, including the elderly and parents with young children. Please refer to our Resource section for magazines, books and websites regarding accessibility in France.

Time Line of the Saints

1st century   St. Mary Magdalene
290–303   St. Foy
422–512   St. Genevieve
5th century   Our Lady of Le Puy
1180–1240   St. Edmund of Abingdon
1412–1431   St. Joan of Arc
1567–1622   St. Francis de Sales
1572–1641   St. Jane Frances de Chantal
1580–1660   St. Vincent de Paul
1591–1660   St. Louise de Marillac
1597–1640   St. John Francis Regis
1623   St. Anne of Auray
1641–1682   St. Claude de la Colombiere
1647–1690   St. Margaret Mary Alacoque
1660   Apparition of St. Joseph
1673-1716   St. Louis de Montfort
1786–1859   St. John Vianney - Curate of Ars
1805–1885   St. Therese Couderc
1806–1876   St. Catherine Labouré
1813–1853   Blessed Frederick Ozanam
1844–1879   St. Bernadette Soubirous
1846   Our Lady of La Salette
1858   Our Lady of Lourdes
1871   Our Lady of Pontmain
1873-1897   St. Therese of Lisieux
1876   Our Lady of Pellevoisin

Resources

INTERNET SITES

The Internet is an enormous resource for travel information. We have included sites for researching the regions, departments and cities of France, plus general travel information to get you started. For the English version of a website, look for the British Flag. Sometimes the British Flag icon is very small or at the bottom of the home page. If the website is in French, look for "Tourisme," "Histoire," "Culture," or "Patrimonie" for information about shrines and churches. Many websites require you to drag your cursor over the category and then a drop-down menu appears. In the ever-changing world of the Internet, websites change, so if one we provide doesn't work, do a search, and let us know about the new site. If you don't want to type in the website addresses below, go to our website www.innertravelbooks.com, and click on "Links" for faster access.

REGION TOURIST BOARDS

Auvergne Regional Council www.cr-auvergne.fr/uk/index.asp

Auvergne Tourist Board www.crt-auvergne.fr

Brittany Regional Council www.brittanytourism.com

Brittany Tourist Board www.region-bretagne.fr

Burgundy Tourist Board www.burgundy-tourism.com

Centre Tourist Board www.visaloire.com

Côte d'Azur & Rivièra Tourist Board www.crt-riviera.fr — Go to: Art & Discovery; Religious heritage.

Il de France Tourist Board www.paris-ile-de-france.com

Midi-Pyrenees Tourist Board www.tourisme-midi-pyrenees.com French

Normandy Tourist Board www.normandy-tourism.org

Pays de la Loire Tourist Board www.paysdelaloire.fr

Provence-Alpes-Côte-d'Azur Tourist Board www.crt-paca.fr

Provence Tourist Board www.crt-paca.fr — Go to "Religious Art" for descriptions of churches.

Rhone-Alps Tourist Board www.france-rhonealps-tourism.com

Western France www.westernfrancetouristboard.com

Western Loire www.westemloire.com

DEPARTMENT TOURIST BOARDS

The department tourist boards below are for the cities listed in this book.

Ain Tourist Board www.ain-tourisme.com — Ars-sur-Formans

Ardeche Tourist Board www.ardeche-verte.com — La Louvesc

Aveyron Tourist Board www.aveyron.com — Conques

Aveyron Regional Council www.conques.com/index1.htm — Conques

Calvados Tourist Board www.calvados-tourisme.com — Lisieux

Eure-et-Loire Tourist Board www.tourisme28.com — Chartres

Haute-Loire Tourist Board www.mididelauvergen.com — Le Puy-en-Velay

Hautes-Pyrénées Tourist Board www.cg65.fr — Lourdes

Haute-Savoie www.hautesavoie-tourisme.com French — Annecy

Paris Ile-de-France www.pidf.com — Paris

Indre http://tourisme.cyberindre.org — Pellevoisin

Lot www.lot.fr — Rocamadour

Manche Tourist Board www.manchetourisme.com — Mont Saint Michel

Mayenne Tourist Board www.cg53.fr/Fr/ French — Pontmain

Morbihan Tourist Board www.morbihan.com French — St. Anne d'Auray

Nièvre Tourist Board www.cg58.fr — Nevers

Seine-Maritime Tourist Board www.seine-maritime-tourisme.com — Rouen

Sâone-Loire Tourist Board www.southernburgundy.com — Paray-le-Monial & Taizé

Var Tourist Board www.tourismevar.com French — Cotignac

Vendée Tourist Board www.vendee-tourisme.com — Saint-Laurent-sur-Sèvre

Yonne Tourist Board www.tourisme-yonne.com — Pontigny

Bouches-du-Rhône www.visitprovence.com — La Sainte-Baume & Saintes-Maries-de-la Mer

CITIES

Conques www.conques.index1.htm

Conques Official Website for the Town www.conques.fr French

Conques Office de Tourisme
www.tourisme.fr/office-de-tourisme/conques.htm French

Lisieux www.ville-lisieux.fr/decouvrirfr.htm French

Lourdes Office de Tourisme www.lourdes-infotourisme.com

Mont Saint-Michel www.abbaye-montsaintmichel.com — Official website for the Monastic Fraternities of Jerusalem at the Abbey of Mont Saint-Michel.

Nevers www.ville-nevers.fr French

Paray-Le-Monial http://perso.wanadoo.fr/richez/Burgundy/Paraye.htm

Paris www.pidf.com

Rocamadour www.rocamadour.com

Rouen www.rouentourisme.com

Saintes Maries de La Mer www.saintes-maries.camargue.fr

TOURIST INFORMATION

There are many websites on France. Any search for "France" and "lodging" will give you more than enough websites to explore. Below are a few to get you started.

All Travel France www.alltravelfrance.com/France/Car_Rental/Driving_Tips.htm — Driving tips for France.

Centre des monuments nationaux www.monum.fr — The National Center of Monuments.

Discover France www.discoverfrance.net/Boutique/Travel/index.html — Travel Center.

Discover Paris www.discover-paris.info/index_aboutparis.htm —Tourist info for Paris.

Dorling Kindersley www.dk.com — Eyewitness travel guides

Fodor's www.fodors.com — Fodor's travel guides.

France Keys www.francekeys.com — Comprehensive tourist info.

France on Foot www.franceonfoot.com — The French trail system consisting of 110,000 miles of foot paths.

French Tourist Offices www.office-de-tourisme.org — General tourist info.

Frommer's www.frommers.com — Frommer's travel guides.

Insight Guides www.insightguides.com — Insight guides, maps and phrasebooks.

Les aéroports Français www.aeroport.fr —French airports.

Let's Go www.letsgo.com — Travel guides written by students for budget travel.

Lonely Planet www.lonelyplanet.com — Lonely Planet travel guides.

Mappy www.mappy.fr — Offers route planning, travel info, and maps for France.

Online Highways www.2hwy.com/fr —Tourist info.

Office de Tourisme et des Congres Paris www.paris-touristoffice.com — Paris Convention and Visitors Bureau.

Rand McNally www.randmcnally.com — Online store for folded maps of France.

RATP www.subwaynavigator.com — Transportation info in Paris.

Rick Steves www.ricksteves.com — Go to: Plan Your Trip/Country Information.

Rough Guides http://travel.roughguides.com — Rough Guides, miniguides and phrasebooks.

Routes International http://routesinternational.com — Transportation links.

SNCF National Rail Service www.ter-sncf.com — Train info in English.

Solo Travel Portal www.solotravelportal.com — Resources for solo travelers.

Stanford www.stanfords.co.uk — Maps, travel guides and unique maps and guides for example: Cistercian Abbeys & Sites in France—A road map with info on abbeys.

TGV Railsystem www.tgv.com — High speed trains.

Travel Guide Warehouse www.travelguidewarehouse.com — Travel guides, maps, phrase books, and language courses.

U.S. State Department www.travel.state.gov — Updated international travel advisories.

Via Michelin www.viamichelin.com — Comprehensive site for driving in France with online store for maps.

Visit Europe www.visiteurope.com — Comprehensive site for touring France.

THE ROAD TO SANTIAGO DE COMPOSTELA, SPAIN

American Association of Friends of Road to Santiago www.geocities.com/friends_usa_santiago — American website with information and resources for pilgrimage to Santiago, Spain.

The British Confraternity of St. James www.csj.org.uk — British website with information and resources for pilgrimage to Santiago, Spain.

The Little Company of Pilgrims www.santiago.ca — Canadian website with information and resources pilgrimage to Santiago, Spain.

SHRINE INFORMATION

Refer to individual chapters under Websites, or visit: www.innertravelbooks.com and click on Links.

Abbaye de Mont Saint-Michel www.abbaye-montsaintmichel.com — Official website for the Monastic Fraternities of Jerusalem at the Abbey of Mont Saint-Michel.

Apparitions of Jesus and Mary www.apparitions.org — Lists apparitions around the world.

Basilique du Sacré Couer de Montmartre www.sacre-coeur-montmartre.com — Official website of The Sacred Heart Basilica of Montmarte.

Centre des monuments nationaux www.monum.fr — The National Center of Monuments.

Chapelle Notre Dame de la Médaille Miraculeuse http://chapellenotredamedelamedaillemiraculeuse.com — Official website for the Chapel of Our Lady of the Miraculous Medal in Paris.

Diocèse de Chartres www.diocesechartres.com/cathedrale — The website for the diocese of Chartres; in French.

Dominicains de la Sainte Baume http://saintebaume.dominicains.com French — Dominican Fathers of Sainte Baume and the Grotto of St. Mary Magdalene.

Espace Bernadette Soubirous Nevers www.sainte-bernadette-nevers.com — Official website of the Sanctuary of St. Bernadette in Nevers.

Lourdes www.lourdes-france.com — Official website for Lourdes.

La Maison du Pelerin www.lourdes-fr.com — Information about the major shrines in France and Europe.

The Montfortian Religious Family www.montfort.org/English/LifeLM.htm — Comprehensive website maintained by the Montfort Missionaries in Rome, with detailed information on St. Louis de Montfort.

Notre Dame Cathedral www.cathedraledeparis.com/EN — Official website for the Notre Dame Cathedral in Paris.

Notre-Dame de Pellevoisin www.pellevoisin.net — Official website for Our Lady of Pellevoisin; in French.

Notre Dame de Reims www.cathedrale-reims.com — Official website for the Cathedral of Reims; in French.

Paray-le-Monial Pèlerinages www.paray.org — Official website for the Sanctuaries of Paray-le-Monial in French.

Regional Council of Aveyron www.conques.com/index1.htm — Comprehensive website about the St. Foy Abbey church in Conques. After you leave the home page, the English buttons will work.

Sanctuarie de Lisieux http://therese-de-lisieux.cef.fr — Official website for the Sanctuary of St. Therese of Lisieux.

Sanctuarie de Notre Dame de La Salette www.nd-la-salette.com — Official website of the Sanctuary of Our Lady of La Salette; in French.

Sanctuaire Notre-Dame de Grâce www.nd-de-graces.com — Official website for Our Lady of Grace in Cotignac.

Sanctuaire Notre Dame de Pontmain www.sanctuaire-pontmain.com — Official website of the sanctuary of Our Lady of Pontmain; in French.

Sacred Sites www.sacredsites.com — Martin Gray's photos and descriptions of sacred sites around the world.

Sanctuaire d'Ars www.arsnet.org — Official website for the Sanctuary of Ars: St. John Vianney. Parts of website are in English.

Sanctuaire Sainte-Anne d'Auray www.sanctuaire-ste-anne-dauray.com — Official website for the Sanctuary of St. Anne d'Auray in French.

Soeurs de Notre Dame du Cénacle http://ndcenacle.free.fr/ — Official website of the Sisters of Our Lady of the Cenacle (St. Therese Couderc) in French.

The Taizé Community www.taize.fr — Official website for Taizé in twenty-six languages.

Villes Sanctuaries en France www.villes-sanctuaires.com — The Association of Shrine Towns in France with suggested tours and contact information.

PILGRIMAGE
There are hundreds of pilgrimage tour operators. Do a search with the words: France/pilgrimage/tours.

LODGING IN MONASTERIES AND CONVENTS
BOOKS
Europe's Monastery and Convent Guest Houses by Kevin J. Wright.

Guide St. Christophe This comprehensive guide for lodging in monasteries and convents is in French and costs 25 euros. It can be paid by check or bank transfer. Email: gsc@mp.com.fr or write: Guide Saint Christophe/163 blvd Malesherbes/75859 Paris cedex 17/France. A website is planned in the near future. You can also purchase the guide in some bookstores in Paris.

WEBSITES
Italia Sixtina www.sixtina.com — A French booking service for lodging in convents and monasteries. You provide a price range and pay them directly. If you don't have time to buy the books or do the research, this is for you.

MEDITATION RESOURCES
BOOKS
Centering Prayer in Daily Life and Ministry by Thomas Keating. Christian contemplative meditation.

The Best Guide to Meditation by Victor N. Davich. Overview of different meditation techniques and their history. Good for beginners wanting to know what is out there.

Discovering Jewish Meditation, Instruction & Guidance for Learning an Ancient Spiritual Practice by Nan Fink Gefen. Jewish Meditation for beginners.

How to Meditate like Jesus: A Guide to Breath Prayer by W. Scott Ragsdale. Christian meditation.

How to Meditate: A Practical Guide by Kathleen McDonald. Buddhist meditation.

How to Meditate: A Step-by-Step Guide to the Art and Science of Meditation by John (Jyotish) Novak. Yoga meditation techniques for beginners.

Meditation for Beginners by Jack Kornfield. Buddhist Vipassana, cassettes.

Meditation for Dummies by Stephan Bodian. Introduction to a variety of meditation techniques.

Meditation for Starters by J. Donald Walters. Meditation techniques for beginners.

Zen Meditation in Plain English by John Daishin Buksbazen, Peter Matthiessen.

WEBSITES

There are many websites on meditation. Search for "meditation," or for "meditation" and your particular religion or spiritual practice, i.e., "Catholic," "Buddhist," etc.

Ananda Online www.ananda.org — Yogic meditation. Click on: Lessons in Meditation: Online meditation support and monthly newsletter.

Beliefnet www.beliefnet.com — Comprehensive info on all religions. Click on: Spirituality, then: meditation and prayer.

Contemplative Outreach www.centeringprayer.com — Christian Centering Prayer as taught by Thomas Keating.

Dharma Net International www.dharmanet.org — See Buddhist Info Web for list of Buddhist Meditation Centers worldwide.

The World Community for Christian Meditation www.wccm.org — Christian meditation as taught by Dom John Main OSB. Click on: Christian meditation.

Vipassana.com www.vipassana.com/meditation — Buddhist meditation in the Theravada tradition. Offers an online course in meditation.

MEDITATION RETREATS - FRANCE

The Sun Centre www.thesuncentre.com — Yoga retreat in the south of France in the Languedoc region. Two hours north of Nîmes and Montpellier airports and Avignon. Phone: 33 (0)4 66 45 59 63 Email: retreat@thesuncentre.com.

La Buissière www.yogafrance.com — A center for yoga and walking holidays in south west France on the outskirts of the village of Duravel in the Lot valley. Phone:33 (0)5 65 36 43 51 Email: labuissiere@wanadoo.fr.

Retreats Online www.retreatsonline.com/guide/meditation.htm — Search for retreats.

Plum Village www.plumvillage.org — A Buddhist monastery for monks and nuns and a retreat center for lay people, in Ste. Foy la Grande, 53 miles (85 km) east of Bordeaux. Founded by the Vietnamese Zen Master Thich Nhat Hanh (Thây). Email: uh-office@plumvillage.org.

Yoga Directory www.self-realization.com/yoga_directory.htm for countries around the world.

RESOURCES FOR TRAVELERS WITH DISABILITIES

MAGAZINES/NEWSLETTERS

Emerging Horizons publishes a quarterly newsletter, lists and reviews accessible hotels, and offers other travel ideas around the world. Phone: 209 599-9409 www.emerginghorizons.com.

Society for Accessible Travel and Hospitality publishes a quarterly magazine. Phone: 212 447-7284 www.sath.org.

BOOKS

Access in Paris: A guide for those who have problems getting around by Gordon Couch and Ben Roberts Access Project/39/Bradley Gardens/West Ealing/ W138HE/United Kingdom www.accessproject-phsp.org Email: Gordon.couch@virgin.net This detailed book is available for free but donations are requested.

A World of Options Mobility International USA/PO Box 10767/Eugene, OR 97440/USA US$45.Phone: 1 541 343-1284 www.miusa.org.

Barrier Free Travel: A Nuts & Bolts Guide for Wheelers & Slow Walkers by Candy Harrington 888 795-4274/215 923-4686 www.emerginghorizons.com

Guide Rousseau H comme Handicapés Les Éditions La Route Robert/14 rue Louis-Philippe/92200 Neuilly/Seine/France Fax: 33 (0)1 46 24 42 13. In French. Available in French bookstores.

How to Travel: A Guidebook for Persons with Disabilities by Fred Rosen 1 636 394-4950.

Touristes Quand Même This guide is in French and describes services in the main towns, with translations in English of common phrases. Available free from CNRH (Comité Naitonal Français de Liaison pour la Réadaptation des Handicapés) or the Paris Convention and Visitors Bureau Headquarters, www.paris-touristoffice.com.

WEBSITES

Access-able Travel Source www.access-able.com — Comprehensive travel info.

Accessible Europe www.accessibleurope.com — Comprehensive travel info.

Disability Resources on the Net www.disabilityresources.org — Links to travel/foreign websites.

Emerging Horizons www.emerginghorizons.com — Comprehensive travel info for France: Go to "Travel Resources," "Destinations," "Europe," "France."

Maison de la France www.franceguide.com — Official website of the French Government Tourist Office. Click on "Special Needs Tourism."

Moss Rehab Resource Net www.mossresourcenet.org — Informative site with many useful links and travel tips.

Routes International www.routesinternational.com/access.htm#organizations — Links to travel websites.

The European Commission
http://europa.eu.int/comm/enterprise/services/tourism/policy-areas/guides.htm — Travel guides for tourists with disabilities.

VEGETARIAN TRAVEL

BOOKS

Vegetarian France: Over 150 Places to Eat and Sleep by Alex Bourke, Vegetarian Guide, Ltd. www.vegetarianguides.co.uk Email: info@vegetarianguides.co.uk.

WEBSITES

Happy Cow's Global Guide to Vegetarian Restaurants www.happycow.net — Vegetarian restaurants around the world.

La Maison du Vert www.maisonduvert.com Vegetarian Hotel and Restaurant in Vimoutiers, near Lisieux, Caen, Bayeux and Rouen. Email: mail@maison-duvert.com.

The Vegetarian Resource Group www.vrg.org/travel — Travel information. Lists books, websites, tour operators, bulletin board, and articles.

Veg Dining www.vegdining.com — Vegetarian restaurants around the world.

Vegetarians Abroad www.vegetariansabroad.com — Establishments abroad that cater to vegetarians.

Rocamadour cat (chat)

Glossary

Abbey – A monastery erected with permission of the church, with a community of not fewer than twelve religious; monks under the supervision of an abbot; nuns under that of an abbess.

Altar – A focus of spiritual devotion; in the Catholic Church altars are the center of focus for the building and where the Eucharist is kept for the celebration of Mass. In large Catholic churches, when there are other altars in side chapels, the main altar is called the "high altar." Personal altars can be made in a home with pictures of saints and symbols of one's faith as a source of focus for meditation and prayer.

Apse – An area of a church that is typically semi-circular and projects out from the building as part of the sanctuary or altar.

Basilica – A Roman Catholic church given certain ceremonial privileges.

Bastille Day – July 14 is commemoration of the storming of the Bastille (prison) in Paris in 1789 and marking the beginning of the French Revolution.

Beatification – The step taken before recognition of sainthood, or canonization, of a deceased Christian. After a local church has organized a strong petition, then with papal approval, beatification takes place, allowing the person to be called "Blessed." With this designation the local church that organized the cause can venerate the Blessed.

Blessed – The title given to a deceased Christian who has passed certain criteria in the beatification process, which is the step taken before recognition of sainthood, or canonization.

Calvinism – The religious doctrines of John Calvin (1509-1564) emphasizing the omnipotence of God and the salvation of the elect by God's grace alone. French Calvinists founded the Huguenot movement, which was suppressed by the Roman Catholic Church.

Canonization – In the Catholic Church, after extensive research, and proof of at least one miracle, the pope declares that a deceased Christian is a saint, allowing for universal veneration.

Cathars – A Christian sect, also known as Albigenses, flourishing in Western Europe in the twelfth and thirteenth centuries that was condemned by the Catholic Church as heretical because of their dualistic belief. The Roman Catholic Church eliminated Catharism by the fifteenth century.

Cathedral – The principal church of a bishop's diocese, containing the Episcopal throne.

Cloister – An area within a monastery or convent to which the monks or nuns are normally restricted.

Convent – The building in which a religious community lives. Usually referred to as an establishment for nuns in the United States, but in France, convent and monastery are used for both nuns and monks.

Crypt – The burial place of a person in a church. Also called tomb, reliquary, mausoleum, sepulcher, and vault. These places usually are under the high altar, or under altars in side chapels, but they can also be in a room downstairs, beneath the high altar.

Ecumenical – The general definition is the bringing together of all faiths in order to find common ground and purpose.

Eucharist – Also called the host, Holy Communion and the Blessed Sacrament. It is a wafer of bread blessed, consecrated, by a priest during the Mass. The consecrated bread is turned into the body of Christ and taken internally during Mass. In the Roman Catholic Church the recipients must be Catholic, but other Christian religions have different criteria for receiving the host. The Eucharistic miracles are instances where the consecrated hosts have been scientifically proven to turn into human flesh, to have shed blood or withstood the test of time by not decomposing.

Feast day – In the Catholic Church saints have a feast day where a special Mass is celebrated in their honor once a year. Usually the day is the date of their death, or near that date. For some saints, there are more festivities around a feast day, birthday or the translation of their relics to the church

French Revolution – The transformation of the society and political system of France, lasting from 1789 to 1799. France was temporarily transformed from an absolute monarchy, where the king monopolized power, to a republic of theoretically free and equal citizens.

Gothic – The style of architecture developed in northern France that spread to Western Europe from the middle of the twelfth century to the early sixteenth century. It is characterized by pointed arches, the ribbed vault, and the flying buttress.

Hugeunots – A French Protestant of the sixteenth and seventeenth centuries.

Hundred Years War – A series of short conflicts between France and England from 1337 to 1453 resulting from disputes between the ruling families of the two countries.

Mass – The ritual that entails recitation of the liturgy of the Roman Catholic Church around the celebration of the consecration of the Eucharist. Mass is celebrated daily at most churches.

Nave – The perpendicular body of a cross-shaped church that connects to the horizontal wings, called the transept. The nave is the main part of the church where the congregation sits.

Novice – A person admitted into a religious community for a probationary period.

Novitiate – The time period that a person is a novice, or a house where novices are trained.

Penance – An act of self-mortification or devotion to show sorrow for a sin or other wrongdoing.

Predestination – The doctrine that God has foreordained every event throughout eternity.

Presbytery – The part of a church reserved for clergy.

Reconciliation – A sacrament in some Christian churches that includes contrition, confession to a priest, acceptance of punishment, and absolution (remission of sin).

Reformation – The creation of the Protestant church by Martin Luther and others who broke off from the Roman Catholic Church in the sixteenth century.

Relic – A part of a saint or blessed's mortal remains, or an object connected to a saint or blessed.

Reliquary – A container or shrine in which sacred relics are kept.

Sacristy – A room in a church where sacred vessels and vestments are kept and where the clergy dresses for Mass.

Saint – A deceased person officially recognized, through the rigorous process of canonization and final approval by the pope in the Roman Catholic Church, as having reached the highest attainment of holiness.

Sanctuary – The most sacred part of a church, typically where the altar is located.

Saracens – The nomadic Arabic tribes that invaded the borders of Western Europe.

Stations of the Cross – There are 14 Stations of the Cross that depict Christ's final journey to Calvary, and prayers are said at each one.

Stigmata – The wounds of Christ's passion recreated in a person desiring to imitate Christ and experience the pain of His wounds. There are the visible stigmata and the invisible stigmata. St. Francis of Assisi was the first known person to experience the stigmata. Since then, hundreds of men and women have manifested the wounds, typically in the hands, feet, side and head.

Tertiaries – Also called "Third Order," a branch of a religious order that is comprised of lay women and men, who live in the world instead of in convents and monasteries.

Transept – The transverse or horizontal wings of a cross-shaped church.

Translation – The removal of a saint's remains from one place to another.

Transubstantiation – The belief that during the ritual of the Mass, the bread and wine are literally changed into the body and blood of Christ.

Tympanum – The decorative panel above a church entrance often containing sculptured or mosaic ornamentation.

Storytelling in Rocamadour

Acknowledgements

To write a book about saints is a great blessing. To work with sweet and soulful individuals is a double blessing. We could not have written this book without the loving help and assistance of many people. To our amazement, many generous individuals gave of their time without compensation. We want to thank Dan Fontugne, a native Frenchman, for the French translations in the book. He saved us an enormous amount of time and energy. Eliane Atwell and Pat Kirby graciously pitched in transcribing and corresponding in French. Durga Smallen, Jeannie Tschantz, Nancy Sexton, John Ernst, Stewart Motyka, John Lenti, Anandi Cornell, Prakash Van Cleave and Susan Deranja, gave of their time, to proofread the final draft. Tout le monde merci beaucoup!

During our travels and afterwards, many Brothers, Sisters, and staff at the shrines cheerfully provided us with the information we needed, and gave us encouragement for writing this much-needed book.

We were lucky again to be able to snag our trusty friend and neighbor, Cathy Parojinog, for her expert editing and thoughtful support in the world of words. She made our job so much easier, and we will be forever grateful. Stephanie Steyer provided cheerful and patient assistance in teaching typesetting, getting our book off to the printer, and introducing us to the world of Mac. Ken Gutierrez, a gifted teacher, Renee Glenn and Tera Antaree offered many helpful graphic design tips.

Also, to all our friends and family who encouraged and supported us through a very long year of endless writing: Jyotish and Devi Novak, Nancy Sexton, Patty McCarley, Ingrid and Eric Glazzard, Jeff and Eleni Rice, Sara, Nakula and Rama Cryer, Jeannie and Tim Tschantz, Julie and Craig Roberts, Keshava and Diana Taylor, Martha and John McDougall, Mary and Mark Perini, Joe and Joan Heater, Mary Ann and Dennis Sundene, Don McDougall, and in memory of Joe and Gerry Heater.

For providing us with a daily example of how to create with Divine inspiration, we thank Swami Kriyananda. We thank God, Paramhansa Yogananda, and all the saints of France for guiding us every step of the way. Bless you all for helping us to share the light and love of these great saints with pilgrims everywhere.

Bibliography

The American Standard Version, *The Holy Bible*, 1901.

Beaumont, Barbara Estelle O.P., *Pellevoisin: A Message of Mercy and a Mission of Prayer*, Monastere des Domincaines, Pellevoisin, France, 1997.

Demouy, Patrick, *Saint-Remi of Rheims Basilica*, (booklet) Editions la Goelette, Saint Ouen, France, 1997.

Bély, Lucien, *Mont Saint-Michel*, (booklet) Editions Ouest-France, Rennes, France, 1999.

Castel, Roger, *La Salette: From the high peaks, Mary calls us to*, (booklet) Editions du Signe, France, 1995.

Comte, Louis, *Le Puy-en-Velay: Cathedral, Cloisters, Penitents*, N.D. de France, (booklet) Le Puy Cathedral, France.

Flinders, Carol Lee, *Enduring Grace: Living Portraits of Seven Women Mystics*, Harper San Francisco, California, 1993.

International Bible Society, *The Holy Bible, New International Version*, 1984.

King, Ursula, *Christian Mystics: The Spiritual Heart of the Christian Tradition*, Simon & Schuster Editions, New York, 1998

Knight, Kevin, *The Catholic Encyclopedia*, Online Edition 2003, www.newadvent.org.

Le Dorze, Jean, *Sainte-Anne D'Auray*, (booklet) Editions Jean-Paul Gisserot, France, 1998.

Fau, Jean-Claude, *Visiting Conques*, (booklet) Editions Sud Ouest, France, 2003.

Macmitchell, Melanie, *Sacred Footsteps: A Traveler's Guide to Spiritual Places of Italy & France*, Opal Star Press, Encinitas, California, 1991.

Miller, Malcolm B., *Chartres: Guide of the Cathedral*, (booklet) Editions Houvet-la Cyrpte, France, 2001.

Perrier, Jacques, *Notre-Dame de Paris*, (booklet) Impex, Rambervillers, France, 1998.

Poux, Didier, *Rocamadour: Great Pilgrimage Centre*, (booklet) Apa-Poux Editions, Albi, France, 1994.

Roux, Julie, Juliette Freyche (trans:), *The Road to Compostela*, MSM, Vic-en-Bigorre, France, 1999.

Sacre-Coeur de Montmartre, (booklet) Lescuyer, Paris, 1997.

Steves, Rick, & Steve Smith, *France 2003*, Avalon Travel Publishing, Emeryville, California, 2003.

Taize: Trust on Earth, (booklet) Macon-Imprimerie, France, 2002.

Thurston, Herbert J. & Donald Attwater (eds.), *Butler's Lives of the Saints*, Christian Classics, Allen, Texas, 1996.

Wright, Kevin J., *Catholic Shrines of Western Europe: A Pilgrim's Travel Guide*, Liguori, Missouri, 1997

SAINTS

ST. BERNADETTE SOUBIROUS

Trochu, Francis, *Saint Bernadette Soubrious*, Tan Books and Publisher, Inc., Rockford, Illinois, 1985.

Harris, Ruth, *Lourdes: Body and Spirit in the Secular Age*, Penguin Compass, New York, 1999.

ST. CATHERINE LABOURÉ

Laurentin, René, *The Life of Catherine Labouré*, Collins Liturgical Publications, Sisters of Charity of St. Vincent de Paul, London, 1983.

ST. EDMUND OF ABINGDON

Paris, Matthew, *The Life of St. Edmund*, Alan Sutton Publishing Limited, United Kingdom, 1996.

ST. FRANCIS DE SALES

De Sales, Saint Francis, *Introduction to the Devout Life*, Kessinger Publishing, LLC, 1934.

Thibert, V.H.M. Péronee Marie, (trans.) *Francis de Sales, Jane de Chantal: Letters of Spiritual Direction*, Paulist Press, Maywah, New Jersey, 1988.

BL. FREDERIC OZANAM

Ramson, Ronald, C.M., *Praying with Frédéric Ozanam*, Saint Mary's Press, Christian Brothers Publications, Winona, Minnesota, 1998.

ST. JANE DE CHANTAL

Thibert, V.H.M. Péronee Marie, (trans.) *Francis de Sales, Jane de Chantal: Letters of Spiritual Direction*, Paulist Press, Maywah, New Jersey, 1988.

ST. JOAN OF ARC

Beevers, John, *Saint Joan of Arc*, Tan Books and Publishers, Inc., Rockford, Illinois, 1981.

Trask, Willard, (trans.), *Joan of Arc: In Her Own Words*, BOOKS & Co., New York, 1996.

ST. JOHN VIANNEY

Trochu, Abbé Francis, *The Curé d'Ars: St. Jean-Marie-Baptiste Vianney*, Tan Books and Publishers, Inc., Rockford, Illinois, 1977.

Lambert, Joel Rev., *Ars Pilgrim Guide*, (booklet), Actes Graphiques, Saint-Etienne, France.

ST. LOUIS DE MONTFORT

Onfroy, Jean-Marie, *Saint Louis-Marie Grignion de Montfort*, Pierre Téqui, Paris, 1991.

De Montfort, Louis-Marie Grignion, *True Devotion to Mary*, Tan Books and Publishers, Inc., Rockford, Illinois, 1985.

De Montfort, Louis, *The Secret of Mary*, Tan Books and Publishers, Inc., Rockford, Illinois, 1998.

ST. LOUISE DE MARILLAC

Dirvin C.M., Joseph I., *Louise de Marillac of the Ladies and Daughters of Charity*, Farrar, Strauss & Giroux, Inc., New York, 1970.

Ryan, France and John E. Rybolt (ed.), *Vincent de Paul and Louise de Marillac: Rules, Conferences, and Writings*, Paulist Press, Mahwah, New Jersey, 1995.

ST. MARGARET MARY ALACOQUE

The Sisters of the Visitation, (trans.) *The Autobiography of St. Margaret Mary Alacoque*, Tan Books and Publishers, Inc., Rockford, Illinois, 1986.

The Sisters of the Visitation (trans.), *Thoughts and Sayings of St. Margaret Mary*, Tan Books and Publishers, Inc., Rockford, Illinois, 1986.

ST. MARY MAGDALENE

Buysson, Father Philippe Decouvoux du, *The Sainte Baume: A Mountain Steeped in Geological and Religious History*, Editions PEC, Marseille, France, 1992.

ST. THERESE COUDERC

Hoover, Rose F. (ed.) *At Prayer with Saint Therese Couderc*, (booklet) Religious of the Cenacle, Chicago, Illinois, 1999.

ST. THERESE OF LISIEUX

Taylor, Rev. Thomas N. Taylor, (trans.) *St.Thérèse of Lisieux: An Autobiography*, Burns Oates & Washbourne LTD, London, 1927.

Flinders, Carol Lee, *Enduring Grace: Living Portraits of Seven Women Mystics*, HarperCollins Publishers, New York, 10022, 1993.

ST. VINCENT DE PAUL

Ryan, France and John E. Rybolt (ed.), *Vincent de Paul and Louise de Marillac: Rules, Conferences, and Writings*, Paulist Press, Mahwah, New Jersey, 1995.

Forbes, F.A., *Saint Vincent De Paul*, Tan Books and Publishers, Inc., Rockford, Illinois, 1998

Index

About the Authors

James and Colleen Heater are longtime practitioners of yoga who teach classes on meditation and inspirational music as members of a spiritual community in Northern California. They combine their interest in the lives of the saints and their love of travel to create this series of soulful travel guides for people of all faiths.

Their honeymoon to Italy in 1998 brought about the idea for writing spiritual travel books. The following year, they returned to Italy to research over thirty-five shrines, and to revisit their favorite gelaterias. *The Pilgrim's Italy* was the fruit of their labors. Shortly thereafter, the Heaters embarked on writing *The Pilgrim's France*, after driving 4,000 miles and exploring thirty French shrines.

Colleen's professional background includes working as a licensed marriage and family therapist, specializing in addiction and codependency, and offering the component of spiritual renewal to her clients. Colleen has lived and traveled throughout Europe for both pleasure and pilgrimage. Currently, she is the publisher for Inner Travel Books.

James, a licensed architect with a gift for the use of space to inspire and uplift, specializes in both religious and secular designs. His background in meditation and music—including being an accomplished guitarist—has prepared him to understand the subtle energies of some of the holiest shrines in Europe. He has also led guided tours of sacred places in the United States and Italy.

The Heaters lecture throughout the country introducing the techniques of meditation outlined in their books, and presenting beautiful photographs of the sacred sites of Italy and France.

For information about presentations, or other publications by Inner Travel Books, visit www.innertravelbooks.com or call toll free 1 866-715-8670.

Plan your next pilgrimage adventure to Italy with help from
The Pilgrim's Italy: A Travel Guide to the Saints!